gwynt – wind

hen – old

hafod, hafotty – summer dwelling

hebog – falcon

hir – long

hydd – stag

hendre – winter dwelling

isa, isaf – lower

las, glas – green or blue

llan – church

llechog – slaty

llechwedd – hillside

llethr – slope

llithrig – slippery

llwyd – grey

llwyn – grove

llyn – lake

maen (pl. meini) – stone

march (pl. meirch) – horse

marchog – armed horseman

nawr, fawr – big

meillionen – clover

mign, mignen – bog

mochyn (pl. moch) – pig

moel, foel – rounded hill

morfa – coastal marsh

mur (pl. muriau) – wall

mynach – monk

mynydd, fynydd – mountain

nant – brook, dingle

newydd – new

ogof – cave

oleu – light

oer – cold

pair – cauldron

pant – small hollow

pen – top, head

penrhyn – promontory

pentre, pentref – village

pistyll – spout, cataract

plas – mansion

pont, bont – bridge

pwll – pool

rhaeadr – waterfall

rhiw – hill

rhos – moorland, marsh

rhyd – ford

saeth (pl. saethau) – arrow

sarn – paved way, causeway

sych – dry

tal – end

tan – under

tarren – hill

teg, deg – fair

tir – land

tomen – mound

traeth – stretch of shore

tre – town, hamlet

tri – three

trwyn – nose, promontory

twll – hole

ty (pl. tai) – house

tyddyn – smallholding

ucha, uchaf – upper

uwch – above

waun – moor

wen, wyn – white

wrach, gwrach – witch

wyddfa – tumulus

y (article) – the, of the

yn – in

ysbyty – hospice

ysfa – itching

ynys – island

ysgol (pl. ysgolion) – ladder, school

ystrad – valley floor, strath

ystum – bend

# On Foot in Snowdonia

*Also by Bob Allen*
ON HIGH LAKELAND FELLS
ON LOWER LAKELAND FELLS
ESCAPE TO THE DALES

# On Foot in Snowdonia

### The Best Hill Walks and Scrambles
### from Cadair Idris to the Carneddau

BOB ALLEN

MICHAEL JOSEPH
LONDON

MICHAEL JOSEPH LTD
Published by the Penguin Group
27 Wrights Lane, London W8 5TZ, England
Penguin Books USA Inc., 375 Hudson Street, New York, New York 10014, USA
Penguin Books Australia Ltd, Ringwood, Victoria, Australia
Penguin Books Canada Ltd, 10 Alcorn Avenue, Toronto, Ontario, Canada M4V 3B2
Penguin Books (NZ) Ltd 182-190 Wairau Road, Auckland 10, New Zealand

Penguin Books Ltd, Registered Offices: Harmondsworth, Middlesex, England

First published in Great Britain 1993

Copyright © Bob Allen 1993

Typeset in 10/11pt Caslon Book ITC by
Goodfellow and Egan Ltd., Cambridge

Colour reproduction by Anglia Graphics, Bedford
Printed and bound in Singapore by Kyodo Printing

A CIP catalogue record for this book is available from the British Library
ISBN 0 7181 3563 6

The moral right of the author has been asserted

*p. i:* Moel Siabod on the skyline, seen over Ffynnon Llugwy from
the slopes of Carnedd Llewelyn.
*p. ii:* Llynau Mymbyr and the Snowdon Horseshoe seen from near Plas y Brenin.

# Contents

Introduction     ix
Acknowledgements     xi

**1: CADAIR IDRIS**
1. Penygadair from the north: the Pony Path
   from Ty-nant     2
2. Penygadair via scramble on the Cyfrwy Arête     5
3. The Round of Llyn Cyri, with Tyrau Mawr, from
   Llynnau Gregennen     8
4. Gau Graig, the north-east spur of Cadair Idris     10
5. Penygadair via Cwm Cau: return via Mynydd Moel     12
5a. Penygadair, returning via Cwm Rhwyddfor     15
6. Scramble to Penygadair from Cwm Cau, return
   via Craig Cau     15
7. The 'Precipice Walk', Dolgellau     16
8. Castell y Bere and Craig yr Aderyn     16

**2: THE ARAN, THE BERWYN, THE ARENIG
AND THE RHINOG**

*Part 1: The Aran*
1. Aran Fawddwy from Cwm Cywarch via Drysgol     20
2. Aran Benllyn from Llanuwchllyn     22
3. Traverse of the Aran from Cwm Cywarch     24

*Part 2: The Berwyn*
4. Pistyll Rhaeadr and the Berwyn     26
5. A Short Round on the Berwyn     30

*Part 3: The Arenig*
6. Arenig Fawr by its west ridge     31
6a. Alternative descent via the south ridge     34

6b. Continuation to Moel Llyfnant     34

*Part 4: The Rhinog*
7. A Round of Y Llethr and Diffwys     36
8. A Round of Rhinog Fawr and Rhinog Fach from
   Cwm Nantcol     39
9. Rhinog Fawr by the Roman Steps     43
9a. Rhinog Fawr by the Roman Steps: return
    via Gloyw Llyn     43
10. Craig Wion and Rhinog Fawr from Cwm Bychan     45

**3: MOEL SIABOD, CNICHT AND THE MOELWYN**
1. Moel Siabod by the east ridge     48
2. Cnicht by the south-west ridge: return by
   Llynau Cerrig-y-myllt     51
3. Cnicht by the south-west ridge: return by Cwm
   Croesor     54
4. Llyn Llagi and the Dog Lakes     54
5. Moelwyn Bach, Moelwyn Mawr and Cwm Croesor     59
6. Cnicht, Moelwyn Mawr and Moelwyn Bach     63
7. Cwm Bychan from the Sygun Copper Mine     64
8. The Ffestiniog Railway Walk     66

**4: EIFIONYDD HILLS: NANTLLE AND CWM PENNANT**
1. Moel Hebog, Moel Ogof and Moel Lefn from
   Beddgelert     70
2. Y Garn, Mynydd Drws-y-Coed and Trum y
   Ddysgl from Rhyd-Ddu     74
3. The Nantlle Ridge     77
3a. Traverse: start at Rhyd-Ddu, end in Cwm Silyn     77
3b. Rhyd-Du to Garnedd-goch and return to Rhyd-Ddu     78
3c. The Round: start and finish in Cwm Pennant     78

4.   Moel Lefn and Moel yr Ogof from Cwm Pennant         80
5.   The Round of Cwm Pennant                            81
6.   A Round over Moel Hebog from Cwm Pennant            84
7.   Mynydd Mawr from Rhyd-Ddu                            86
8.   Scramble on Sentries' Ridge, Craig y Bera           88

5:   THE CARNEDDAU

*Part 1: Northern Carneddau*
1.   Aber Falls and the Northern Circuit                 93
2.   Tal y Fan and the Standing Stones                   98

*Part 2: Southern Carneddau*
3.   The Cwm Llafar Horseshoe                            103
4.   Scramble to Carnedd Dafydd by the Llech Ddu
     Ridge                                              104
5.   Cregiau Gleision, Llyn Cowlyd and Pen Llithrig     105
6.   Penyrhelgi-du and Pen Llithrig-y-wrach from
     the A5                                             108
7.   Pen yr Ole Wen and the Carneddau from Llyn
     Ogwen                                              108
7a.  Carnedd Dafydd from Ffynnon Llugwy                 111
7b.  Carnedd Dafydd via Cwm Lloer                       111
7c.  Carnedd Llewelyn and Carnedd Dafydd from
     Ffynnon Llugwy                                     112
8.   Scramble on west face of Pen yr Ole Wen by the
     Horned Ridge                                       113
9.   Scramble in Cwm Lloer                              114
10.  Cwm Eigiau Horseshoe                               117

6:   TRYFAN
1.   Tryfan by the South Ridge from Bwlch Tryfan        122
2.   Tryfan by the North Ridge, descent by the
     Heather Terrace                                    124
3.   Tryfan by the Heather Terrace and the South Ridge  126

4.   Scrambles from the Heather Terrace                 128
4a.  The central route by Little Gully                  129
4b.  The north buttress route                           131
4c.  The south rib route                                133

7:   THE GLYDERS AND GALLT YR OGOF
1.   Glyder Fach, from the north by the east ridge      136
2.   Bristly Ridge and the Devil's Kitchen              139
3.   Scrambles on Glyder Fach                           141
3a.  Glyder Fach Main Cliff: scramble on East Gully
     Ridge                                              142
3b.  Glyder Fach Main Cliff: scramble on Dolmen Ridge   144
4.   Gallt yr Ogof from Ogwen Valley                    146
4a.  Scramble on Gallt yr Ogof                          148
5.   Glyder Fawr                                        149
5a.  Glyder Fawr via Twll Du (Devil's Kitchen) and
     Llyn y Cwn                                         149
6.   The Glyders via the Gribin Ridge (Y Gribin)        152
7.   The Glyders via scramble on the Cneifion Arête     152
8.   Glyder Fawr via scramble on north-west face
     and Senior's Ridge                                 155
9.   The Glyders from Pen-y-pass                        157
10.  Glyder Fawr via scramble in Bryant's Gully         159

8:   WEST WALL OF THE NANT FFRANCON
1.   Y Garn via the Sheep Walk                          164
2.   Y Garn via scramble on east-north-east ridge       166
3.   Round of Y Garn and Foel-goch                      169
4.   Scramble on Foel-goch by Needle's Eye Arête        169
5.   Scramble on Carnedd y Filiast via Atlantic Slab    171
6.   A Round of Y Garn and Elidir Fawr from
     Llanberis Pass                                     172
7.   A Round of Carnedd y Filiast and Elidir Fawr
     from Marchlyn                                      174

9: THE SNOWDON GROUP

1. Snowdon by the Miner's Track ... 179
2. Scramble to Snowdon by Cribau (The Gribin) ... 181
3. Snowdon by the Pig Track ... 182
4. Snowdon by the Watkin Path, return by the south ridge ... 185
5. Moel Eilio and the round of Cwm Dwythwch ... 188
6. Snowdon by Moel Eilio and Moel Cynghorion ... 190
7. Llanberis Path to Snowdon (with optional scramble on Clogwyn Du'r Arddu) ... 190
8. Snowdon from Rhyd-Ddu, return by Moel Cynghorion ... 193
9. Snowdon by the Snowdon Ranger Path ... 195
10. Crib Goch by the East Ridge ... 197
11. Crib Goch via Cwm Glas Mawr and Bwlch Coch ... 199
12. Crib Goch via the North Ridge ... 201
13. Garnedd Ugain via Cwm Glas ... 203
14. Garnedd Ugain by scramble on Clogwyn y Person Arête ... 205
15. Scramble on Llechog Buttress to Clogwyn Station ... 206
16. The Snowdon Horseshoe ... 209

10: THREE CLASSICS AND TWO OUTLIERS

1. The Cwm Bochlwyd Horseshoe ... 211
2. The Idwal Skyline ... 212
3. The Welsh Three-Thousanders ... 213
4. A Round over Moel Famau in the Clwydian Hills ... 217
5. The Limestone Edges of Llangollen ... 220

Index ... 224

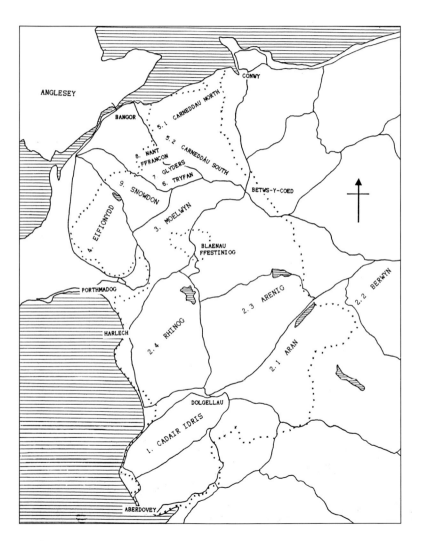

# Introduction

This book describes 102 of the best walks and scrambles on the Welsh mountains from Cadair Idris to the Carneddau, plus a few others. I have deliberately included a few low-level walks suitable for easy days or the family excursion. Much of the area is that covered by the Snowdonia National Park, although there are some walks outside it. They are split up into chapters which coincide as far as possible with geographical features such as main roads and valleys.

## The Walks

I firmly believe that most mountain-walkers prefer to return to their starting-point at the end of a day on the hills and so, of the sixty-six walks covered, all but two – the traverse of the Aran (2.3) and the Welsh Three-Thousanders (10.3) – are 'rounds'. The walks are all graded by a *star system* to indicate overall quality, with three stars marking the best. This is necessarily subjective; some people may say that it is completely misleading but, on the whole, mountain-wayfarers are usually in general agreement as to what gives a good day in the hills: continuous interest, fine scenery and a sense of achievement are all part of it. From comments made to me about my earlier books, most people find the system useful.

'*Approximate times*' given for walks are just that. They are intended as a guide based on my own times but do not allow for lengthy stops (i.e. more than about twenty minutes). The biggest factor in these times is not the mileage but the combination of height gained with the ease or roughness of the terrain. The '*highest elevation reached*' is the altitude above sea level of the main peak or area of higher land being visited. The '*height

Winter sunset from Bwlch Meillionen looking down Cwm Pennant.

*gained'* is the sum total of all the ascent involved in the day's walk: on an undulating round this can add up considerably. The *'approximate distances'* are based on map miles, i.e. running a map-wheel or a piece of cotton along the line of the route and converting to miles/km at the scale involved. On the level, these distances will be fairly accurate; on a walk involving the ascent of slopes they will be under-stated, of course.

## Maps and Place Names

My debt to the superb maps of the Ordnance Survey will be obvious and it is always imperative to have the relevant map with you on a walk. My own maps are intended to focus on particular features and places mentioned in the descriptions. I have put numbers on the maps, corresponding to the chapters and numbers of the walks, **at or near the beginning of walks.** (When the numbers are circled, they indicate scrambles.) I have made frequent use of compass points and grid references to establish direction and position and would always recommend that a compass be carried as well as the map. There are slight variations in the spelling of place names from one edition of the maps to another, and between the 1:25,000 and 1:50,000 scales also. So far as possible, I have used those on the 1:25,000 scale maps.

## Access

I have taken particular trouble to try to ensure that any walker or scrambler following my directions should have no problems of access, but situations do change, particularly in details, so commonsense also needs to be used if the situation on the ground is not always exactly as I have described.

## The Scrambles

'Scrambling' is mountaineering as it was before the almost separate skill and sport of 'rock-climbing' developed. It is finding the easiest way up reasonably continuous rock, whether it be in a gully or on a ridge or crag: it is the area of mountain activity midway between hill-walking and rock-climbing. For the mountain-wayfarer in much of Snowdonia, hill-walking and scrambling are inextricably mingled, simply because of the nature of the terrain. Many thousands of people have by now enjoyed what are probably the two most popular routes in North Wales, namely the North Ridge of Tryfan and the Snowdon Horseshoe. Both routes involve the use of hands as well as feet, even in perfect conditions; they are scrambles, or at least they are 'scramble-walks' i.e. walks with sections of scrambling on them. People who have enjoyed those, can and do enjoy similar experiences elsewhere and my purpose is to draw to their attention some of the best possibilities.

**'Scramble difficulty grade'**: Here, as in my book *On High Lakeland Fells*, I have used a numerical grading system, with grade 1 as the easiest and grade 3 as the hardest. Grade 1 scrambles will involve the occasional use of the hands on steep ground, e.g. Bristly Ridge on Glyder Fach (7.2) or the scramble to Carnedd Dafydd by the Llech Ddu Ridge (see 5.4). Grade 2 scrambles will have individual passages which are a bit harder, e.g. the scramble on the Dolmen Ridge of Glyder Fach's main cliff (7.3b) and a rope *may* be useful to protect inexperienced members of a party. Grade 3 scrambles are those verging on the lowest grades of rock-climbing, namely Moderate and Difficult and in any party of mixed ability, it is advisable that some of the members have some rock-climbing and rope-handling experience. For experienced scramblers, a rope will be often more of a hindrance than a help and I have done all the scrambles described without using a rope at all, most of them solo, in fairly stiff-soled boots and with a rucksack.

For the major scrambles only, I have added a short summary at the beginning of the description which, once the start of the route has been identified, may be all that is needed by an *experienced* party. Where some short scrambling sections are really only incidents on what is essentially a walk, then I have covered the details in the text only.

The little sketches are intended to help in locating the start or line of the scramble; once that is found, the rest usually follows fairly logically, but it is essential to get the start right. The heights given in the scrambles are based on readings using two altimeters, not pitch-lengths as in rock-climbs.

The scrambling grades assume dry rock, not too much wind and air temperatures that enable you to use hands without gloves. These are of course conditions found generally more in summer than in winter. A change in weather conditions can completely alter the character of a scramble, as it can a walk, and only judgement based on experience can tell you when to retreat or continue. A vital part, and indeed one of the most rewarding parts of the whole hill-walking/mountaineering experience, is the making of the decisions about whether to continue or turn back, and to do it safely.

If I have omitted your own favourite walk or scramble, I apologise. On the other hand, there are some places which I have deliberately avoided, particularly for scrambles, because I think they are potentially too dangerous. Such a place, for example, is the great cliff of Lliwedd. The problem is that the crags on Lliwedd lack obvious distinguishing features so that route-finding is very tricky. In addition, the rock seems particularly greasy in all but perfect conditions; in short, it is not a cliff for scramblers. On the other hand, I have also deliberately avoided cliffs, crags and situations where there is what I consider to be too much loose rock in exposed positions.

So far as the walks are concerned, I do not deny my dislike of conifer forests and I have consequently avoided those isolated hill areas such as Rhobell Fawr and Dduallt, where the walking is too complicated by forestry.

## Acknowledgements

I would like to acknowledge the help and companionship of my old friend Trevor Jones who was full of ideas for walks and scrambles and who accompanied me on some of the best. His daughter, Victoria Coghlan, joined me on several others and her enthusiasm was a tonic. Hamish Nicol rightly insisted that I should go scrambling on Carnedd y Filiast, with great results. (I am sure there are other scrambles there that I have not yet had time to find.) The Head Wardens and Wardens of the Snowdonia National Park (SNP), have been particularly helpful on matters to do with points of access and rights-of-way, and I am very grateful to them; also to Nigel Warren, of Gilfach Farm in Cwm Pennant for the same reason.

Steve Ashton's very good little pocket-sized guide book on *Scrambles in Snowdonia* has been the starting-point for quite a few scrambles that were previously unknown to me, while I have scoured numerous Climbers' Club rock-climbing guides for routes in the very lowest grades which, although largely consigned to oblivion by the modern rock-climber, are proving quite capable of resurrection as scrambles. I was greatly helped by Terry Marsh's excellent *Mountains of Wales* in some areas that were relatively unfamiliar before I started this book.

My long-suffering wife Lin and my son Jonathan accompanied me on a couple of walks but, much more importantly, have put up with my early departures and late arrivals with stoicism. Last but not least I have to thank my editor, Jenny Dereham, who always looks at my walks, scrambles, maps and drawings with the needs of the first-time as well as the regular visitor in mind; the eventual result is undoubtedly better than it would have been.

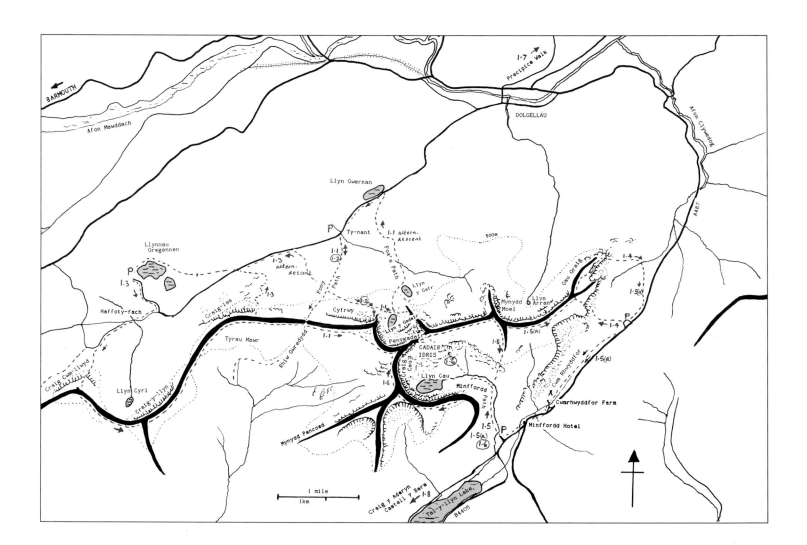

# 1:  Cadair Idris

| BEST MAPS: OS 1:50,000 Landranger 124 Dolgellau & surrounding area<br>OS 1:25,000 Outdoor Leisure 23 Snowdonia: Cadair Idris area | | | | | | |
|---|---|---|---|---|---|---|
| Approx Distance | Approx Time | Highest Elevation Reached | Height Gained | Star Rating | Scramble Difficulty Grade | Scramble Height Gain |
| **1.1 Penygadair from the north: The Pony Path from Ty-nant** | | | | | | |
| 6½ miles/10.4km | 4–5 hours | 2930ft/893m | 2404ft/733m | */** | — | — |
| **1.2 Penygadair via scramble on the Cyfrwy Arête** | | | | | | |
| 6½ miles/10.4km | 5 hours | 2930ft/893m | 2404ft/733m | *** | 3 | 500ft/152.4m |
| **1.3 The Round of Llyn Cyri, with Tyrau Mawr, from Llynnau Gregennen** | | | | | | |
| 8½ miles/13.6km | 4 hours | 2169ft/661m | 1381ft/421m | ** | — | — |
| **1.4 Gau Graig, the north-east spur of Cadair Idris** | | | | | | |
| 3½ miles/5.6km | 3–3½ hours | 2241ft/683m | 1355ft/413m | ** | — | — |
| **1.5 Penygadair via Cwm Cau: return via Mynydd Moel** | | | | | | |
| 6 miles/9.6km | 5 hours | 2930ft/893m | 3117ft/950m | *** | — | — |
| **1.5(a) Penygadair, returning via Cwm Rhwyddfor** | | | | | | |
| 9½ miles/15.5km | 7–8 hours | 2930ft/893m | 3117ft/950m | *** | — | — |
| **1.6 Scramble to Penygadair from Cwm Cau, return via Craig Cau** | | | | | | |
| 5 miles/8km | 4–5 hours | 2930ft/893m | 2867ft/874m | */** | — | — |

| Approx Distance | Approx Time | Highest Elevation Reached | Height Gained | Star Rating | Scramble Difficulty Grade | Scramble Height Gain |
|---|---|---|---|---|---|---|
| **1.7 The 'Precipice Walk', Dolgellau** | | | | | | |
| 3½ miles/5.6km | 2 hours | 820ft/250m | — | */** | — | — |
| **1.8 Castell y Bere and Craig yr Aderyn** | | | | | | |
| 3 miles/4.8km | 3 hours | 764ft/233m | 699ft/213m | ** | — | — |

Cadair Idris, the 'chair' of the legendary Idris – giant, mythical hero, close relative of King Arthur, or simply a delightful figment of folk imagination – is an isolated mountain massif, exposed to all the good and the bad weather and only rivalled by Snowdon itself in the National Park. A tremendous escarpment, nine miles of it above about 1600ft (488m) with deep cwms scooped out of its northern edge and a particularly dramatic one scooped out of its southern edge, it is the most southerly mountain group of the Snowdonia National Park and is unquestionably one of its finest. To the south-east, it is well-defined by the long wooded valley containing Cwm Rhwyddfor, Tal-y-llyn Lake and the Afon (river) Dysynni, along which the road leads to the small seaside resort of Tywyn. To the north-west, wooded foothills running from the ancient inland market town of Dolgellau to the seaside resort of Barmouth tiptoe into the waters of the beautiful estuary of the Afon Mawddach.

For mountain-walkers and scramblers, the area has everything, including some interesting projects for easy days, so I have added three of those as well. Dolgellau and Barmouth were the traditional starting-points for assaults on Cadair's great battlements, for that is what they resemble when seen from the slopes just north of Dolgellau or from the 'Precipice Walk', of which more later. But nowadays, there are several excellent

Snowdonia National Park facilities which have made car parking much easier and have greatly improved access to some wonderful walks.

### 1.1 Penygadair from the north: the Pony Path from Ty-nant
*6½ miles/10.4km        4–5 hours*

Under settled weather conditions, this is the easiest and probably most popular route, a good 'family way' to the highest point of the massif, especially if the return is to be made by the same way. This path has a history going back at least as far as our enterprising Victorian ancestors who used it to ferry supplies up to a stone-built refreshment hut situated immediately below the highest rocks. A hut is still there, re-built by the National Park Authority. The roof is now modern 'wriggly-tin' but its inside has bench seats round the walls providing a good spot on a bad or windy day to enjoy your sandwiches. Deliberately, it is not a comfortable enough place to tempt anyone to bivouac, except in emergency.

There's an excellent SNP car park at Ty-nant at grid ref 698153 about 3 miles/5km south-west of the centre of Dolgellau and 1½ miles/2.5km beyond Llyn Gwernan. (The car park at the Gwernan Lake Hotel is for residents only.) On leaving this,

turn right and in a hundred yards beside a telephone box there's a path signed 'Cader Idris'. This Pony Path leads up through bushes, then slants up rocky and brackeny fields with occasional stone steps. There are fine views of the great escarpment ahead, particularly of the splendid crags forming the north wall of Cyfrwy with its superb notched left-hand skyline. This soon disappears from view as a couple of zigzags are negotiated, with more steps, on this obvious path, climbing to reach the col, the lowest point on the escarpment (Rhiw Gwredydd). A path from Tyrau Mawr to the west joins here and if you just crossed the col and went down the other side you would descend broad slopes to the Afon Cadair. The way upwards however is obviously to turn left (ESE) here at a couple of stiles where a well-worn peaty track, with many cairns, climbs at an easier angle and skirts the rocky stone field which forms the west shoulder of Cyfrwy.

The track is too far back from any edge to give good views until it swings north-east over much stonier ground and starts to climb the broad and rocky ridge which quickly leads to the trig point and stone shelter on Penygadair's summit. The view to the south is very impressive, down steep slopes to the black waters of Llyn Cau and the awesome vertical rocks, the great cliffs of Craig Cau, which almost plunge into it. To the north, it is no less grand, peering over a great void to see the lovely pool of Llyn y Gadair sparkling at the bottom of a deep cwm whose left-hand (W) arm is the long rocky arête of Cyfrwy and whose right arm is a broad, shaly slope used by the Fox's Path. To the east, the contrast could hardly be greater for the view is of a high, broad and mostly grassy plateau, with more cwms scooped out of its edge; this stretches for just over a mile (1.6km) to the summit of Mynydd Moel.

The great wall of Cadair Idris seen from the north-west.

To return, the easiest way is to reverse the ascent and that is particularly true if you have youngsters in your party. However, an alternative descent for competent parties is to use the Fox's Path, reached by descending to the north-east from the summit rocks (skirting the edge of a boulder field) to the grassy plateau and then turning northwards downhill. Here a couple of cairns mark a slaty trench and beyond it there is an obvious path. This has been described elsewhere as 'notorious', 'desperately loose and dangerous' etc. There is an element of truth in this, but I think it is exaggerated and I can think of many much worse paths elsewhere. The real problem is that the erosion is considerable and can only get worse unless either fewer walkers make use of it, or it is stabilised by some technique such as 'pitching', that is flat stones laid in the bed of the path and locked together. But, except in icy winter conditions or high wind, so long as you have proper boots and keep well to the right on the descent and use the little rock ledges, it is perfectly easy, with just a bit of stony scree for the last thirty yards.

The Fox's Path leads to the shore of Llyn y Gadair lying in the hollow of the cwm, and then it descends, with a few kinks in the path, roughly northwards past Llyn y Gafr to reach the road at the Gwernan Lake Hotel. That's a perfectly good way to go if you don't mind the half-mile walk back to Ty-nant along a narrow walled (and potentially dangerous) lane, for there's no link from the hotel to the very overgrown right-of-way path that skirts the other (N) side of Llyn Gwernan.

Fortunately, there is a good, though not as obvious, alternative. Go round to the north-west corner of Llyn y Gadair and then, initially over some large stones and boulders beside the Llyn, a path will be found leading down a rocky little moraine ridge to the north-west. It passes under those splendid great crags of Cyfrwy and then crosses the moor to link up with the Pony Path again at a wall junction where there is a little stream. The return to the car park is then straightforward.

## 1.2. Penygadair via scramble on the Cyfrwy Arête

SUMMARY: 500ft/152.4m of Grade 3 scrambling, east-facing; 6½ miles/10.4km, 5 hours. The route takes the notched eastern skyline edge of Cyfrwy as seen from the Pony Path, starting from the obvious flat top of Table Buttress. A steep arête leads to the top of the Table and then, with more exposed moves on the ridge above, to easier ground and the top of Cyfrwy.

*Opposite:* Cyfrwy and Llyn y Gadair from Fox's Path.

I can't miss out this route, first climbed solo by O.G. Jones (probably the most famous of the Victorian pioneer rock-climbers) in 1888 before he became well-known, and on which Sir Arnold Lunn had an accident that turned him from climbing to skiing. It is really a traditional 'mountaineering route', right on the borderline between scrambling and rock-climbing (and in climbing guides is graded 'difficult' – which, I should add, is very low on the scale of difficulty). Walkers with rock-climbing experience (a rapidly growing number) should find this a splendid outing. I enjoyed it greatly as a solo, done on a fine, dry but windy day, although I was a bit put off by the wind. I wouldn't do it under wet conditions at all and it is normally rightly tackled as a roped party of two.

Evening light on the cliffs of Cyfrwy.

Clearly seen on the notched eastern skyline ridge from the lower part of the Pony Path, there is a flat-topped pillar called The Table, about two-thirds of the way up. This is a key feature, well seen as you approach from the west but not easy to pick out from Llyn y Gadair where the scramble starts. At the lowest section of the crag and well below The Table itself, however, is a steep rock buttress called Table Buttress, and that is easy enough to distinguish. The route itself starts at the top of Table Buttress, a point which from Llyn y Gadair looks as though it is about half way up the main cliff.

To get there, the best way is from the Ty-nant car park at grid ref 698153 and then take the Pony Path for its initial stages until a junction of walls and a little stream is reached (grid ref 695143) and a sketchy path then leads south-east across the moor and below the Cyfrwy crags to reach Llyn y Gadair (the reverse of the return in (**1.1**) above). Seen from here, the Table Buttress consists of very steep rock dropping away to the right (N) but its top, seen from the llyn, consists of broken grassy ledges, bounded on their far left by a big wide gully. The aim is to go up these much easier-angled ledges to the left of the almost vertical walls of Table Buttress itself and these are reached by walking up a scree chute and then trending right. Little tracks lead over the ledges to the top edge of the Buttress and almost overlooking it, but below more steep rock pinnacles leaning together higher up: these collectively make up the Cyfrwy Arête. To be absolutely sure, the initials 'C A' are marked on a large vertical slab at the bottom of the route itself.

Directly above the slab, a steep rock arête with big holds leads to a corner and then onto another arête above which, in turn, leads upwards to the top of The Table, about 130ft/40m from the start. The Table is speckled with quartz, tilted at about 30° towards Penygadair, and to proceed you must crawl over its top to the corner with the shortest drop; from here you scramble down to the little col which links The Table to the main ridge. Now step left and go up a short groove to a small pinnacle, only 30ft/9.1m or so away from the col. The broad arête above is steep and probably the most exposed bit of the route; it is certainly the section which most justifies the use of a rope for protection. I was in shorts and the ripping sounds made by the wind as it gusted around the pinnacles made me feel I was about to be even more exposed; I was glad I wasn't wearing a kilt. Fortunately the holds are good and, after about 40ft/12.2m, I was able to step left to a ledge and then up a short corner to rejoin the main ridge again. Two short walls with a midway ledge follow and then about 200ft/61m more of easier scrambling, up more ledges, short walls and spikes of rock, leads to the top of the route. The top of Cyfrwy is reached by trending left round the head of a deep-cut shaly gully and scrambling just a few feet higher.

This is a fine viewpoint for Penygadair, seen from here to consist of four broad bands of granitic rock which are steep and fairly clean, but these are separated by other bands of very vegetated and slaty rock. From the top of Penygadair, the strata tilt top left to bottom right into a wide cwm and then curve up again towards Cyfrwy, whose summit rocks have a very distinctive columnar structure.

The columnar rocks at the cop of Cyfrwy.

When I climbed this route, I had left my little dogs, Henry and Freddie, guarding my rucksack at the bottom and so had to descend the last bit of the Arête and then the broad gully on the right (NE) to retrieve them all. For those without such complications, the way round this cwm to Penygadair is now very obvious, with an eventual descent either by the Fox's Path or the Pony Path back to Ty-nant car park as described above.

### 1.3 The Round of Llyn Cyri, with Tyrau Mawr, from Llynnau Gregennen

8½ miles/13.6km        4 hours

This is a fine walk along the western end of the great Cadair Idris escarpment as it declines towards the sea, with less of the drama of the great cwms and greater heights further east. It has its own cwm, nevertheless, enfolding the lovely Llyn Cyri. Walking here offers mostly easy going with splendid views, together with a quietness and solitude sometimes absent on the main peaks, though the easy going is not without its moments of excitement on the direct descent from Tyrau Mawr. There is an easier alternative descent if preferred.

The two Llynnau (Lakes) Gregennen are probably best approached by car from Dolgellau along the secondary road below the Cadair Idris escarpment, since they lie in a fold between it and the wooded foothills above the Mawddach Estuary. Owned by the National Trust, they are a popular beauty spot, and the large car park there at grid ref 658143 is a good place to start the walk. It's worth mentioning that the land between the lakes and the Mawddach Estuary is made up of numerous little outcrops, rocky knobbles covered with heather, fine viewpoints and lots of picnic places: just right for young kids.

For the walk, go back south-east along the metalled track skirting the larger lake, with the steep slopes and crags of Tyrau Mawr clearly visible ahead on the skyline. Stay on the tarmac, ignoring the walking-man footpath sign for our objective is the obvious grassy north ridge of Braich Ddu, fringed by the rock of Craig Cwm-llwyd, to the SSW. Go back through a gate to reach the secondary road again, then turn right (W) to pass the derelict farmhouse of Hafotty-fach (grid ref 660134) and then reach a junction of road and tracks. The one heading south-west and signed 'Unsuitable for Motors' is the one needed. Beyond a gate, a solitary standing stone on a hillock stares over the Mawddach Estuary to the Rhinog; then there's another gate, after which this pleasant track winding upwards reaches yet one more gate and then levels out at the foot of the ridge.

There's no path up the ridge, but it is easy going up grassy slopes towards an obvious outcrop of grey rocks just below the skyline, Craig Cwm-llwyd. As height is gained, there are good views to the east across the wide cwm where Llyn Cyri lies as yet unseen: to the sharp upthrust of Tyrau Mawr, with Cyfrwy and Penygadair just visible beyond it, and to the west a superb view down to Barmouth and the estuary. A scramble through a little boulder field leads to a last pull onto a broad grassy moor crossed by a wire fence. Head south now and a gentle descent to a col (a 'bwlch') brings views at last of Lyn Cyri, like a single teardrop four hundred feet below and with a tiny sheepfold at its edge.

A short climb, now on a path, leads up to the shattered rock edge of Craig-y-llyn and along its grassy top beside a protective wire fence. A gentle descent follows, down to a col near which are the scars of a rather intrusive farm track, then a longer climb leads to the highest point of the walk, the summit of Tyrau Mawr. Step over the fence for a tremendous panoramic

Llyn Cyri from the edge of the escarpment of Tyrau Mawr.

view beyond Penygadair to the Aran, to the Arenig, to central Snowdonia and even to the Lleyn Peninsula. Below your feet, very steep grassy-topped cliffs drop sheer almost to the minor road at their foot. You can trace a farm track, which is used as the footpath, leading from the right-hand end of the slopes below the foot of the crags, across a cattle-grid to the road and back to the Llynnau Gregennen and the car park. The question is how to get there?

If you lack confidence in your ability to descend these steep slopes safely – and remember that most mountain-walking accidents occur as a result of slips on wet grass – you could continue the walk eastwards to join the Pony Path at the lowest point of the escarpment, at Rhiw Gwredydd, descend to the north-east and then take the left fork once below the steeper section and so reach the minor road. You will then have about a mile or more of road before reaching the turn off at the cattle-grid (678144).

There is a quicker and more interesting way, which I believe was used by miners from Dolgellau as their route over the escarpment, and it uses a series of ancient grassy zigzags descending to the NNE from the north-east end of the crags, marked Craig-las on the maps. These are clearly seen from below, so long as you are looking for them, but not so easily seen from above. To locate them, stay on the crag side of the fence (N) and then, keeping well right of the steepest part of the cliffs, descend into a little grassy cwm to the north-east when they will become evident, leading gracefully down for quite a long way until the terrain looks easy enough to veer left and head for the cattle-grid in the valley bottom. Once reached, the farm track leads west and a footpath, indicated by marker posts, bypasses the farm and leads to the north side of the Llynnau Gregennen and the start.

*Opposite:* The ridge rising to Gau Graig from the north-east.

## 1.4 Gau Graig, the north-east spur of Cadair Idris
*3¹⁄₂ miles/5.6km        3–3¹⁄₂ hours*

A glance at the map will show that Gau Graig is at the north-east end of the great Cadair Idris escarpment and as such can obviously form part of a long traversing walk, say from west to east: from Craig Cwm-llwyd over Craig-y-llyn, Tyrau Mawr, Cyfrwy, Penygadair and Mynydd Moel to Gau Graig: this is a distance of just over 9 miles/14km excluding the ascent or descent at either end. Such would be a superb day's walk, but it would involve making perhaps awkward transport arrangements. This proposed walk only climbs to the last of these high points. It is a short round, but a good one, sheltered a little from the prevailing south-westerly weather and ideal for a half day, or even a fine evening in summer. If weather, time and energy permit, it can easily be extended to include the higher top of Mynydd Moel.

There's a good view point towards Tal-y-llyn Lake and a useful car parking spot in a layby on the west side of the A487 near the top of Cwm Rhwyddfor, marked at grid ref 753136. Now walk up the road for three or four hundred paces out of the defile and over the brow of the hill to where a footpath sign points across the slope beyond, to the north. Don't take this path now; it's for the return. A less obvious and unsigned path (at grid ref 757140), not on the OS maps, leads from almost the same point, uphill and to the west, beside the only wire fence seen climbing the hillside. Going this way leads to the top of a rise and discloses a good view of the hump of Gau Graig, seen across a grassy hollow. The fence turns north and the path follows, through a gate and then through heather and bilberry, continuing up steeper slopes. When an area of rock and boulders, beneath some little crags facing down Cwm Rhwyddfor, is reached the fence continues in a straight line. The path, however, goes to the right to skirt the obstacle, up a scruffy little gully onto more open heather slopes above, then swings back to

rejoin the line taken by the fence. This now leads directly to a broad, grassy shoulder, from where there is a fine view of Mynydd Moel.

Turning to the north-east, however, leads to a big cairn perched just above the great cwm and cliffs of Gau Graig, a fine viewpoint, particularly towards the Rhinog and with Trawsfynydd Power Station just visible about fifteen miles away to the north-west. The fine cwm seen below one's feet has a scree-filled middle with a noticeable vertical rib of white quartz rising from it at the top. The right-hand wall, as one looks down, has plenty of heather but also some steep rock slabs. The north (left) arm of the cwm consists of a line of fierce vertical crags but they all have flat tops, making a fine knobbly ridge covered in a profusion of heather. A delightful path (not shown on the OS maps) leads down this, close to the edge of the drop, over a couple of ladder-stiles where walls protect sheep from straying too close to the crags, but when another ladder-stile leads over to the south side of the wall (right) and the path almost immediately veers north (not the way you want at all), it must be left for a less-used and not always obvious one going east. This trends downhill into the much lower reaches of the cwm, over rough pasture with many boulders and little rock outcrops, to meet a wall and fence alongside which goes the footpath shown on the maps (from Bwlch-coch to the milepost (MP) on the A487). This leads south, then follows marker posts to a broad green track that takes you rapidly back to the A487. All that remains is to walk back the short distance along the road to the car.

## 1.5. Penygadair via Cwm Cau: return via Mynydd Moel
*6 miles/9.6km        5 hours*

The approach to Cadair Idris from the south-east, almost from Tal-y-llyn Lake, is steep and unremitting, leading up through mature woods and with consequent restricted views, but it leads as directly as possible to Cwm Cau. To be in Cwm Cau is an experience in itself, for it is one of the finest mountain cirques in Wales. To complete a circuit of its rim, climb easily to Penygadair and look over into the northern cwms before traversing the high plateau to Mynydd Moel, makes for an exceptional day's mountain walking. There are few things better than this anywhere in Britain, let alone Wales. Don't throw it away on a day of indifferent weather.

The start nowadays is from the very good car park and facilities amongst trees just west of the Minffordd Hotel, where the B4405 from Tal-y-llyn Lake meets the A487 from Corris and Machynlleth (grid ref 732116). Then a good track with marker signs leads along an avenue of fine horse chestnut trees, past a ruin and to a gate at the foot of made steps which lead steeply up through woods to the NNW. The steps soon deteriorate into a bouldery path and after about twenty minutes of uphill effort, gaining about 700 feet/213m, the woods are left behind. Emerging from the woods, another path crosses the stream and heads off right (NE) and is used for the descent from Mynydd Moel. So stay with the main path which curves round to the west, now sloping over a boulder-strewn and grassy moor and into the arms of the great Cwm Cau, with the tremendous precipice of Craig Cau looming above a rocky shelf ahead. A little further and the waters of Llyn Cau come into sight, below the crags.

Seen from the main stream outlet, the precipice is fan-shaped, a line of terraces run across from bottom left to top

Craig Cau and Llyn Cau, in one of the finest cwms in Wales.

right, with steep crags leaning to the left, apparently prevented from slipping sideways and into the waters of the llyn by the great vertical Pencoed Pillar which buttresses them at the left side. On the right side of the Pillar, seen from here, is the deep gash of the Great Gully, a route which held immense fascination for the early rock-climbing explorers a century ago. Nowadays it is not considered a good summer route at all because there have been rock-falls and it is normally wet, loose and vegetated. It looks as though the whole precipice is likely to be the same, since the slanting terraces are covered with vegetation, but, on closer acquaintance, it becomes apparent that there is a great deal of excellent rock to be climbed.

From the elegant final cone of Craig Cau, the edge of the cliff declines gently to a col on the right, beyond the point where the crags taper off into hillside, then the slope rises again to the higher bulk of Penygadair's summit. The direct route from Cwm Cau to Penygadair takes a slanting line just below the most rightward of the great pale buttresses and, following a scattering of white quartz outcrops and slaty gutters, climbs to the col. It can also be reached by walking round the llyn: the left side path rises higher above the water and has a couple of rocky steps, while the right-hand path goes round almost at water level. It's an easy enough way to go up in dry conditions but the slate would be slippery in the wet, and care should be taken. The most interesting walking way, however, is to climb up to the lowest point of the ridge forming the left-encircling arm of the cwm: a good path leads there and a better one (the Minffordd Path) is joined on the ridge itself. This is now becoming well worn, keeps well back from the edge of the cwm and passes to the left below two large quartz-speckled and banded rock outcrops (the edges of which give entertaining short and easy scrambles and also views otherwise denied). Nearing the high point of Craig Cau, the path passes close to the top of Great Gully, seen steepening and narrowing in its upper part – a very grand but dank and dismal place – then reaches a wire fence and stile on the actual top of the crag, which proves a fantastic viewpoint. Peer down only with great care, for the drop is vertical, an awful long way and very impressive.

The path continues due north from here to Penygadair, firstly with the slight descent to the col already mentioned and then an easy climb over grassy and then rockier ground to reach the trig point, a circular unroofed windbreak and the hut mentioned earlier.

In the early 1800s, there was a fashion for moonlight mountaineering, suitably fortified by copious draughts of strong liquor, of course, and hampers being carried with additional supplies. Penygadair appears to have been a particularly favourite peak for this pastime, very probably because of the legend about the 'Chair of Idris'. There is a rock hollow near the summit (although I must admit I couldn't be sure which it is, or whether it is the whole of the summit) and it is said that whoever passes the night in the giant's (Idris's) chair will either go mad, die in the night or become a genius.

From Penygadair, the summit plateau slopes down towards the north-east; a short rocky descent skirting a boulder field leads to a broad grassy ridge where sheep graze in summer, then gives way to a gentle ascent towards more rocky ground seen in the distance ahead. There is about a mile of easy and delightful walking along this with fine retrospective views to the west. The rocks, which you might easily assume to be those on top of Mynydd Moel, prove not to be so, for the highest point is just a little further, beyond a wire fence and stile and has a boat-shaped stone windbreak. There's a much greater surprise, however, particularly for a first-time visitor. That easy stroll along the broad grassy ridge leading to Mynydd Moel could lead you to expect that the land beyond will simply decline gently into moorland. Nothing of the kind: here is yet another great cwm, with the tiny Llyn Arran glinting below a fringe of broken crags and another great vertical cliff, black against the western light. Far from being a moorland stroll, the continuation of the edge would be an exhilarating descent for another mile down to Gau Graig.

For most walkers, however, a descent from Mynydd Moel back to Cwm Cau will seem the most appealing way now, but to avoid any difficulties, particularly in deteriorating conditions, return to the fence and stile crossed just before reaching the top of Mynydd Moel and turn downhill, roughly south, following the fence. The path is indistinct but you can't lose the fence. Don't cross by the ladder-stile reached shortly but continue the descent to another simple step-stile, cross the fence here and a zigzag path then leads downhill quite steeply. It re-crosses the fence but always follows the general line of the collapsed wall and fence, with splendid views into Cwm Cau, until, just above the tree line, another ladder-stile leads back towards Cwm Cau. This joins the main path at a little ford just before the descent into the woods and the easy return to the start.

## 1.5 (a) Penygadair, returning via Cwm Rhwyddfor
*6 miles/9.6km      5 hours*

If the challenge of extending the walk and returning from Gau Graig appeals and time, weather and fitness are on your side, may I suggest enthusiastically that you follow the line of the fence from the top of Mynydd Moel down to Gau Graig. From here, it is perfectly feasible to descend directly down to the top of Cwm Rhwyddfor using the path described as the ascent route in Walk 1.4 above; this will be the quickest (and steepest) route. But, for a more delightful descent, follow the northern-bounding arm of the cwm below Gau Graig, as described in Walk 1.4, and reach the A487 by the mile-post at spot-height 285 (or a metre higher on the OS 1:50,000 map!). Take to the road for the very

short distance to the signed car park almost at the top of the pass and, just beyond it, turn off right down the old road. This turns out to be a delightful grassy track, at a lower level than the newer road, and it leads easily and most pleasantly beside the stream and down to the excellent camping/caravan site of Cwmrhwyddfor Farm, where it rejoins the main road for the last third of a mile back to the car park.

## 1.6 Scramble to Penygadair from Cwm Cau, return via Craig Cau

Scrambling, that grey area between roped/technical rock-climbing and simple fellwalking, where hands may be used as well as feet, can be a particularly satisfying way of gaining height, simply because it is more absorbing and requires more concentration than that needed for the simple act of putting one foot in front of another. It also needs more care and judgement, particularly about when to retreat or seek an easier alternative; it is essentially 'mountaineering' as it was before rock-climbing became a separate and increasingly specialist sport.

This scramble to Penygadair is very low in the order of difficulty and is really not much more than a walk up slabs but, by adding a little more detail, I hope I have made it worthwhile. I spotted the line as I sat beside Llyn Cau on a glorious morning while the mists cleared and instead of looking all the time at that grand cliff ahead, I looked instead at the rocky flanks sweeping down to the llyn from the area near Penygadair itself, or more specifically to the right of the summit from where I sat near the outflow.

From a point about one hundred yards/91m nearer to Craig Cau than the outflow from the llyn, I looked north-west to see an obvious line of easy-angled, pale-coloured slabs descending from Penygadair, not quite to the water's edge. A wide shallow gully with scree at the bottom separates these slabs into two halves, the right side being quite a bit steeper. Keeping to the left of this central gully I worked my way up perfect rock. It was so gently angled that my hands were hardly ever needed and even when the easy slabs ended and a steeper little buttress reared up ahead it was only pretending to bar the way, for grassy ledges took me easily around the obstacle. Above these, the rock was less continuous, just little outcrops of it, but it was bilberry time, the views over Llyn Cau to the great crag were magnificent and I was in no hurry to reach the ridge and swing left (west) up the last few boulders to the summit. That day, I returned by taking the anti-clockwise route round Craig Cau but there would be plenty of time for other and longer descents if you chose, *see* **1.5** and **1.5a**.

## 1.7 The 'Precipice Walk', Dolgellau
*3½ miles/5.6km        2 hours*

This is the first of three low-level excursions that I would recommend in the Cadair Idris area for off-days or indifferent weather.

The 'precipice' is pretty tame but the walk itself is certainly well worth doing and is sign-posted, except, rather curiously, right at the beginning where you most need it. Much of the walk rambles gently along the 250m/820ft contour, on good paths, and is consequently excellent for smaller children; Dad can carry the smallest. The views are outstanding.

The start is at a good car park about three miles/4.8km roughly north of Dolgellau at grid ref 745212, then turn west along the road and take the first turn on the left (south) down a ride through a wood. At the end, turn right, follow the path between hedges to a couple of ladder-stiles and into a little open valley cradling the small reservoir of Llyn Cynwch, with a distant view of Cyfrwy and Penygadair. The walk returns to this point, but now turn right (north) and follow the walk anti-clock-

wise, leading round a circuit of the little hill of Foel Cynwch, once site of an ancient, pre-Roman, hill-fort. There are lovely views over gentle wooded country to the north, towards the village of Llanfachreth, and more down to the delightful Afon Mawddach, meandering along the bottom of a deeply glaciated, wooded valley, as the level path above the 'precipice' is followed to a further vantage point. From here the great wall of the Cadair range, from Craig Cwm-llwyd in the west to Gau Graig in the east, together with a splendid view of the Mawddach estuary, comes into sight. The circuit is completed as the path now swings north-east, this time alongside the west bank of the little reservoir to rejoin the outward route. The Precipice walk was created and intended for visitors: I enjoyed it and I think you will too.

## 1.8 Castell y Bere and Craig yr Aderyn
*3 miles/4.8km        3 hours*

The fascinating ruins of Castell y Bere are at grid ref 667085, in a superb position on a crag standing above a broad and green valley down which the waters of the Afon Dysynni meander to the sea near Tywyn.

Building was started in 1221 by Llewellyn the Great but the castle only survived sixty years before being taken and razed by the (Norman) English. However, what remains has been restored, gives a poignant glimpse into the past and is well worth visiting. Then a gentle ramble of less than half a mile/0.8km north-eastwards, on the metalled track up the valley, towards the endless slopes of Mynydd Pencoed (who would ever guess that they ended in the great precipice of Craig Cau?), leads to the hamlet of Tyn-y-ddôl and the touching memorial to Mary Jones who, in the year 1800 at the age of sixteen, walked the long road to Bala barefoot in order to obtain a Welsh Bible.

Returning to Castell y Bere, Craig yr Aderyn is visible from

The ruins of Castell y Bere, Mynydd Pencoed in background.

the battlements in the south-west, a sheer sea cliff thrusting above the green fields miles from the sea. It is an inland breeding site for cormorants: the sea receded about five miles during the late eighteenth century and the birds haven't forgotten.

After a short drive from Castell y Bere, there is an excellent little walk onto its airy top: about 1.7miles/2.7km round trip. Half a dozen cars can park at grid ref 651076, at the end of a little lane. Walk perhaps four hundred yards/366m up the lane alongside a wall and then, when the main track goes through a gate, forsake it for a grassy track on the right (south) leading to the saddle between high rock outcrops on the left and the greater heights of Bird Rock on the right. The remains of a Stone Age or Celtic fort are to be found on the top and the cormorants are very much in evidence. There are superb views particularly up and down the valley, and to the Tarren Hills to the south. The return is much the same way, or make your own variations. It's an excellent place for a picnic.

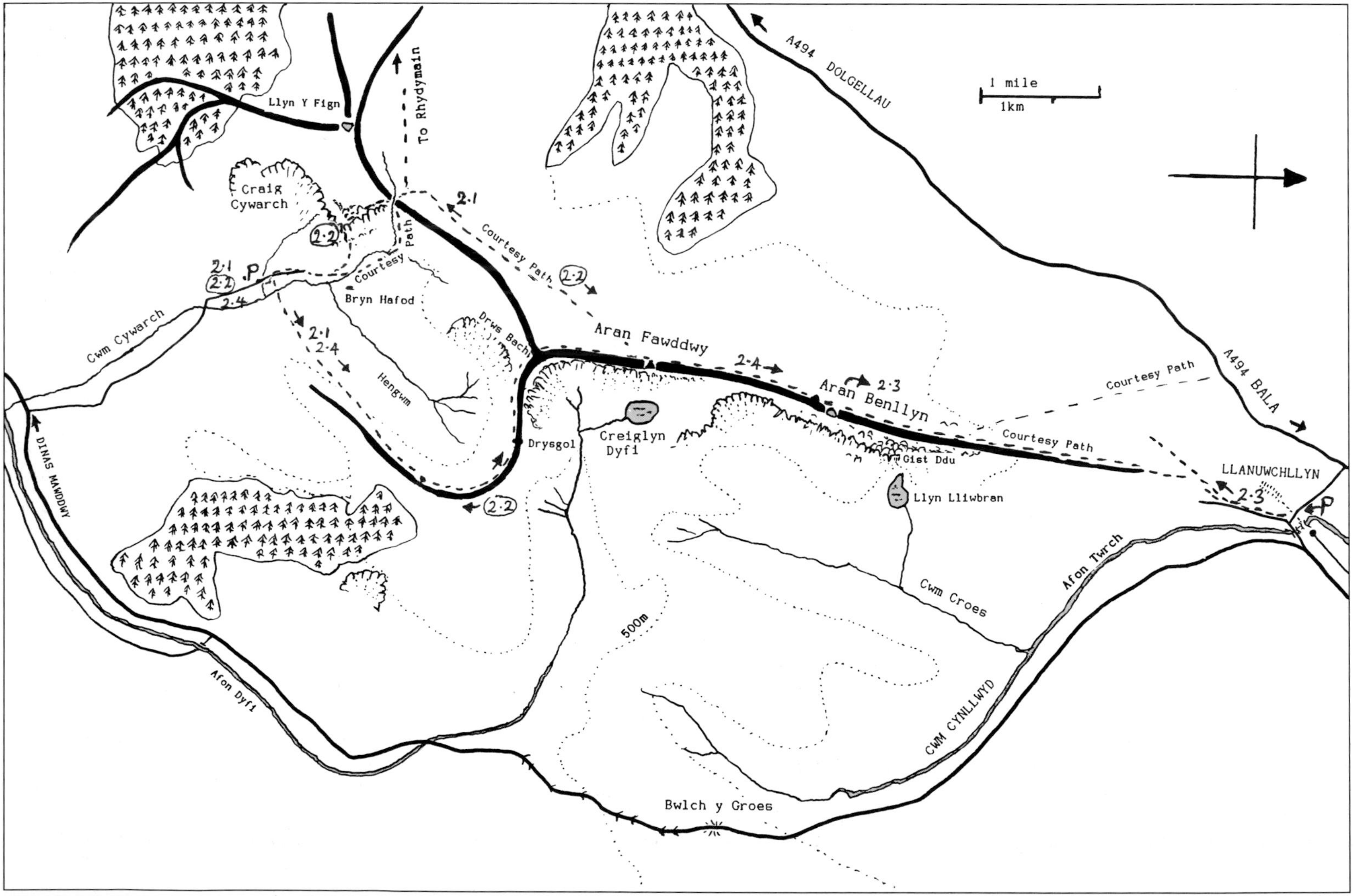

Llyn Y Fign

To Rhydymain

A494 DOLGELLAU

1 mile
1km

Craig
Cywarch

2.1

Courtesy Path

2.2

2.1
2.2
P
2.4

Courtesy Path

Bryn Hafod

Drws Bach

Aran Fawddwy

2.2

2.4

2.3

Aran Benllyn

Courtesy Path

A494 BALA

2.1
2.4

Hengwm

Courtesy Path

Cwm Cywarch

DINAS MAWDDWY

Drysgol

Creiglyn
Dyfi

2.2

Gist Ddu

Llyn Lliwbran

LLANUWCHLLYN

2.3

Afon Dyfi

Cwm Croes

Afon Twrch

500m

CWM CYNLLWYD

Bwlch y Groes

# 2: The Aran, The Berwyn, The Arenig and The Rhinog

## Part 1: The Aran

| BEST MAPS: | OS 1:50,000 Landranger 125 Bala & Lake Vyrnwy & surrounding area | | | | | |
|---|---|---|---|---|---|---|
| | OS 1:25,000 Outdoor Leisure 23 Snowdonia: Cadair Idris area | | | | | |

| Approx Distance | Approx Time | Highest Elevation Reached | Height Gained | Star Rating | Scramble Difficulty Grade | Scramble Height Gain |
|---|---|---|---|---|---|---|
| **2.1 Aran Fawddwy from Cwm Cywarch via Drysgol** | | | | | | |
| 7¹⁄₂ miles/12km | 4–5 hours | 2976ft/907m | 2484ft/757m | ** | — | — |
| **2.2 Aran Benllyn from Llanuwchllyn** | | | | | | |
| 7 miles/11.3km | 4–5 hours | 2900ft/884m | 2277ft/694m | */** | — | — |
| **2.3 Traverse of the Aran from Cwm Cywarch** | | | | | | |
| 9 miles/14.5km | 5–6 hours | 2976ft/907m | 2680ft/817m | **/*** | — | — |

When seen from Cadair Idris, the Aran look dull and uninteresting, just miles of forest and bogs, but they are a continuation north-eastwards of the great escarpment of Cadair Idris and are, in fact, of great interest to the mountain-walker. There are two paths (public paths extended by 'courtesy paths') from Rhydymain on the A494 on this western flank to the main ridge, but these do traverse rather dull ground, so I won't bother you with them. The boring impression from this side is far from the whole story, for on their eastern sides the Aran are much more precipitous, with steep crags just below their sharp crests,

one of which, Gist Ddu overlooking Llyn Lliwbran, gives some of the finest rock for climbing in mid Wales.

More good walks would be possible on the eastern side but not at present because the area is complicated by Access Problems. This is undoubtedly the result of thoughtless parking and other aggravations in the past; the consequence is that legal access is essentially limited to the summit ridge from either end (or from Rhydymain, see above) and that is only as the result of painstaking negotiation. Nobody is keener on unrestricted access to open mountain and moorland than I am: considerate walkers cause no damage and only ever take away photographs, tired bodies and memories. But to upset local farmers again is only to risk this grand ridge being legally denied to others, so please bear this in mind. Permission to walk over hills where you know there is a problem of access is almost never denied to small parties who take the trouble to ask for it; although it is sometimes very difficult finding out who the landowner is. In order to avoid problems myself, this is the only mountain area anywhere in Britain where I leave my own two little dogs in the car, although I invariably keep them on a lead until we are well out of the 'ffridd' and up onto the 'mynydd' or high mountain land. Initially, because of this, I found the 'welcome in the hill-sides' here somewhat diluted, but I must immediately add that, once you've left the valley bottoms, most of the walking is good and the mountain scenery splendid. The SNP wardens are nego-tiating to improve access and, by the time this book is in print, expect the complete traverse of the range, from Bala to the pass at the top of the A470, will be legally possible once more.

Motorists can obtain some fine views of the eastern crags by travelling what must be one of the most spectacular roads in Wales, the minor road from Llanuwchllyn at the southern end of Lake Bala to Dinas Mawddwy, via Cwm Cynllwyd. The descent from Bwlch y Groes down to the valley of the Afon Dyfi has some of the most breathtaking views I have ever seen from a road in these islands.

## 2.1. Aran Fawddwy from Cwm Cywarch via Drysgol
*7½ miles/12 km        4–5 hours*

The Aran ridge divides at its southern end and its arms enclose the unsuspected but impressive Cwm Cywarch, with two streams flowing into it. A narrow single-track road between walls and hedges winds up the valley, revealing a cirque of fine buttresses separated by wide gullies at its head, then crosses a large open field. The accepted car parking area is at the far side of this field, just before the road re-enters a walled lane and where several tracks converge (grid ref 853185). Please do not park anywhere else unless there are clear signs so instructing you.

From here, go forward (NW) along the walled lane for 200 yards/183m to where there's a sign for the footpath. This leads over a footbridge and up another walled lane (littered with crab apples and rowan berries in September), to a cart track and then a footpath climbing steadily north-east (with a couple of stiles) up the east flank of the grassy valley of Hengwm. Less than an hour should see you out of its confines, swinging north-west up a broad slope on the shoulder of Drysgol, then west along an almost level grassy ridge and so up to the little summit of Drws Bach. This is unmistakable as it is crowned by a monu-ment (a plaque set into a cairn of rocks and quartz lumps) to a member of the RAF St Athan Mountain Rescue Team sadly killed by lightning. There's a grand view down Hengwm to the south from here, and to the north are views of the Creiglyn Dyfi (source of the River Dovey) and the cliffs of Aran Fawddwy; the sterner crags of Aran Benllyn are a good mile further north but partly seen. Continuing beside the wire fence, the path now leads north-west and, after crossing the fence in a corner by a ladder-stile, make your way up what is now very rocky ground (occasional cairns) to the large cairn on the south summit. The main summit lies a little further across more rough ground, with a prominent trig point and a view of Creiglyn Dyfi almost direct-ly below your feet. If you are peak-bagging, you will of course want to continue over to Aran Benllyn, but it's a good mile further and I expand on this later.

Cwm Cywarch and the memorial cairn on the summit of Drysgol.

*Above:* The Aran ridge-top; Aran Benllyn seen from Aran Fawddwy.

*Opposite:* The east face of Aran Benllyn seen from Cwm Cynllwyd.

To get back to base, return from the main summit to the lower south summit, from there to the ladder-stile in the corner and then trend south-westwards. It would be more interesting to return to Drws Bach and follow the rim of the head of Hengwm out to Gwaun y Llwyni, but a line of regimented posts, alongside a wire fence, and with planks bridging bits of bog, is there to ensure that you do not wander from the official way. I'm afraid it's a dull section and notice boards defining the 'courtesy paths' block you from continuing over the height of Glasgwm, where Llyn y Fign lies almost on the top of the hill and which could give a longer, more logical finish. Fortunately, the official descent is an exhilarating one as you sharply change direction to the south-east at grid ref 839202, heading steeply down a major gully or defile, skipping along beside a torrent and passing below some of Cywarch's steepest crags. You are soon back at the car after an excellent walk.

### 2.2 Aran Benllyn from Llanuwchllyn
*7 miles/11.3km        4–5 hours*

Because of the access problems, you'll have to return the same way on this walk. Don't let that put you off for it's a grand, rough and knobbly ridge with fine views when you reach it, and it's easy going to get there.

The start is at grid ref 879297 (on the 1:50,000 map, just off edge of 1:25,000 map) where there is a good car park at the south end of the village of Llanuwchllyn, near the south end of Lake Bala, just before the point where the road turns sharply over the Afon Twrch. From here, take the metalled track beyond a gate and stile, heading south on the west side of the river. In a quarter of a mile/0.4km just past the second cattle-grid, a bridleway (stile and sign) is taken to the right, slanting across a field and around a little hill. After a couple of stiles, the bridleway veers to the right and you should leave it for the

grassy path alongside the wire fence. This leads almost due south now, climbing steadily over grassy moorland, with the occasional stile and unfortunately keeping just below the line of the ridge itself, so that the views are restricted until more height is gained. Having climbed about a thousand feet/305m since joining this path, the ground becomes much rockier and the path goes over a few rock slabs, climbing more rigorously now, to reach a noticeably steeper section of quartz-speckled hillside. The edge of steep crags shows on the skyline (Gist Ddu) and, as you climb the slope and look back, you get your first view of Llyn Lliwbran lying in a hollow below the precipice.

Just over the top of the slope is a little plateau, a tiny llyn, with a slightly bigger one nearby (Llyn Pen Aran), and a large cairn. You need to continue another couple of hundred yards and gain a little more height, however, to find the true summit cairn on a rocky eminence whose rocks are liberally splashed with quartz. These veins of protruding quartz are very noticeable here, and I've found them helpful in deciding my precise position in bad visibility.

The return is a simple reversal of the way up, quite straightforward but this time with fine views to Arenig Fawr and the Rhinog, with Snowdon in the distance.

## 2.3 Traverse of the Aran from Cwm Cywarch
*9 miles/14.5 km      5-6 hours*

There can be little doubt that the best long walk on the Aran is the complete traverse of both Aran Fawddwy and Aran Benllyn, although transport would have to be organised, of course. Ideally this would begin in Dinas Mawddwy but there are still access problems there. The Snowdonia National Park Wardens advise, however, that, by the time this book is in print, a complete traverse from Llanuwchllyn to the pass at the top of the A470 (grid ref 803170), about 3½ miles/5.6km west of Dinas

Mawddwy will be officially possible. Or in reverse, of course. I do not have the final details at time of writing.

A shorter alternative that has no problems is to start from Cwm Cywarch (grid ref 853185, *see* **2.1** above). You would then either reach Aran Fawddwy via the courtesy path up the long ravine at the north-east end of Craig Cywarch (which leads initially towards Rhydymain), swinging east along the main ridge to Aran Fawddwy or, as a better alternative to the boring bogtrot along that part of the main ridge, reach Aran Fawddwy exactly as in 2.1 above, via Hengwm and Drysgol. The summit is on top of a steep little rocky pyramid and you descend this by going north to an old wall, fence and ladder-stile on a small col. Then a steady, undulating climb over rocky ground regains most of the height lost to reach a big collapsed cairn on a subsidiary top, Erw y Ddafad ddu. Two ladder-stiles lead to the quartz-veined rocks and the cairn on the highest point of Aran Benllyn, then two more ladder-stiles lead to the biggest of the little llyns on the ridge, Llyn Pen Aran, with the large cairn of the false summit nearby. The steep descent from the rocks of the summit ridge down to the grass of the moorland follows immediately and then it's simple walking down to Llanuwchllyn.

Craig Cywarch seen from the path up Hengwm.

# Part 2: The Berwyn

| | | | | | | |
|---|---|---|---|---|---|---|
| BEST MAPS: OS 1:50,000 Landranger 125 Bala & Lake Vyrnwy & surrounding area | | | | | | |
| *Approx Distance* | *Approx Time* | *Highest Elevation Reached* | *Height Gained* | *Star Rating* | *Scramble Difficulty Grade* | *Scramble Height Gain* |
| **2.4 Pistyll Rhaeadr and the Berwyn** | | | | | | |
| 7½ miles/12km | 5 hours | 2713ft/827m | 1729ft/527m | ** | — | — |
| **2.5 A short round on the Berwyn** | | | | | | |
| 5 miles/8km | 3 hours | 2713ft/827m | 1729ft/527m | ** | — | — |

Lying about 10 miles/16km east of Lake Bala, the vast rolling moors and sheep-runs of the heather-covered Berwyn are just outside the Snowdonia National Park and most of them are of little interest to the hill-walker because of the sheer difficulty of making progress in the heather. The main Berwyn ridge, however, gives easy walking and though there are no crags as dramatic as those on the Aran, for instance, their eastern slopes are steep enough to give real dramatic interest. Add to this the famous waterfall of Pistyll Rhaeadr, one of the 'wonders' of Wales, which pours over a crag near the southern end of the main ridge and you have the ingredients for good walking.

## 2.4 Pistyll Rhaeadr and the Berwyn
*7½ miles/12.1 km        5 hours*

The best walk of all would probably be a traverse of the main ridge from north to south, starting at Hendwr (grid ref 042385, about 1½ miles/2.4km south of Cynwyd on the B4401) then by a minor road beside the telephone box leading to a right-of-way path with a succession of gates and marker-posts over boggy land, over the minor top of Moel Pearce and so to the col (Bwlch Maen Gwynedd) on the main ridge, between Cadair Bronwen and Cadair Berwyn. To do this does assume that you have transport organised at the far end, but since this is difficult for most walkers, my preferred walk starts at the southern end, at Pistyll Rhaeadr and returns much the same way.

There's a good car park (charge for parking, but also toilets and restaurant facilities) at the farm of Tan-y-pistyll (grid ref 073295). The waterfall itself (seen in the distance as you drive up the narrow approach road) is in a deep tree-girt gorge and plunges in a most impressive leap, landing in a natural rock basin with a circular arch about two-thirds of the way down, spume and spray exploding through the gap, before making a further leap to the river bed. It's an exciting sight.

Pistyll Rhaeadr, one of the traditional wonders of Wales.

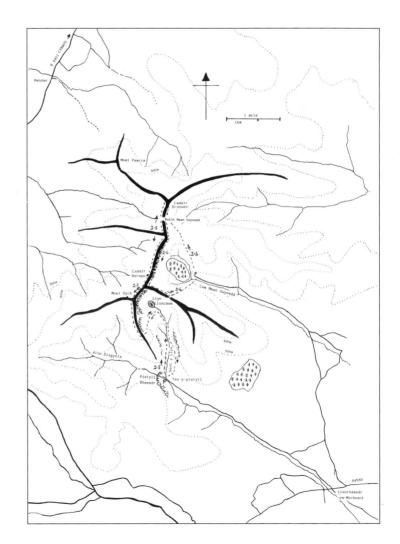

From the bridge at the foot of the falls, head right (north-east, arrow and public footpath sign) on a path through a couple of gates to the edge of a plantation, then head north on a good track up the wide valley of the Nant y Llyn, which has a fringe of little crags high up on both sides. The main track soon swings back sharply left (leading to the top of the falls) but a path beside a wire fence continues up the west bank of the stream into a more open grassy bowl where there is a sheep-fold. Just beyond the stream forks. Here cross the main stream and follow the right fork until you join another path coming up the right side of the valley. This path climbs steadily now, heading north, re-crossing the stream and heading over peaty moor to reach Llyn Lluncaws. This lies in a grassy cwm with steep slaty sides stretching directly up to Moel Sych, about 650 feet/198m above and the highest point of the Berwyn. The lake is unusual in that it is almost completely covered with a pondweed whose leaves allow only sluggish ripples, even in a breeze.

The east ridge of this cwm gives the most interesting ascent and a sketchy path up easy ground leads to and then around the rim. It skirts just below the almost unnoticed top of Moel Sych, however, so you'll need to turn off west for a few paces to touch the cairn, found piled on flat open moorland by a fence-junction. Continuing north-east, a gentle down-slope then an easy climb leads to the twin tops of Cadair Berwyn. Here there is a fringe of crags (with a good view down to Llyn Lluncaws), a large circular stone windbreak and then, across a little dip, the trig point itself. At 2713ft/827m, it is just one foot lower in height than Moel Sych but certainly much more of a summit. Beyond the trig point, the ridge continues north-east with a little dip and then a rise up to a grassy high point, shadowing a wire fence. A second cwm (Cwm Maen Gwynedd) is now visible on the east side, this time holding a conifer plantation rather than a llyn. From a junction of fences and a metal gate, a longer descent follows (about 300ft/91m), heading north and still

alongside the fence, to reach the pass at Bwlch Maen Gwynedd, where an ancient path crosses the main ridge. It's not far now up the other slope to reach the huge cairn, looking just like the prehistoric beehive-shaped stone houses of Co Kerry in southern Ireland, on the third main Berwyn summit, Cadair Bronwen. Except for another junction of wire fences there's not much else, although the top is marked on the maps as 'Bwrdd Arthur' (Arthur's Table) and there are certainly fine, long-range views to the Aran, the Rhinog and the Arenig as well as the western sector of the Snowdon group.

There is really only one way back and that is to reverse the route of approach back to Moel Sych. From here it looks tempting to stay on the ridge (along the fence line) going due south to reach the Afon Disgynfa above the falls at Pistyll Rhaeadr and I did try it for a way. The heather gave such difficult walking however (and I'm not that easily put off), that I soon traversed back to the path coming up from Llyn Lluncaws and thankfully followed it back to the llyn. From here, the path leading down the east side of the Nant y Llyn gives a delightful walk on a grassy track and the way is perfectly obvious until you are opposite the plantation again. The track continues to the tarmac road below and beyond Tan-y-pistyll and you may go this way and then walk back up the road, but most walkers will prefer to ford the stream and scramble up the opposite bank to reach the path by the plantation again, with the car park just beyond.

Looking south from Cadair Berwyn towards Nant y Llyn.

## 2.5 A short round on the Berwyn
*5 miles/8 km        3 hours*

This is a cheating way of doing the best of the main ridge, although you won't see Pistyll Rhaeadr at all. For a short day, however, it is an ideal walk.

The secret is to drive from either Llanarmon Dyffryn Ceiriog, or from Llanrhaeadr-ym-Mochnant, up Cwm Maen Gwynedd itself, gaining a lot of height to about 1640ft/500m at a point virtually at the edge of the plantation at grid ref 084326 where a car or two can park. The ancient path already mentioned (**2.4**) leads fairly steeply but easily from here to the Bwlch Maen Gwynedd, from where it is just a further short climb to the north to Cadair Bronwen. Returning to the col, the longer climb up to the metal gate and fence follows and then the easier walk across to Cadair Berwyn's two tops. Press onwards for the short descent and climb back to collect Moel Sych and then return to the dip before the re-ascent to Cadair Berwyn. From the dip, a grassy ridge, forming the northern encircling arm of Llyn Lluncaws, descends to a col at grid ref 076318 and it is then a simple descent north-eastwards to the edge of the plantation and the car.

Looking down on Llyn Lluncaws from the edge on Cadair Berwyn.

# Part 3: The Arenig

| | | | | | | |
|---|---|---|---|---|---|---|
| BEST MAPS: OS 1:50,000 Landranger 125 Bala & Lake Vyrnwy & surrounding area<br>OS 1:25,000 Outdoor Leisure 18 Snowdonia: Harlech & Bala areas | | | | | | |
| Approx Distance | Approx Time | Highest Elevation Reached | Height Gained | Star Rating | Scramble Difficulty Grade | Scramble Height Gain |
| **2.6 Arenig Fawr by its west ridge** | | | | | | |
| 6½ miles/10.5km | 4–5 hours | 2802ft/854m | 1686ft/514m | ** | — | — |
| **2.6(a) Alternative descent via the south ridge** | | | | | | |
| 11 miles/17.7km | 6 hours | 2802ft/854m | 1686ft/514m | */** | — | — |
| **2.6(b) Continuation to Moel Llyfnant** | | | | | | |
| 12 miles/19.3km | 6–7 hours | 2802ft/854m | 2484ft/757m | */** | — | — |

About 25 miles/40km to the north-east of Cadair Idris and 15 miles/24km north of the Aran ridge, the two Arenig rise above miles of wild heather moorland. They are well seen from the secondary road linking Bala to Ffestiniog on the south side of the reservoir of Llyn Celyn. The much smaller Arenig Fach has a fine llyn below north-east-facing crags but is virtually trackless and seldom visited. I found the battling with deep heather was exhausting and don't recommend the experience. On the other hand, Arenig Fawr, the higher and the much bigger of the two, is a fine mountain of five long ridges, like an octopus emerging from the heather, gradually leading to a final summit cone. Perhaps because it is so isolated, it is largely ignored; it deserves to be better known.

## 2.6 Arenig Fawr by its west ridge
*6½ miles/10.5 km        4–5 hours*
Start at grid ref 831393, about one mile from the junction of the Ffestiniog road (B4391) with the A4212. Here you can park on a large open space at the end of the dismantled railway and opposite the disused quarry. Now walk east along the quiet road for just under a mile until Llyn Celyn comes into view. On the right, a gate and stile will be found at the end of a track (grid ref 846396) slanting back, initially south-west but veering south-east across rough pasture and quickly climbing to reach Llyn Arenig Fawr. This lies below impressive crags: good-sized two-tier buttresses on the right, a wide and shallow gully down which a stream drains in the middle and a single-tiered buttress on the

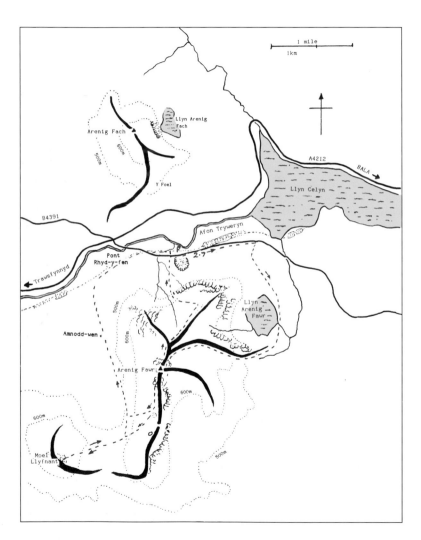

left. The summit is 2 miles/3.2km away and as yet out of sight.

The walking route chooses the best line anyway, up the long ridge seen curving round the llyn's southern shore. So cross the little dam to where a fair path (not shown on the maps) winds up over alternately rocky and peaty ground just to the left of the craggy edge of the ridge. On a level with the top of the crags on the right, cross over the remains of a wall and, keeping west, continue on the path up broad slopes, with the summit now in view, to reach the mountain's main ridge. There was once a wall along this; now little more than the posts and remains of a fence are to be found, but they lead over quartz-speckled rocks to within a very short distance of the summit trig point. Here there is also a circular stone windbreak, a few scraps of aircraft metal and a memorial to the eight crew of a US Flying Fortress 'which crashed on the Arenig 4th August 1943'.

To get the best out of the mountain and in the shortest distance I think the best way to go now is to head north-east, back over the quartz-speckled rocks by the old fence posts, along the line of the nearest ridge which curves like a sickle towards the north-west. Very little height is lost until you reach a newer fence but then descend grassy moor, still north-east, towards a broad plateau littered with large rocks and boulders and on which lie three or four little tarns. You are now on the high land due west and above Llyn Arenig Fawr and, by just walking east a little, you can find suitable vantages from which to peer down the crags to see it, and look at the grand views north-east to Llyn Celyn. The main ridge itself ends in a blunt nose of steep rocks, so that is no way down. And the wire fence, which has been your guide so far, ends abruptly at a gully. This could be descended, but not without some trepidation. So, before the slope gets too steep and rocky, it is better to swing left west into the broad cwm drained by several little streamlets and make an easy though

The windbreak and memorial on the summit rocks of Arenig Fawr.

pathless descent, keeping just left south of the Arenig quarry. There are then no obstacles and you'll reach a grassy track just before it joins the road opposite where you left the car.

### 2.6(a) Alternative descent via the south ridge
*11 miles/17.7 km      6 hours*

From the summit, the ridge continues to the south, first down a little dip to a ladder-stile over a transverse fence, then back up to another small top with a cairn. From here the view, apart from that over to the separate mountain of Moel Llyfnant to the WSW, is down a slope and to a broad and rocky ridge with about six little llyns sprinkled along it. If you descend the slope to the first of these, it is then an easy continuation to the west to pick up a good track heading north. This leads down the valley past some forestry and the derelict Amnodd-wen until, just beyond a little disused quarry, another track veers north-east and gives pleasant walking parallel to the old railway and then the road, joining the latter just before the parking place.

### 2.6(b) Continuation to Moel Llyfnant
*12 miles/19.3km      6–7 hours*

A continuation can easily be made to 'bag' Moel Llyfnant by carrying on down the south ridge and swinging south-west to the broad and boggy hause separating Moel Llyfnant from Arenig Fawr. It is then a trudge up trackless rough ground to the top and as a walk I don't think it has much to commend it.

The descent is best made by returning to the col and then taking the valley route as in **2.6(a)** above.

Looking south from the summit of Arenig Fawr.

# Part 4: The Rhinog

| BEST MAPS: | OS 1:50,000 Landranger 124 Dolgellau & surrounding area |
| | Harvey Walker's Map 1:40,000 Snowdonia South |
| | OS 1:25,000 Outdoor Leisure 18 Snowdonia: Harlech & Bala areas |

| Approx Distance | Approx Time | Highest Elevation Reached | Height Gained | Star Rating | Scramble Difficulty Grade | Scramble Height Gain |
|---|---|---|---|---|---|---|
| **2.7 A Round of Y Llethr and Diffwys** | | | | | | |
| 11 miles/17.7km | 5 hours | 2480ft/756m | 2283ft/696m | ** | — | — |
| **2.8 A Round of Rhinog Fawr and Rhinog Fach from Cwm Nantcol** | | | | | | |
| 6½ miles/10.5km | 5–6 hours | 2362ft/720m | 2854ft/870m | *** | — | — |
| **2.9 Rhinog Fawr by the Roman Steps** | | | | | | |
| 4¾ miles/7.6km | 3½ hours | 2362ft/720m | 1854ft/565m | ** | — | — |
| **2.9(a) Rhinog Fawr by the Roman Steps: return via Gloyw Llyn** | | | | | | |
| 4½ miles/7.2km | 3½ hours | 2362ft/720m | 1854ft/565m | *** | — | — |
| **2.10 Craig Wion and Rhinog Fawr from Cwm Bychan** | | | | | | |
| 7 miles/11.3km | 5 hours | 2362ft/720m | 2000ft/610m | *** | — | — |

Separated from Cadair Idris by the beautiful Mawddach estuary and valley, the ridge of the Rhinog is most extraordinary in that it contains both the wildest, roughest walking in North Wales as well as some of its easiest and grassiest. Y Llethr and Diffwys, at 2480ft/756m and 2461ft/750m respectively, are the main peaks on the southern, grassy part of the ridge, which extends all the way to Barmouth. Rhinog Fach and Rhinog Fawr, at 2336ft/712m and 2362ft/720m respectively, are the main ones on the northern part of the ridge, where simple walking is an adventure in itself.

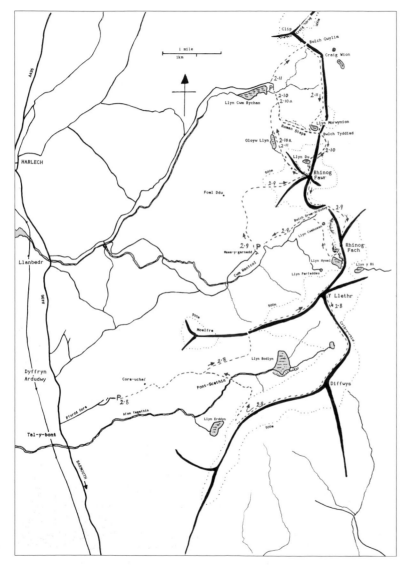

I don't know anything about the geology of the southern half but the northern is made up of hard gritstones, all that remains of an upthrust in geological aeons past called the Harlech Dome. What remains of it now is an ancient landscape sprinkled with lakelets, where bare rocks and little crags are like bones sticking up out of a wrinkled skin of heather. This heather on the Rhinog is famous for exacting excessive effort in order to make progress over it. The stories exaggerate, but not much. In fact, the heather itself is not the problem; it is that it conceals a tremendous variety of underlying rocks, from huge boulders to sharp-edged slabs and spikes of rock waiting to trap the unwary ankle. Good solid boots are essential. Despite this, the rewards of walking here are great, including splendid and very dramatic mountain scenery, hidden llyns suddenly seen and a great sense of achievement at the end of the day. And there are some paths. Many paths are admittedly made by sheep (and on the two Rhinog by feral goats as well), but sheep and goats don't build cairns, so you should be able to spot the difference.

## 2.7 A Round of Y Llethr and Diffwys
*11 miles/17.7km        5 hours*

This very good round of the southern part of the range is essentially a circuit of the wide cwm containing the Llyn Bodlyn Reservoir, whose outflow is the Afon Ysgethin. The walking is mostly on good tracks and grassy paths, with fine views. There are no access problems, although some paths are permissive and may be officially closed for one day a year just to maintain that status.

The start of this walk is near Tal-y-bont, about 6 miles/9.6km south of Harlech on the A496 coast road. As soon as you see the

Looking north from Diffwys over Crib-y-Rhiw to Y Llethr.

The two Rhinog seen beyond Llyn Hywel from Y Llethr.

sign for 'Tal-y-bont' on the northern edge of the village, turn left (coming from Harlech) off the main road (there is a letterbox on the wall as well) and onto a metalled road, signed Fford Gors, between two stone pillars. Drive up this past a caravan site to reach two more pillars where you turn right and follow the metalled road round the farm buildings and hall at Cors y Gedol until you reach two gates, one ahead and one on the right, grid ref 603231. There is plenty of parking space in the lane although you can't drive any further beyond the gate ahead.

A walled bridle-way continues eastwards beyond the gate, passes by the ruins of Cors-uchaf and continues north-east, with the isolated hill of Moelfre ahead. The skyline to the right, roughly east, is the long ridge running from Diffwys to Barmouth; Y Llethr is still hidden behind Moelfre. Keep on this track towards Llyn Bodlyn, also still out of sight at present, and stay on it when (at grid ref 628237) a footpath marked by yellow arrows leads off to the right, slightly downhill: this will be used on the return. (This path leads to the old stone packhorse bridge of Pont-Scethin, which carried the old London to Harlech main road, and then, after crossing the Afon Ysgethin, it winds up onto the ridge and will be used on the return.) A little further along the track, Y Llethr comes into sight, a rounded, grassy and unexciting looking hump seen from here, with a wall running up to its top. Don't let that put you off.

The track continues to Llyn Bodlyn which can now just be glimpsed below steep crags, but you should now leave it, going north to reach the low col between Moelfre and Y Llethr (grid ref 638246). Either take the sketchy track that turns off the bridleway or, if you miss that (and it is not obvious), wait until the bridleway takes a sharp turn right as it meets a wall coming down the hillside from the left and then turn left (north) alongside it. You will soon meet the long wall coming down from Y Llethr and can gain height steadily alongside that, heading north-east up long grassy slopes to reach a wall junction on the main ridge just south of and below the summit. The grassy top is about 250ft/76m higher and there is a cairn and another wall junction.

It's a grand place with views west to the sea and south to the great wall of Cadair Idris but you must make a point of walking a little to the north-east alongside the wall on the broad summit ridge; you will get a fine view of Rhinog Fach, with the dramatic Llyn Hywel below its crags. Rhinog Fawr can be seen beyond, its overlapping rock strata looking grey and almost bare of vegetation from here. To spot the tiny Llyn y Bi on the right side (east) of the sharp ridge connecting Y Llethr with Rhinog Fach,

you will need to continue a little further along the ridge, beyond the cairn marking the point where a rough path descends towards Llyn Hywel.

Returning to the summit cairn, descend to the south, down the grassy slope to the wall junction and then follow the line of the ridge, south, beside the wall, towards Diffwys, whose strata look like many saucers piled up one on another. There is a path and it leads along the rocky little ridge of Crib-y-rhiw but, although Llyn Bodlyn is in view, you won't catch sight of the much smaller Llyn Dulyn until you take a backward look as you are scaling the slope towards the trig point found just over the wall on the top of Diffwys.

Leaving the top, the ridge continues generally towards the south-west, still with its accompanying wall, and a gentle descent beside it, now on grass again, crosses a shallow col and then up and over two more slight eminences to reach another wall junction (grid ref 639225). Either continue just beyond the junction to a cairn marking the point where a green path crosses the ridge, then turn back sharp right (north) down this path, or cut the corner alongside the wall to reach the same path. It skirts high above Llyn Erddyn, avoiding steeper rocky ground, and winds down to reach Pont-Scethin. All that remains is the short climb up the hillside beyond to link up with the outward route.

## 2.8 A Round of Rhinog Fawr and Rhinog Fach from Cwm Nantcol

*6½ miles/10.5km        5–6 hours*

Drive up the lovely valley of Nantcol from Llanbedr, a few miles south of Harlech on the A496, and park at the road end, just outside the last bit of driveway to the farm, at Maes-y-garnedd

(grid ref 642270). Here you are at the head of a wide cwm, with three mountains on the skyline. Y Llethr is on the right (south-east), Rhinog Fach is in the centre and, beyond the deep gap of the Bwlch Drws-Ardudwy, which is one of the only two passes across the range, Rhinog Fawr lies on the left. This circuit goes north to the col between Foel Ddu and Rhinog Fawr, east over Rhinog Fawr and then over Rhinog Fach. It is not a walk for misty weather or for anyone wearing fancy footwear. It's tough: it's superb.

After paying your car-park fee at the historic farmhouse (which was, I understand, the birthplace of Colonel John Jones, the regicide, who signed the death warrant of King Charles I and later paid for it with his own life, being hanged, drawn and quartered in 1660), take the track going north from the parking place. (The other track to the north-east goes to Bwlch Drws Ardudwy and is the return route.) Go through the gate ahead and turn left (footpath sign) just in front of the house of Nantcol, then quite steeply up the grassy field beyond to the north-west, to reach a gap in its wall with a hurdle-gate. Immediately beyond the gap, turn right onto a grassy way just outside the wall and slant upwards to the north-west, with occasional white marker posts, towards the col between the hilltops of Foel Ddu and Rhinog Fawr. (On the maps two paths are shown going up onto the high land behind Nantcol but neither of them is very clear on the ground and the way described does become clearer once you start spotting the white posts.)

Beyond a transverse wall with an iron gate, continue over sheep pasture (more posts) to reach a ladder-stile in a field corner and then swing north over much rougher pasture towards a solitary cairn clearly seen on the skyline ahead. In fact, the sky-line is further away, as you will realise once you have crossed another transverse wall by a stile to reach the cairn, and what

The dramatic crag-top view down to Llyn Hywel from Rhinog Fach.

signs of a path there were now disappear, but Rhinog Fach is now much nearer and only about 1000ft/305m higher. Slant eastwards towards a transverse wall; on this side is rough pasture, on the other the slopes are quite definitely heather and they rise towards Rhinog Fawr, with what appears to be a subsidiary top and a cairn in the intermediate distance. There is a gap in the wall near the lower corner of the field and beyond that is a path, or sheep-track, almost disappearing in the heather and leading towards Rhinog Fawr. If you don't spot this path, it doesn't matter, for the heather is no worse here than on many a Yorkshire moor or Scottish hillside; it is about calf-deep but the underlying ground is not the tumbled mass of rocks that is yet to come.

Head for Rhinog Fawr over the heather and you will find cairned paths on the upper slopes which, used with common-sense, will lead you quite nicely to the top. If you should find yourself on a fairly good path traversing along the 600m contour towards Llyn Du but below the final steep slopes, that too could be used, for it reaches a shoulder above Llyn Du and intersects with the path from the Roman Steps and you can complete the last rough scramble up that route (see **2.9** overleaf). There is a trig point on a pile of rocks, a rock shelter and a large cairn, with a fine view to the north, over a steep drop down to Llyn Du. The path from Cwm Bychan and the Roman Steps comes up this way.

To the south-east of the trig point there are two more cairns on the edge of a short descent down to a shoulder, from where there's a good view to Rhinog Fach, the next objective. An obvious path leads down a first stony slope onto the shoulder but then forks. The right-hand path leads to the edge of a steep and unattractive looking gully which is in fact the top of a fault-line leading virtually to the bottom of the long face to be descended and there is no doubt but that you *could* go down this way, but it is inadvisable. Better to take the left fork, going further east, where a none-too-obvious path descends to avoid a first belt of steeper, broken rocks and then, having outflanked that, swings back right along the top of another band of chaotically jumbled rock. Either keep going right and then descend a little gully with some simple scrambling near the end of this rock-band or, more easily, go left again to find a longer but easier descent. The terrain is so rough on this flank of the mountain, jumbled rocks, spikes, boulders, scree, slabs, that only the occasional cairn will keep you on course; aim south-east towards the gap of the Bwlch Drws-Ardudwy nearly 1200ft/366m below. At about 300ft/91m above the Bwlch, the way goes down a last gully, a chaos of blocks and sharp-edged rocks partly hidden by the heather, yet clearly in regular use by at least one herd of feral goats that moved away as I clattered down myself. Below this gully, the path (or goat-track) leads to a hogget-hole through the wall and it is certainly easier to crawl through than climb over, leading to the large cairn on the Bwlch just below. On the descent, you will have been able to see the path going up the opposite slope towards Rhinog Fach. Fortunately it looks infinitely easier than the descent of the Fawr, which must be one of the few mountains in Snowdonia which need more time to go down than to go up, and so it proves.

A steep runnel through the heather leads directly upwards from the col (and even slipping backwards one step in every three seems easy now) leading shortly to a shoulder. From here the easiest line (although a direct one up the ridge on the right is feasible) is to follow the path slanting across the cwm below the ridge which then curves back rightwards to reach its top. This point, where there is a cairn, proves to be on the northern end of the summit ridge and there's a good view from here back to the Fawr. It might also be worth mentioning that there is a descent from here also, a path going down through heather to the south-west which could prove useful if you are running out of time. The main top, however, is a little higher and further

away along the ridge and must be visited, for just beyond it is a most dramatic view.

Continue only a hundred paces or so beyond the summit cairn towards Y Llethr, seen clearly ahead, and a path leads directly to where you are perched on a rock platform, on the very edge of steep crags with a terrific vertical drop to the waters of Llyn Hywel below. Until you reach this platform, although you see Y Llethr clearly enough across the divide. Llyn Hywel itself is not seen until the very last instant and then it is with a gasp of surprise. It is especially memorable because great slabs of rock on the narrow ridge between Y Llethr and Rhinog Fach plunge at an astonishingly steep angle into its waters. On the other side of the ridge, where there is an almost identical cwm, lies the smaller Llyn y Bi.

Perched here on these crags, it seems unlikely that there is any direct descent to the shore of Llyn Hywel and indeed the easiest descent is possibly to return the few paces to the summit and then go leftwards (east) to descend alongside a wall built down a steep and shaly slope to the south. But there is a direct descent starting from the rock platform, almost 600ft/183m down a path on the very right-hand edge of the crags. This looks and *is* very steep and there are two little bits of grade 1 scrambling down two small gullies, but the path is clearly there. Further down, this path trends to the right away from the rocks and walking down some scree is unavoidable, but it is soon over.

From the outlet of the lake, a well-marked path leads besides the stream down a depression, heading slightly to the west of north. The stream soon disappears below ground, although you can hear it gurgling below the stones nearby, but the path continues, descending towards the tiny Llyn Cwmhosan. Don't take the path which forks off to the left about half way down towards the valley for it peters out in rough ground very quickly. The main path is tough enough, like walking down Cwm Tryfan, but it soon reaches the lower valley and here you can pick up the Bwlch Drws-Ardudwy path. This now leads more easily, over occasional gritstone slabs like those on the Roman Steps path (*see* **2.9** below) to arrive precisely at the parking place. You'll look back up this lovely valley, its two tough guardians at its head, not only with pleasure but with a real sense of achievement.

### 2.9 Rhinog Fawr by the Roman Steps
*4³/₄ miles/7.6km        3¹/₂ hours*

The thought of Roman legions tramping over the Bwlch Tyddiad, however unlikely, does stir the imagination and no doubt helps to make this walk the most popular one in the Rhinog. The normal route is straight up and back by the same way but in **2.9(a)** I suggest a more interesting and a shorter return.

Take the attractive but very narrow road to the head of Cwm Bychan, with good views of the rugged country ahead in the last two miles, until Llyn Cwm Bychan comes suddenly into view. The car park is at the far end of the lake; you pay a small fee into the tin box on the entrance gate.

Climb a ladder-stile from the car park onto a good footpath signed 'Roman Steps Bwlch Tyddiant' (sic). In about 100yds/91m, cross another stile, then the obvious path leads gently up through a wooded valley of oak and silver birch to reach a last ladder-stile over the enclosing fence. Almost immediately the trees end and you are out onto open heather-covered mountainside, crossing a little pack-horse bridge and then climbing gently up towards a narrow defile ahead. The path quickly becomes a causeway on stone slabs laid to form a footway across the heather, particularly once you have passed through a break in a wall, although there are very few slabs laid

in the manner of a staircase; indeed, almost all of them are laid flat on the ground. After about half an hour, you pass through a gap in a second wall, where there is a small standing stone and a wooden post; in a further ten minutes, you should be at the top of the pass, the Bwlch Tyddiad, an exceptionally stony place where there is a large cairn and a good view down the other side. You will have gained just under 1000ft/305m in height so far, with slightly less still to win.

Continue downhill on the east side of the bwlch for about 200yds/183m and a small cairn marks the place where a much narrower path leads off to the right (south). This gives very much rougher walking now, hopping from boulder to boulder over bog and heather, gaining height and swinging from south to south-west to reach Llyn Du, cradled beneath the terraced buttresses of Rhinog Fawr whose summit is still 700ft/213m above.

About 500ft/152m of part-walking part-scrabbling on a poorly-defined path up a wide and boulder-choked gully, just to the right of the summit, leads to a broad shoulder and a temporary easing of the angle. (A path from the direction of Foel Ddu reaches this same point.) Here you may pause for breath before tackling the last steep 200ft/61m to reach the trig point, the stone shelter and the various cairns on the summit. The views are very extensive and well worth the effort.

The return is a straightforward reversal of the ascent and should give no problems.

### 2.9(a) Rhinog Fawr by the Roman Steps: return via Gloyw Llyn
*4¹/₂ miles/7.2km        3¹/₂ hours*

Given good visibility, this return from the summit of Rhinog Fawr is both shorter in distance and surprisingly free from the ankle-cracking terrain found on the southern slopes of the mountain.

From the summit, return towards the Llyn Du as far as the shoulder 200ft/61m or so below the top. From here, you can look down to the north-west to the Gloyw Llyn, with Llyn Cwm Bychan in the valley beyond. In the near distance, there is a much smaller llyn, only shown on the OS 1:25,000 map. Linking your position on the shoulder with the Gloyw Llyn is a discontinuous line of overlapping rock slabs and edges slanting down in just the direction you need, and the great advantage of these is that you can walk much of the way on flat and visible rock and not have to worry about sharp-edged boulders hidden in the heather. At the level of the Llyn Du, follow the edge of the wall near its west end and stay on the faint path that leads north-west down a defile (grid ref 653295) until it goes through a gap in a wall. Here, turn left immediately and scramble up onto the edge of more splendid slabs that then lead downhill again, almost without break, to the basin where the lovely Gloyw Llyn lies. From the northern tip of the llyn (I doubt if you will find the path shown on the maps), you will find a well-used path descends directly towards the east end of Llyn Cwm Bychan. Turn right (east) when you reach the trees and wire fence again and follow it down to a metal gate. A little further on, on the right, is the ladder-stile on the main path and the car park is close by.

## 2.10 Craig Wion and Rhinog Fawr from Cwm Bychan
*7 miles/11.3km      5 hours*

If you have by now acquired a taste (and respect) for the magnificently rough and rugged Rhinog, you may like to try this longer round covering some of the wild country to the north of Rhinog Fawr. You will have no problems with crowds of people, I assure you.

Looking down to the Gloyw Llyn from Rhinog Fawr.

Start from the car park at the head of Llyn Cwm Bychan (grid ref 646315), then, from the barn at the side of the road by the car park, go over a ladder-stile next to it and up the field to the north-east. There is a finger-post pointing to 'Clip', the eye-catching, domed mountain-top ahead, which you can see from the road. Its summit cone looks from here as if it is almost completely bare rock, although if you scramble on it you will find that the bare rock walls are separated by broad heather terraces. Beyond the stile, white painted arrows lead you slanting up the steep sheep pasture, curving left then right again, onto what soon becomes an obvious and easy path, with finger-posts, heading just to the east of the steep crags (Craig Ddrwg) on the flank of Clip towards the Bwlch Gwylim. Just before reaching the top of the pass (the path continues to link with Llyn Trawsfynydd), you will reach a transverse wall. Here turn south-east, for you are now on the main ridge-spine of the Rhinog; the easy walking is over, the adventure begins.

Shadow the wall over the rugged ground to Craig Wion, with two little llyns hiding just on the eastern side of the ridge. After the wall ends, it is simply a case of working out your own route to the south. Rhinog Fawr is an obvious objective, since it fills the skyline ahead, but the way is far from direct and you will be dodging and weaving over and round heather and rocks in profusion, continually gaining a little height only to lose it again. It is tough, but greatly satisfying going. When Llyn Morwynion comes in sight, make for its eastern edge and then continue round the little rise beyond to join the Roman Steps path on its last rise to Bwlch Tyddiad. This stony pass, with its evidence of human passage, will feel like a return to civilisation after a journey in the wilderness. Go 200yds/183m over the top of the pass to the east but then turn off and follow the narrower path to Llyn Du and Rhinog Fawr, as in **2.9** above. Complete a very good round by descending via Gloyw Llyn to Cwm Bychan, as in **2.9(a)**.

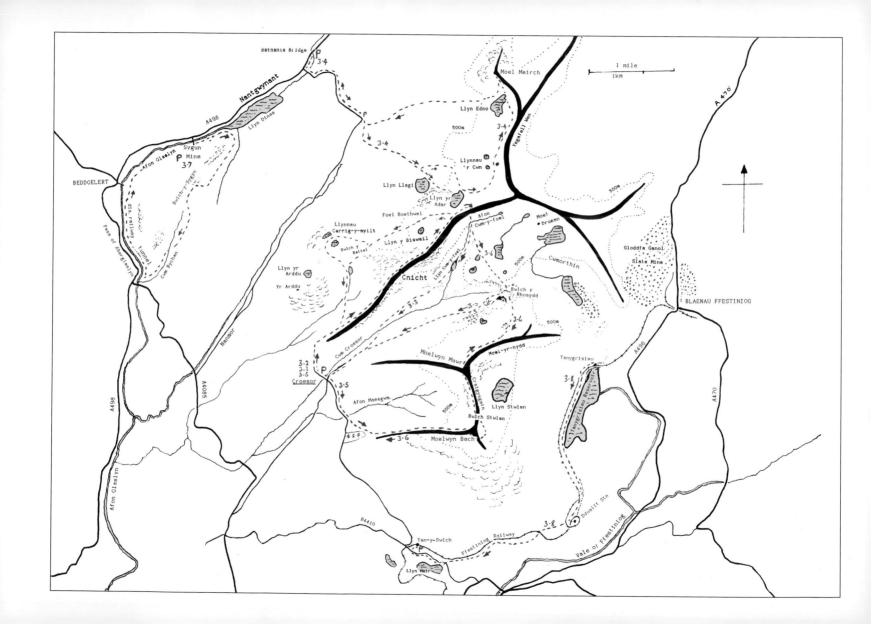

# 3: Moel Siabod, Cnicht and The Moelwyn

| | | | | | | |
|---|---|---|---|---|---|---|
| BEST MAPS: | OS 1:50,000 Landranger 115 Snowdon & surrounding area, plus sheet 124 Dollgellau & surrounding area (both needed) OS 1:25,000 Outdoor Leisure Sheet 17 Snowdonia: Snowdon area; Sheet 18 Snowdonia: Harlech & Bala areas. At this scale, Sheet 16 Snowdonia: Conwy Valley is also needed for walk 3.1 only | | | | | |

| Approx Distance | Approx Time | Highest Elevation Reached | Height Gained | Star Rating | Scramble Difficulty Grade | Scramble Height Gain |
|---|---|---|---|---|---|---|
| **3.1 Moel Siabod by the east ridge** | | | | | | |
| 5 miles/8km | 4 hours | 2861ft/872m | 2237ft/682m | *** | — | — |
| **3.2 Cnicht by the south-west ridge, return by Llynnau Cerrig-y-myllt** | | | | | | |
| 6½ miles/10.5km | 4–5 hours | 2260ft/689m | 1699ft/518m | *** | — | — |
| **3.3 Cnicht by the south-west ridge, return by Cwm Croesor** | | | | | | |
| 6 miles/9.7km | 4 hours | 2260ft/689m | 1699ft/518m | ** | — | — |
| **3.4 Llyn Llagi and the Dog Lakes** | | | | | | |
| 7½ miles/12km | 4 hours | 2132ft/650m | 2067ft/630m | **/*** | — | — |
| **3.5 Moelwyn Bach, Moelwyn Mawr and Cwm Croesor** | | | | | | |
| 7 miles/11.3km | 5 hours | 2526ft/770m | 2375ft/724m | *** | — | — |
| **3.6 Cnicht, Moelwyn Mawr and Moelwyn Bach** | | | | | | |
| 10 miles/16km | 6 hours | 2526ft/770m | 3507ft/1069m | *** | — | — |
| **3.7 Cwm Bychan from the Sygun Copper Mine** | | | | | | |
| 6 miles/9.6km | 3½ hours | 1043ft/318m | 869ft/265m | **/*** | — | — |

| Approx Distance | Approx Time | Highest Elevation Reached | Height Gained | Star Rating | Scramble Difficulty Grade | Scramble Height Gain |
|---|---|---|---|---|---|---|
| **3.8 The Ffestiniog Railway Walk** | | | | | | |
| 5 miles/8km | 2½ hours | 623ft/190m | n/a | ** | — | — |

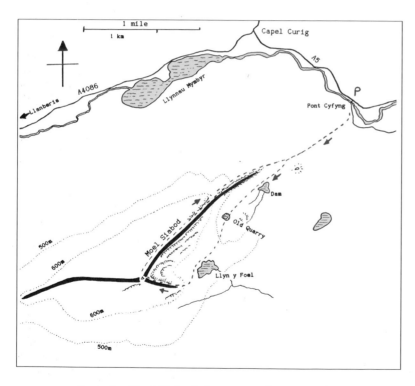

*Opposite:* Moel Siabod: the eastern flank seen from the dam.

This area of high land, bounded by the beautiful wooded valley of the Nantgwynant on the west and the Vale of Ffestiniog and the slate mines of Blaenau Ffestiniog on the east, contains in my opinion some of the most attractive walking country anywhere in the whole of North Wales. Particularly in the area between Cnicht and Moel Siabod there are few signs of the quarrying that has ravaged the eastern flanks. What paths there are seem to weave around little outcrops of knobbly volcanic rock; there are more little lakes to be found here than elsewhere in Snowdonia and they lie like jewels on grassy ledges or hidden in rocky caskets; the land has a wrinkled and crinkled appearance. It is also, in general, less frequented, perhaps because access is not always obvious. If my descriptions fall short, I hope my pictures will give some idea of how delightful it is.

### 3.1 Moel Siabod by the east ridge
*5 miles/8km        4 hours*

A view of Moel Siabod from the A4086 heading from Capel Curig towards Snowdon would suggest that it consists of bland and boring grass slopes, but there is a good glimpse of Moel Siabod from the A5 going west just beyond Betws-y-Coed, when it can be properly seen for what it is, a bold and impressive mountain with a great corrie or cwm on its flank. It is justly popular either as a straightforward ascent and return or, more interestingly, by way of Llyn y Foel and Moel Siabod's east ridge, which gives

some short sections of good but very easy scrambling.

Parking is possible in either of two laybys beside the A5 just south of Pont Cyfyng, where the gorge of the beautiful Afon Llugwy is bridged near some fine waterfalls (grid ref 734572).

Having crossed the bridge, take the second tarmac lane on the right which leads steeply uphill through woods. Turn sharp right where an old quarry railway line reaches the road, continue past farm buildings onto the shoulder of the moor and Moel Siabod comes into view ahead. Just beyond the last derelict house, the track forks. The left-hand one veers towards extensive and interesting derelict quarry workings and dwellings but the other goes straight ahead, still almost on the level, towards the mountain and is followed to the next parting of the ways. Then, if all you want is a quick dash to the top, just swing to the right over a ladder-stile and keep going uphill. (This is my recommended *descent* route.) For the much more interesting east ridge approach, take the turn off to the left (gate and ladder-stile). The good track quickly skirts below the rocky north-west end of Moel Siabod, alongside the dam which soon appears, then climbs gently past spoil heaps and a few derelict buildings to reach the water-filled upper quarry. The track ends here, but a path leads over sometimes very boggy ground to a broad col. Beyond it, straight ahead, is a good view of the rocky east ridge, rising at a fairly constant angle of about 30° but in two steps. Llyn y Foel lies in a rocky hollow at the foot of the ridge. It's not so grand as Llyn y Cau below Cadair Idris, but it is almost in that class; there is a fine atmosphere about the place, with the summit of Moel Siabod still 1100ft/335m above.

Descending slightly towards Llyn y Foel, the path skirts it on its north side and then goes round the toe of the ridge itself to the left (south) before actually joining it about 200feet/61m

Nearing the top of the East Ridge on Moel Siabod.

higher. From here, the path twists and turns up the ridge: around outcrops, up little grooves and across little rocky ledges. It is fairly polished here and there, and occasionally hands are needed for assurance; under icy or very wet conditions, it could be more awkward, but there is little sense of exposure and in the dry it is most enjoyable.

At about 2450ft/747m, a shoulder is reached; this is in fact the top of a buttress whose steep side faces towards Llyn y Foel. The summit is still about 400ft/122m higher but the going becomes more straightforward and easier, although there is one last slabby bit just before the final pull up to the trig point and, about a hundred paces away, a large circular stone windbreak.

Reaching this point on one occasion, in high wind and thick cloud, I was intrigued to see a large, shapeless orange-coloured mound near it. Looking closer, I spotted rucksacks sticking out from under the edge, heard voices and realised that I was looking at a huge bivouac sack sheltering a group of kids.

Looking from the summit to the south-west, a ridge-line can be distinguished, leading for 5 miles/8km or so to the delightful rocky top of Moel Meirch; this gives an enjoyable traverse, eventually to the Nantgwynant. It is worth considering for another occasion when you can organise transport. But the outstanding view from the summit is due west to Snowdon; that to the Glyders on the other hand is dull and uninteresting.

The return to Pont Cyfyng is to the north-east, along the splendid summit ridge. This, like that of Cnicht, is virtually level for almost a mile/1.6km and is quite rocky, with steep crags dropping away to the east (right) and stony boulder-fields to the west. The rock is in great slabs, many of them laid across the spine of the ridge and jumbled on each other so that you progress up and down little grooves, steps and slabs; in bad conditions or high wind it needs treating with respect. Suddenly the rock ends and a steeper descent follows down grass and then down a long shallow groove or gutter, only returning to the last

few spiky bits of the ridge proper just before it fades into moorland. The path now leads obviously back down to the farm buildings and the way of ascent.

### 3.2 Cnicht by the south-west ridge: return by Llynnau Cerrig-y-myllt
*6½ miles/10.5km          4–5 hours*

(Note that the best maps for this walk and 3.3 are 1:50,000 Landranger 115 and 1:25,000 Outdoor Leisure 17 but the starting place, Croesor, is just off both these maps. It can be found on Landranger 1:50,000 124 Dolgellau.)

This splendid mountain is frequently referred to as the 'Matterhorn of Wales' and its elegant cone-shaped profile seen from the south is certainly reminiscent of that of the Matterhorn seen on the approach to Zermatt. But from almost any other direction it is seen to be more a long ridge than a cone. It rears up amidst some superbly wild mountain country, with a profusion of little tarns or llyns lying in rocky hollows all around its northern arc, while its relatively low height (2260ft/689m) means that it is accessible even on a short day. It even has a delightful north-west ridge which is, for some odd reason, largely ignored.

The start is in the little village of Croesor at grid ref 632447, reached by driving north-east off the A4085 between Penrhyndeudraeth and Beddgelert and up Cwm Croesor (with the 'Matterhorn' view ahead). Turn left at the crossroads and the car park is just on the right. From here, go north-west over the stream next to the car park, up the village street past the school, over a hump and down to a gate and stile, after which a stony walled track leads uphill through a wood. Leaving the wood and

just before another gate/stile, a 'walking-man' marker points the way to the north-east, and there's your mountain, more or less straight ahead. A good slaty track now leads up the west side of the long south-west ridge, which you see end on, and when the slates run out, a flooded level can be spotted going into the hillside just on the right of the track. Ahead and to the left (north-west) just across the intervening valley is the fascinating ground that will be visited on the return, little cliffs and outcrops of rough, knobbly rock separated by ledges of heather and holding little pools. A further sign points you onto the ridge itself, with a view to the Moelwyn across Cwm Croesor. Just above some old workings, the path goes over a wall and wire fence by a stile to reach the foot of the final ridge proper. Gaining about 700ft/213m in the process, you climb steadily now to reach a shoulder and a little col. From here, a steeper slanting rock buttress rises and the way up is by its lower edge, an easy 50ft/15m scramble (hands needed) with easier ground above, leading to the first of several tops of Cnicht. This little scramble should not give any problems but in adverse conditions or in descent there should be no doubts about the competence of the party.

*Opposite:* From Llynnau Cerrig-y-myllt looking north up Nantgwynant.
*Below:* The south-west ridge of Cnicht, on the approach from Croesor.

The view towards Snowdon is very fine in good weather; to the west can be seen the hills of the Nantlle Ridge on the skyline and, hidden until now, the glint of light on the Llynnau Cerrig-y-myllt. Continue along the north-east ridge which is broad and rocky, that marvellous, rough, solid, knobbly rock that has given little purchase to the heather and is a delight to walk over. There are four separate tops on the ridge, but no cairns on any of them, and after the fourth the ridge begins to decline gently, Llyn y Biswail is passed on the left below and ahead shines Llyn yr Adar. Just before reaching this latter, swing left (north-west) towards the little rocky height of Foel Boethwel and then make your way down largely untracked ground to the south-west, below the ramparts of Cnicht, to reach a col, the Bwlch y Battel. A little-used path goes through this pass and you will return to it shortly, but first you must not miss seeing the Llynnau Cerrig-y-myllt which are near at hand.

From the Bwlch y Battel go west, winding a way round little craglets and through the defiles between them and you will soon reach the upper of the two llynnau, hiding in a rocky hollow. This is delightful, enchanted mountain country; a host of Welsh pixies could be hiding here. Looking up that broad north-west ridge to Cnicht high above, bathed in evening light, you may spot all their tiny battlements and redoubts chiselled from the bare rock. Before heading back to Croesor wander over to the south-west, over more of this fantastic rock landscape, to discover Llyn yr Arddu cupped in another rocky goblet and giving you yet more glimpses of the haunting beauty of this delightful mountainscape.

You will have to leave eventually, of course, so just wend your way eastwards and find the path that runs from Nanmor over the Bwlch y Battel and which you reached earlier. This path goes through an obvious gap between Cnicht's south-west ridge and Yr Arddu and as you follow it to the south-west you will soon realise that you have linked up with your outward journey.

### 3.3 Cnicht by the south-west ridge: return by Cwm Croesor
*6 miles/9.7km        4 hours*
*(Map: OS sheet 18 at 1:25,000 scale is also needed)*

This is the more usual way of traversing Cnicht, with a return down Cwm Croesor. The ascent to Cnicht is precisely as described above, but then continue along the ridge to the north-east almost as far as Llyn yr Adar (trying to descend earlier will lead onto very steep ground high above Llyn Cwm-y-foel). The old path from Nantgwynant to Blaenau Ffestiniog curves round the north-eastern side of the llyn and can be used for about 300yds/274m from the edge of the llyn until it crosses the little Afon Cwm-y-foel. This drains into the Llyn Cwm-y-foel in upper Cwm Croesor and you can traverse along its south-eastern shore to the dam at its end. From here, you will see a pipeline going down to the valley below while a path, from the same point, takes a higher, slanting line across the lower flanks of Cnicht, keeping well above the valley floor for more than a mile, but joining it eventually. All that remains is a walk down the stony track at the bottom to the car park.

### 3.4 Llyn Llagi and the Dog Lakes
*7½ miles/12km        4 hours*

This is a marvellous excursion into more of the rugged terrain of the Moelwyn, visiting Llyn Llagi, the 'Dog Lakes' (Llynnau'r Cwn) and the beautiful Llyn Edno. The highest land visited, the undulating ridge of Ysgafell Wen, is comparatively low. This could be awkward country to navigate in mist, although if you are lucky enough to be here on one of those mountain days when the mist is drifting around but clearing occasionally, so that the landscape emerges and then dissolves before your eyes, it would be even more delightful.

The south-eastern cwms of Snowdon seen from a shoulder on Cnicht.

Parking is virtually assured in the big car park in the Gwynant valley at Bethania Bridge (grid ref 627506), then walk south-west down the A498 beside the Afon Glaslyn until you can cross and turn left, south-east, up the single-track road which climbs up to the higher Nanmor valley. It is about a mile/1.6km up the winding lane until, just past a house called Bryn Bedd, the road reaches a level and turns sharply right, south-west, in front of a wood. During the week, or on an off-season visit, it may be possible to park up to three cars at this point, just before the bend (grid ref 637494) but there is no other parking possibility.

There are two footpath signs on the bend. One is marked 'Edno' and points down a track which you should take for about a hundred yards/91m. When it turns sharply back left (another footpath sign), go straight forward instead, round a bend and through a gate and towards a building with two gables (Llwyhyrhwch). (You can also reach this same point by following a right-of-way path eastwards from the converted chapel at grid ref 635490, although it is not as obvious as the way described.) Immediately before reaching the gabled house, turn left (east) on the footpath directly in front of it (sign) and go up the field to its top right-hand corner and through a gate immediately below a little rock outcrop. Follow the path up through the rocks to reach a boggy basin at the top, cross the little stream and then continue south-east, gently climbing on a grassy path through a delightful terrain beside a lively stream. This stream actually flows from Llyn yr Adar (out of sight from here), and it can be seen on the skyline ahead, tumbling in a series of falls down steep and craggy mountainside into the almost circular Llyn Llagi below which, although also out of sight at present, is soon reached.

The path swings east, slanting towards a col on the skyline to the left, avoiding the steep hillside in front and then turning south towards Llyn yr Adar, but an interesting way can be found directly up this same hillside. It is too precipitous to follow the precise line of the stream, even for a confirmed gill-scrambler, but you can weave an easy way up little ledges and tongues of grass to the left of the series of waterfalls. When you get to the top, there's Llyn yr Adar (and a view of Cnicht) immediately ahead, while below and to the north-west, is a fine view of Llyn Llagi and of Snowdon (looking up the Watkin Path route).

Here you are at an altitude of about 1900ft/579m and a broad rocky ridge now stretches to the north-east from near Llyn yr Adar to where the Llynnau'r Cwn lie hidden about half a mile away. The first of these to be reached, and the most attractively situated, is surrounded by little crags. At a lower level, visible from the first, is a second lake, this time encircled by grass. The third is just a bit further away, also in a grassy basin but backed by part of the Ysgafell Wen ridge. From the ridge, which is not particularly well-defined, but has a line of old iron fence posts along its top and a sketchy path beside them, the rocky height of Moel Meirch can be seen to the north, with the glint of light on the waters of Llyn Edno before it. This is the next objective; it is the largest of those visited on this walk, but in my opinion is the most attractive, surrounded not only by little craglets but having a superb view to the south side of Lliwedd and Snowdon.

Going round by the north tip of the lake a path will be found winding round towards Moel Meirch, the highest of the nearby rocky eminences, but ending before it gets there at a little col with a large cairn. Beyond and below this, a path comes up a sort of wide, grassy runnel which opens into a wider grassy basin lower down. This is the descent path to the west and its line is obvious enough, but first do go over to the delightfully spiky little top of Moel Meirch which is only a short distance away. It is surrounded by peachy-grey rocks and gives a wide panoramic view, including Moel Siabod.

From Cnicht looking west towards Llynnau Cerrig-y-myllt.

Returning to the little col, the cairn and the runnel, the path rapidly becomes more definite, descending to the west. It crosses over the stream that has developed just before reaching a sheepfold and then the path becomes less clear on the ground, veering away from the stream although the general direction is always towards Llyn Dinas, clearly seen in the valley bottom below. Now the path finds a slanting way across the top of a belt of crags, snaking back right down a wet gully to get to their foot and apparently heading once more for the bank of the stream below, but veers away above it again, heading towards walls and small enclosures. A ladder-stile leads over the wall and just beyond is a post with a walking-man sign carved on it. Follow the direction indicated towards a second post 150yds/137m away and a long-derelict farm. Immediately in front of this, turn downhill on a green way which leads through two gateways to skirt around the farm buildings and join the farm track itself. After two further gates, you reach the wood you passed at the beginning of the walk and all that is needed is to follow the track round the end of the wood and you are back on the road corner at the start of the walk proper. If you are parked in the Nantgwynant, it is now downhill all the way.

### 3.5 Moelwyn Bach, Moelwyn Mawr and Cwm Croesor
*7 miles/11.3km     5 hours*

Seen from Croesor, apart from a rocky lump between them, the two highest peaks of the Moelwyn appear as grassy rounded humps at each end of a wide grassy cwm, promising an easy ascent or descent. This is a misleading indication of their true character, for their eastern and north-eastern sides are as strikingly craggy and dramatic as the others are bland. The lower of the two, Moelwyn Bach, in particular demands respect and care

From Llyn Edno to Moel Meirch, with Snowdon in the background.

as there is a vertical crag on its summit and the descent is down a slaty path traversing a steep slope with a long drop below. This gives no trouble in dry conditions but can be like walking down wet soapflakes in the rain.

The ruins of the slate quarries on Bwlch y Rhosydd.

It is, of course, the presence of the slate in such quantity which makes this part of the Moelwyn so different from those areas just south-west of the Nantgwynant. The quarrying and mining of the slate in these hills was a colossal enterprise, as any drive through the dereliction of Blaenau Ffestiniog will quickly show, but time is softening the harsh outlines of the affected landscape and the increasing interest in industrial archaeology is beginning to turn what were regarded as monstrosities into attractions instead. This fine round could be completed as a simple circuit of the two main tops but going just a little further than is strictly necessary allows a few glimpses into a fascinating industrial past.

Be warned, however, that while it is easy enough to see the lie of the land under clear conditions, in mist it is very confusing, the maps are very difficult to read and the paths used on the ground do not always correspond with those shown on the OS maps. If overtaken by mist on Moelwyn Mawr, a simple descent down the ridge to the north-west, which quickly curves to the south-west, would be the best way to go as a path is soon picked up which leads back to the valley.

The best start is from the car park in the little village of Croesor (grid ref 632447) settled on a lip at the end of the unusually steep-sided Cwm Croesor. *See* **3.2** for instructions to reach car park. Walking back to the crossroads, go south-east along the gated minor road which climbs uphill, with a couple of sharp little rises, then crosses the Afon Maesgwm. A little further on from the bridge, having gained about 300ft/91m in height from Croesor, a grassy track turns left off the road onto the open moorland. Go along this, but only for a hundred yards or so, then turn south-east, slanting across rough pasture to the corner of a conifer plantation and continuing beyond it to get onto the broad ridge thrown down to the south-west by

Moelwyn Bach. There's very little sign of a path lower down and what paths there are are more likely to have been made by sheep anyway, but it is easy walking with views over miles of wooded country to the south-east and to the Rhinog.

As you gain height and approach Moelwyn Bach, the edge of the prow of vertical rock high on its summit comes into view, and the summit cairn is fairly near to it. Walk just a few paces north of the cairn, at the edge of the crag, and there is a fine view to the north to several other shapely tops, including Alltfawr, beyond Moelwyn Mawr across Cwmorthin. But there is also an astonishing and very dramatic view down to the hideous Stwlan Dam and lake, the upper reservoir of the Ffestiniog pumped storage system. It's like looking into a pit of horror; you wouldn't be too surprised to see some mutated monster rear out of the waters. Beyond are miles of terraces carved out of the hillsides round Blaenau Ffestiniog and millions of tons of slate spoil. It is not surprising that this side of the ridge was excluded from the National Park.

Between Moelwyn Bach and Moelwyn Mawr is a wide col, but it is blocked by an intervening and sharply upthrusting ridge of slaty rock. This is Craigysgafn and, although to traverse it looks improbable from a distance, there is a perfectly straightforward path up and over it. However, you must reach the col first and to do this it is necessary to go east from the summit cairn to outflank the summit crags and descend slightly to a shallow depression. Here a cairn marks the top of the shaly path that now slants across the north-east face of Moelwyn Bach overlooking Llyn Stwlan and descending almost 500ft/152m. As mentioned above, great care is needed under wet conditions.

The path up Craigysgafn has two little rocky steps giving some scramble-walking and it remains rocky and rough along its crest, but it is straightforward and soon reaches the last slope where a 400ft/122m pull zigzags up grassy slopes to the summit trig point of Moelwyn Mawr.

Moelwyn Mawr and the Stwlan Dam from the summit of Moelwyn Bach.

To the north and east the land slopes down into a wide basin or plateau, its eastern edge rimmed with crags. Down there you can see slate spoil-heaps, causeways, flat areas of grey-blue slate and roofless buildings. Make your way down the grassy ridge to the north-east; a faint path soon swings west down the cwm and around the rim of an enormous crater, a disused slate quarry in the open moor. From here a path can be discerned going north-west, roughly towards Cnicht, and then trending

From Moelwyn Mawr over the ridge of Craigysgafn to Moelwyn Bach.

north over acres of spread-out slate spoil. Streams gurgle and disappear; at one point, one dives down an unfenced hole that is just like a pot-hole on a Yorkshire moor. There are numerous spoil-heaps, but a rough track winds down an incline to a cluster of roofless buildings, bits of rusting machinery and quarry work areas on the wide and almost level Bwlch y Rhosydd.

Cwm Croesor and the way home is to the west and a level grassy track, with remnants of railway sleepers buried in its bed, leads in that direction. Follow it for just a short distance until it reaches an embankment on the lip of Bwlch y Rhosydd, from where you can look down the long valley of Cwm Croesor below. Here (grid ref 661462) leave the old railway track, which continues to contour round the fearsomely steep head of the valley for about a quarter of a mile and then comes to a dead end at a disused incline; take instead the very stony path which descends to the south-west and can then be seen traversing down the southern flank of Cwm Croesor. This quickly crosses the stream tumbling down from the bwlch, passes underneath overhanging crags where a waterfall pours over the top, continues just below the foot of some more enormous spoil tips from the former Croesor slate quarry high above and crosses the line of another of these ferociously steep man-made inclines. Thankfully for your feet, it shortly becomes a delightful grassy path, then runs alongside a fence, crossing one more incline, to reach a metal gate. Slant down through this to reach a track beside farm buildings and then the metalled road quickly leads back to the car park.

### 3.6 Cnicht, Moelwyn Mawr and Moelwyn Bach
*10 miles/16km       6 hours*

This fine round of the Cwm Croesor skyline, taking in the three major tops of the Moelwyn, should be reserved for a fine day as it involves some fairly strenuous walking, and navigation can be tricky on the middle section in less than good visibility. Most of the ground covered has been mentioned already in Walks **3.2.** and **3.5** but a few other comments may be helpful as well, since the ascent up to the two Moelwyn tops is being undertaken in the reverse direction.

Park in Croesor (grid ref 631447): *see* Walk **3.2** for instruc-tions to reach car park. Then take the road leading north-west out of the village, and as described in Walk **3.2**, proceed to the top of Cnicht at 2260ft/689m, a height gain of 1745ft/532m. Continue north-eastwards along its broad ridge in a gentle descent towards Llyn yr Adar, with splendid views down to rugged craglets, little lakes glinting in rocky basins and across the Nantgwynant to the greater peaks of the Snowdon massif. On the boggy plateau just before reaching the llyn, veer to the east to pick up a path which crosses the little stream of Afon Cwm-y-foel and then heads south-east. (An escape could be made here, following the stream to the dammed Llyn Cwm-y-foel, which is in upper Cwm Croesor; a path can then be picked up making a descending traverse of the north-western flank of Cwm Croesor back to the start.) Assuming this is not necessary, continue on the path which points to the south-east, undulating and twisting but gently descending to reach the extensive former slate quarry workings on the wide Bwlch y Rhosydd (not named on the 1:50,000 map, grid ref 665462).

Behind the ruins of the roofless buildings, an old incline climbs between spoil tips, heading south; then a path continues in the same direction over rock and shale towards the moor above. Skirt round to the left (east) of the huge quarry-pit (grid ref 665453) and head for the lowest point on the skyline ahead where you join the grassy north-east ridge. A path leading up this soon takes you to the summit of Moelwyn Mawr.

Moelwyn Bach, with a black and near-vertical crag just below its summit, will be well in view now to the south and is the final objective. An initially easy zigzag descent to the south from Moelwyn Mawr leads to the rugged ridge of Craigysgafn and a path runs along its crest. This is mostly very easy although particular care may be needed on the way down the rockier section, with its two little steps, to reach Bwlch Stwlan. The shaly path slanting from the bwlch up and across the face of Moelwyn Bach will have been well in view on the descent and its ascent should give fewer problems than it can in descent so that the summit will soon be reached. The return to Croesor is very straightforward: simply pick up the path descending the grassy west ridge (the reverse of Walk **3.5**), to reach the road leading back northwards to Croesor and the end of an enormously satisfying day.

## 3.7 Cwm Bychan from the Sygun Copper Mine
*6 miles/9.6km     3<sup>1</sup>/2 hours*

For a short or 'family' day, this walk could hardly be bettered and a visit to the Sygun Copper Mine, which offers a most entertaining conducted tour, is a welcome addition to the outing.

There are signs for the Sygun Copper Mine just off the A498 Capel Curig to Beddgelert road, where the Afon Glaslyn is bridged (grid ref 604490) and a track leads across to a large car park. Return to the river bank (on the south side), then turn left (east) down the track (footpath sign) alongside the river. This soon becomes a footpath, shadowing the river across fields, until it enters some rhododendrons just by a footbridge at the outlet from Llyn Dinas. Stay on the south side of the river and then, rounding the corner, immediately start to climb an obvious stony track which, in places, is 'pitched' i.e. has large flat stones set into its surface. It soon swings back right then left again to reach an easier angle, from where there is an enchanting view back to Llyn Dinas in its setting of little crags with birch trees, scree, bracken on the lower slopes and heather on the higher ones. Keep going up the easier slope (south-west) until, near the top of the slope, the path forks. It doesn't matter here which you take because they join up again shortly before the rise up to the col of Bwlch-y-Sygyn.

They soon separate again, however, still before the bwlch is reached and although the left-hand path is more direct and leads over into Cwm Bychan itself more quickly, it is a less interesting way. So take the right-hand one, which has some laid stones in its course; it leads uphill to a level space almost on the col itself where there are the remains of buildings, reddish mine spoil and the slits of old mine levels. In fact, although the scars are rapidly vanishing in the heather, the remains of extensive workings can be spotted. Ignore the level path going off to the left (south-east) and go through the levelled area and beyond it. The path kinks left and then immediately right again to arrive at the lip of a sheltered rocky bowl with dwarf rhododendrons and fringed by reddish crags. The path makes a slanting descent into this bowl and then forks again, the right-hand one heading south-west for Beddgelert, while the left-hand one heads south and almost immediately reaches a little llyn at a slightly lower level; this is the one to take for Cwm Bychan.

The grassy way reached soon curves gently to the south-west and joins the other path, the more direct one, just above a line of what look remarkably like four pylons in the bed of the grassy gully lower down. When reached, this is exactly what they prove to be; they supported a cableway for former mining operations and the wheel round which the cable ran is there on the last pylon. There is mine spoil and bits of metal; all a little incongruous in this delightful valley.

A little lower down, beyond a sheepfold, the path crosses a stream and then turns more sharply over a rocky lip where you can see the remains of more iron stanchions for pylons. It continues to descend the valley, in an almost Chinese landscape of tumbling stream, little cypress trees and silver birches dotting the hillsides, with the misty grey bulk of Moel Hebog towering ahead.

A gate leads through a wall into a more wooded area until a short tunnel is seen ahead below the line of the dismantled Welsh Highland Railway. Turn right (north-west) here and enter the mouth of the tunnel itself. This must be about three hundred yards/274m long, but it is largely dry underfoot and you can just see daylight at the far end. It emerges right next to the river in the spectacular Pass of Aberglaslyn, almost immediately goes under an archway and another short section of tunnel and then leads easily along the old trackway towards Beddgelert. When it curves to cross the river by an old iron bridge, take the path on the right (east) bank instead, then on the approach to the Bryn Eglws Hotel on the southern outskirts of Beddgelert, keep left alongside the river's east bank. Don't cross any bridges into the village but follow footpaths beside the river, through a zone of rhododendrons, until the paths end at a ladder-stile leading onto a minor tarmac road at the point where it crosses the river (grid ref 593484). Turn right here, away from the main road, and follow this quiet road until the tarmac ends at a gate. A short way beyond it, the track leads directly to the Sygun Mine and the car park.

Looking north-east along the summit ridge of Cnicht.

## 3.8 The Ffestiniog Railway Walk
*5 miles/8km      2¹/₂ hours*

A steam engine on the Ffestiniog Railway near Tanygrisiau.

The railway originally constructed to bring slate down from the great mines and quarries of Blaenau Ffestiniog to Portmadoc nowadays carries tourists in large numbers who enjoy a delightful journey above the beautiful Vale of Ffestiniog. The line runs through miles of wooded country out onto more open land on the edge of the massif of the Moelwyn and by using it as trans-port in one direction an equally delightful walk can be made out of returning to the start. It is a splendid family walk, or suitable for a shortish day, perhaps when the higher hills are shrouded in mist. In autumn, the trees are particularly fine.

The start is at Tan-y-bwlch Station (grid ref 650415) where there is a large car park (and a big sign, next to the tea-room and ticket office, that says 'Repent and turn to God'). You should book a single ticket, not to heaven just yet, but to Tanygrisiau (grid ref 682450) at the north end of Tanygrisiau Reservoir. The trains are quite frequent during summer months and the actual journey for this stretch takes about 25 minutes (not included in the 'approx $2\frac{1}{2}$ hours' given for the walk itself).

Having alighted, turn west along the road beside the reservoir, pass the café and information centre and take the right fork, which crosses the railway line and heads for a large car park. Before reaching this, there is a path signed off to the right to the Stwlan Dam but the one you want is just a little further on, beyond the car park. Signs lead you south, across the railway again, behind the power station and alongside the lake. Keep on across a sort of causeway to the end of the lake and then, when the railway line goes into a tunnel, you stay on the track which follows the tunnel overland (the path on the map crosses and recrosses the line unnecessarily). When the line reappears, you find yourself walking between it and an abandoned spur of the line that ends in a tunnel entrance but doesn't come out of it; presumably there were geological problems with the tunnel. When the track ends in a field, take to what is now a green way and follow it easily until it reaches a dilapidated signal box at Dduallt Station. Here walk along the station platform – it's not like King's Cross, it's out in the middle of green fields and woods and with a little lake on the right-hand side – to a ladder-stile at the far end. If you choose you can turn left, before reaching the stile, to visit the Golygfan viewpoint and picnic spot, from where there are views of the Moelwyn and also a surprising one of Trawsfynydd power station, looking huge and incongruous on this rural skyline.

Turn left as soon as you have crossed the stile and go alongside the line above the cutting (footpath sign just beyond it), onto a pleasant green path through bracken and sheep pasture which leads over a slight shoulder and reaches the railway line again, crossing it by ladder-stiles. The path beyond, with views along the Vale of Ffestiniog, leads down through clearings surrounded by trees and onto a track leading to the substantial house of Plas y Dduallt. Take care not to go wrong here: don't continue down the track but turn slightly up a little rise in front of the house (there's currently a footpath sign high on a huge conifer tree in front of it) to reach a stile over a wire fence just beyond a gate. The grassy path now winds along through bracken, curves round a little hollow, alongside a fine wood of mature sessile oaks and then up into the wood itself, emerging from it beside the railway line again. The path continues alongside the line for a way now, dropping down to cross a stream by a footbridge when the line uses a viaduct. This is all through lovely countryside: steep hillsides of heather and bracken above the line and mature woodland mostly below it and, except when you are actually close to the line or get a whiff of smoke from the steam trains, you are hardly aware that the railway line is there at all.

When the path forks (grid ref 665417), the right-hand branch is the way to go: through a gate and alongside a wall down a green ride through a larch wood, until the path merges with a track at a cattle-grid. This track gently declines to reach the B4410 opposite Llyn Mair, placid amongst conifer woodlands. Walk along the road a little way beside the lake to reach a parking place-cum-picnic spot at the far end, then take the second of two paths slanting uphill through the woods; the one you want is not the signed 'Nature Trail' but has some wide steps at the start. This leads easily up the wooded slope, enables you to avoid a bit of road-walking, and ends in the car park at Tan-y-bwlch Station again.

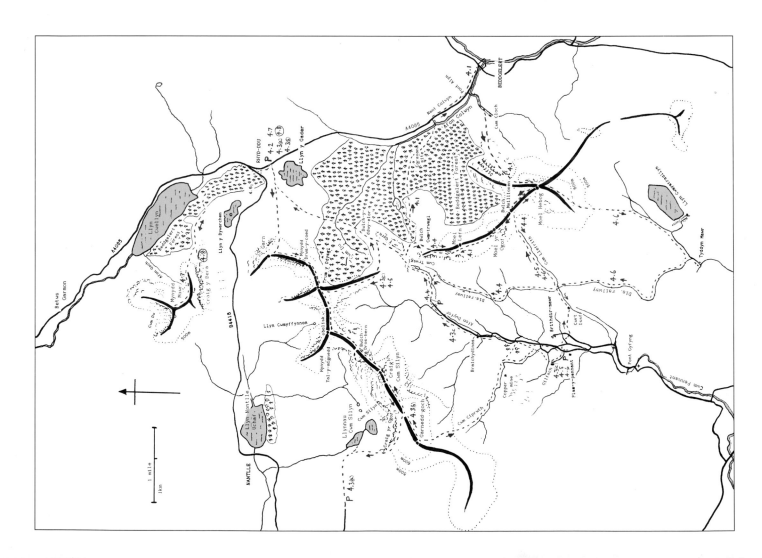

# 4: Eifionydd Hills: Nantlle and Cwm Pennant

| BEST MAPS: | OS 1:50,000 Landranger 115 Snowdon & surrounding area | | | | | |
|---|---|---|---|---|---|---|
| | OS 1:25,000 Outdoor Leisure 17 Snowdonia: Snowdon area | | | | | |
| Approx Distance | Approx Time | Highest Elevation Reached | Height Gained | Star Rating | Scramble Difficulty Grade | Scramble Height Gain |
| **4.1 Moel Hebog, Moel Ogof and Moel Lefn from Beddgelert** | | | | | | |
| 8 miles/12.9km | 5–6 hours | 2566ft/782m | 2441ft/744m | ** | — | — |
| **4.2 Y Garn, Mynydd Drws-y-coed and Trum y Ddysgl from Rhyd-Ddu** | | | | | | |
| 6½ miles/10.5km | 3½–4 hours | 2326ft/709m | 1945ft/593m | ** | — | — |
| **4.3 The Nantlle Ridge** **4.3(a) Traverse: start at Rhyd-Ddu, end in Cwm Silyn** | | | | | | |
| 7 miles/11.3km | 4½ hours | 2408ft/734m | 2838ft/865m | *** | — | — |
| **4.3(b) Rhyd-Ddu to Garnedd-goch and return to Rhyd-Ddu** | | | | | | |
| 10½ miles/16.9km | 6–7 hours | 2408ft/734m | 3881ft/1183m | *** | — | — |
| **4.3(c) The Round: start and finish in Cwm Pennant** | | | | | | |
| 10½ miles/16.9km | 6 hours | 2408ft/734m | 3461ft/1055m | *** | — | — |
| **4.4 Moel Lefn and Moel yr Ogof from Cwm Pennant** | | | | | | |
| 6½ miles/10.5km | 4½ hours | 2149ft/655m | 1896ft/578m | ** | — | — |
| **4.5 The Round of Cwm Pennant** | | | | | | |
| 13½ miles/21.7km | 7–8 hours | 2566ft/782m | 4901ft/1494m | *** | — | — |

| Approx Distance | Approx Time | Highest Elevation Reached | Height Gained | Star Rating | Scramble Difficulty Grade | Scramble Height Gain |
|---|---|---|---|---|---|---|
| **4.6 A Round over Moel Hebog from Cwm Pennant** | | | | | | |
| 8 miles/12.8km | 4–5 hours | 2566ft/782m | 2172ft/662m | */** | — | — |
| **4.7 Mynydd Mawr from Rhyd-Ddu** | | | | | | |
| 6 miles/9.7km | 3–4 hours | 2290ft/698m | 1663ft/507m | */** | — | — |
| **4.8 Scramble on Sentries' Ridge, Craig y Bera** | | | | | | |
| 6 miles/9.6km | 4–4¹/₂ hours | 2290ft/698m | 1663ft/507m | *** | 2 | 499ft/152m |

Mynydd Mawr, occasionally called 'the elephant mountain' because of its shape seen from Snowdon, the fine chain of peaks to the south-east of the quarrying village of Nantlle and known generally as The Nantlle Ridge, and the three peaks to the north-west of Beddgelert, which collectively form the skyline of the lovely Cwm Pennant, are the subject of this chapter. It is a delightful area, though comparatively neglected, possibly because of an earlier history of conflict over access. Walkers on the splendid Nantlle Ridge were considered trespassers until the end of the 1970s, when some access routes were negotiated. The atmosphere is much friendlier nowadays but some useful paths are permissive only and thoughtless or careless use of them, or of any public rights of way for that matter (for some walkers have been known to be aggressive too) could lead to unnecessary conflict. There should be no problems for walkers respecting this situation.

### 4.1 Moel Hebog, Moel Ogof and Moel Lefn from Beddgelert
*8 miles/12.9 km        5–6 hours*

There is a good, although distant, view to be had of Moel Hebog

from the road in Nantgwynant, from where it is seen as a conical and almost isolated peak with an obvious appeal to any mountain walker. Seen from Beddgelert, it looks quite different: more a dominating broad lump with a line of crags, Y Diffwys, just below its summit on its eastern flank; it also becomes clearer that it is part of a ridge. The ascent and descent of Moel Hebog on its own gives a good short day but the addition of the other two high points on the ridge gives a longer and more variable walk and so it is this one which is described. Don't underestimate the care needed to navigate through the forest on the descent and do not forget your compass. It looks easy enough on the 1:25,000 map and in good conditions is straightforward enough, if you are careful, but the forest trails are for extracting timber, not extricating walkers. If those comments put you off, many walkers are content to go up and down Moel Hebog by the same route, a height gain of a respectable 2441ft/744m and a distance of 4¹/₂ miles/7.3km. And in Walk 4.4 a first-class round of the two lower peaks is suggested from Cwm Pennant which does not involve going into any forest at all.

*Moel yr Ogof seen from a shoulder on Moel Hebog.*

There is a large and well-signed car park in Beddgelert just down the A498 road to Porthmadog (grid ref 588481) and from here you should make your way to the front of the Royal Goat Hotel (next to the car park) and head for the mountain by going immediately to the right of the hotel up a tarmac drive which leads into a small housing estate. Before going into the estate, look for a footpath sign and then another (which just cuts off a corner of the estate) leading immediately to a bridge over the old Welsh Highland Railway, with a stile at the far side of the bridge. More footpath signs now point SSW directly at the mountain, which is encouraging but misleading and many walkers, including the writer, have gone astray here. Instead, turn right on a footpath between walls to join a lane where you turn left; follow this along the edge of a little plantation to farm buildings at grid ref 581478. If that sounds too complicated, make your way to the junction of the A498 with the A4085 (i.e. the bridge in the centre of Beddgelert), walk 700 yds/640m to the north-west towards Caernarfon and then turn left on a track over Pont Alyn (signed) leading to the farm at Cwm Cloch Isaf and more farm buildings just beyond.

Signs now lead you to the west over a stile, across a boggy field towards a second stile, and then a green way snaking up through bracken to reach the broad north-east ridge of the mountain. This is grassy with odd stony outcrops but becomes rockier and steeper as height is gained. At about 1900ft/579m the path reaches the left-hand end of the belt of crags (Y Diffwys, the precipice) and goes further left to skirt round and above them, over what is now very rocky but well-cairned ground. I thought that a scrambling route might have been found up Y Diffwys and no doubt a persistent scrambler will do so, but it is probably better left to the rock-climbers.

At about 2400ft/731m a shoulder with two large cairns is reached, and a reward: a surprise view of Moel yr Ogof and the hills of the Nantlle ridge. From this shoulder, the path swings south up more fairly steep and rocky ground, emerging onto an almost level top above a line of crumbling crags on the left (east) side. The trig point is just a little further on.

From the trig point, a steep descent on grass beside a wall heads directly for Moel yr Ogof, but it definitely is steep and you'll find an easier line by returning to the shoulder on the main path and then descending the softer angled slopes westwards for about 700ft/213m to the pass of Bwlch Meillionen. Moel yr Ogof, Hill of the Cave (a hiding place of Owain Glyndwr), rises about 350ft/107m ahead now, with a bold crag on its west (left) skyline and the wall running right up to a cleft at its right-hand end. Beyond the cleft lies a scramble over more rocky ground to the cairn on the top at 2149ft/655m. The cave itself is situated on an overhanging and vegetated cliff facing south-east below the summit (see **4.4** for fuller details) but unless you are prepared to take a little time to seek it, you would be better advised to press on now.

The continuation to Moel Lefn is straightforward. Having left the big boulders on the summit of Moel yr Ogof, grassy slopes lead down, with little loss of height, over a stile to a col and then an easy climb back up to the last rocky high point of this ridge. On leaving it, head for a cairn just left (west) of what looks like the obvious line of descent. From here you will get a good view of the best way down towards the old slate workings in Cwm Trwsgl, 1000ft/305m below, although the objective now is the Bwlch Cwm-trwsgl, which is just a little higher. A faint path leads from the cairn, descending fairly steeply down grassy slopes, veering left and down a short stony gully to skirt below some rocky ribs, then swinging back rightwards to continue the descent down the broad ridge. Just a little higher than the bwlch, you meet the wall enclosing the forest, here at its highest point on the Beddgelert slope. Complete the descent alongside the wall to the lowest point of the bwlch (grid ref 553496) where there is a break in the wall. Just beyond the break, on the forest side, is a wire fence and stile: here the path begins which leads down through Beddgelert Forest.

Follow this path down a break to reach a track, turn left along this for about 100yds/91m and then leave it at a cairn for a path going down eastwards through more forest to reach a stile and open ground (grid ref 557496). A path leads across this open ground, with rough mountainside on your right-hand side, to re-enter the forest at another stile. This path leads in about

The site of Owain Glyndwr's cave on Moel yr Ogof.

300yds/274m to a track. The 1:25,000 map shows the path cutting across the next two bends in this track but it is better to follow the track which makes a wide bend to the right and then a sharper one back left. Just round the second bend, leave the track and take the path descending through more trees to meet another forest track. Here I have found it best to follow this track south for 300yds/274m and then, at the fork, turn back north-east (left) and continue on this new track, descending all the time, to cross a wide stream and then meet with a major track. Turn right (south-east) here and follow it down into the forest caravan and camp-site. From here a metalled track leads east to a bridge over the Afon Colwyn and a 3/4 mile/1.2km hike down the main road to Beddgelert. After getting out of the forest, you will now better appreciate why that famous African tribe, the Fukawi, are reputed to jump up and down in the long grass to find out where they are.

From my own experience, I would caution against trying to take short cuts down what may look like fire-breaks through the forest; all too often they turn out to be full of brash, the decaying brushwood left after the logs have been removed, and are virtually impassable. The forest roads will get you out, eventually, but they were made to contour through the forest to harvest timber, not to provide weary walkers with a quick way home.

## 4.2. Y Garn, Mynydd Drws-y-coed and Trum y Ddysgl from Rhyd-Ddu

*6¹/₂ miles/10.5km        3¹/₂–4 hours*

This fine short walk is essentially a traverse of the northern part of the Nantlle Ridge and a useful spur descending to the south from Trum y Ddysgl, above the line of the forest to the col (the Bwlch-y-Ddwy-elor) between Cwm Pennant and Nant Colwyn, enables a return to be made to Rhyd-Ddu without too much difficulty. It is useful for a short day.

There is a large Snowdonia National Park car park at Rhyd-Ddu (grid ref 571525) reached from Beddgelert or Caernarfon along the A4085; here there are toilets and information boards etc.

Go directly out of the car park at the end nearest to the village, cross the A4085 and make use of the footpath leading on slate slabs across a field and directly towards the slopes of Y Garn ahead. Where the path meets the secondary road going towards Nantlle (grid ref 567525) turn left through a metal gate (sign for horse-riders) and follow the path alongside a wall. It leads to a ladder-stile and then forks at a big stone, the left fork going to Cwm Pennant (and will be the return journey) and the other straight ahead, marked by white arrows on rocks, continuing steeply towards Y Garn. After crossing a double ladder-stile, the path deteriorates into a series of slaty runnels and footholds except near the top where cairns mark a way across a stony slope to a wall and a huge pile of stones forming a windbreak. The 1450ft/442m of ascent to the summit of Y Garn will have been quite taxing and you can console yourself with the thought that it is the uphill bits that are doing you good. There's a good view of Mynydd Mawr and the pinnacles of Craig y Bera across the upper Nantlle valley and the continuation of the ridge ahead looks quite exciting.

A short descent on grass leads to a grassy col, beyond which rises the rocky ridge of Mynydd Drws-y-coed. Beyond that is a view across a deep cwm to the ridge of Trum y Ddysgl, while yet further away can be seen the proud obelisk on Mynydd Tal-y-mignedd. This rocky ridge gives about 200ft/61m of easy scrambling past an obvious leaning rock finger on the skyline to reach a ladder-stile on the summit ridge. If it's clear you can see from here to Caernarfon Castle.

The Nantlle Ridge: from Y Garn to Mynydd Drws-y-coed.

The ridge now swings sharply to the west and descends about 250ft/76m to a col followed by a simple climb up the other side to the grassy top of Trum y Ddysgl, your third and last summit. Go along the almost level ridge to the south-west but as soon as it begins to descend it forks and you should take the narrow path leading off to the left (south-east) down a fairly steep grassy ridge. (The main path at the fork swings to the right (west) to complete the descent to the col and the climb beyond up to Mynydd Tal-y-mignedd.) The grassy ridge curves above the forest below to reach the broad and rather boggy col of Bwlch-y-Ddwy-elor and you here meet the path rising from the old slate workings at the head of Cwm Pennant. Turn left

Y Garn and Llyn y Gader seen from the Rhydd-Ddu path to Snowdon.

(north-east) here, over a stile, and follow the path into the forest until it intersects with a forestry track.

Take the track, and after only a few yards go left at a fork for about a quarter of a mile to reach a bridge over a stream. Turn right on a major track here but, as before, only for a few paces, then turn left again onto a rough path, heading NNE. This soon leads away from the woods and across the lower slopes of Mynydd Drws-y-coed, with some stony and boggy ground en route, to reach the big stone which was the parting of the ways on the outward route.

## 4.3 The Nantlle Ridge
### 4.3(a) Traverse: start at Rhyd-Ddu, end in Cwm Silyn
*7 miles/11.3km          4½ hours*

This traverse assumes you can make the necessary transport arrangements: either two parties start from opposite ends and exchange keys when they meet; or leave a car at the finish and drive another to the start; or, if you're lucky, you may have a willing driver prepared to pick you up.

In Cwm Silyn, the accepted parking place for climbers and walkers is on the moor just west of the two Llynnau Cwm Silyn at grid ref 503511. Go up the lane and continue a little beyond the gate, when it becomes an unfenced track, then park just off the track.

Back in Rhyd-Ddu the parking and start of the traverse is exactly as for Walk **4.2.** above (to Y Garn, Mynydd Drws-y-coed and Trum y Ddysgl). From the grassy ridged top of the latter, the stone pillar on Mynydd Tal-y-mignedd is seen ahead and is the next objective. After a short and very gentle descent to the south for about a hundred yards, swing right (west) and complete this 328ft/100m descent down the main ridge to the col ahead, with the tiny Llyn Cwmyffynnon visible below, deep in the cwm on the north side of the ridge. There are a few rocky steps to be negotiated on the lowest point of the col and then a grassy slope leads easily up the short rise beyond to the obelisk. This was erected to commemorate Queen Victoria's Jubilee; it is beautifully made, square and about 12ft/3.6m high.

The continuation of the ridge to Craig Cwm Silyn changes somewhat in character from here onwards, the sharp up-and-down giving way to a much longer gradual and boggy descent on grass beside a fence and then, as the ridge sharpens again, more steeply down a slaty path to the next col, Bwlch Dros-bern. Ahead the ridge is apparently barred by two rock buttresses, part of Craig Pennant, and there is a choice of ways. Firstly, a direct route goes from the col to the bottom of the nearest buttress where a line of large holds slants to the left towards a wall built right on the sharp edge of the crag. Reaching this wall the route goes straight up a steep little slab on quartz holds and then more easily to the top of the buttress. This pitch is about 70ft/21m long but the only bit that might be awkward, particularly in the wet, is that up the steep slab, which is approximately scramble grade 2. Alternatively and more easily, instead of approaching the rock buttress from the col, veer rightwards about 300yards/274m before it to find some cairns which mark a vague path leading back left up easier angled, although still rocky, ground to join the 'direct' route at the top of the first buttress.

The second buttress is hardly noticed since it is by-passed on a straightforward path. This has an occasional rockier and steeper bit and keeps fairly close to the left edge of the crags lower down but finishes up a broad shoulder of mixed rocks and grass to reach a big circular stone shelter, with a tiny one beside it, on a wide and rocky plateau. Just a little further on is a large rectangular cairn, the highest point of the plateau of Craig Cwm Silyn. Just beyond, as the ground slopes to the south-west, there are two more smaller square cairns, like partly-completed pillars, then the rocks underfoot give way to grass and the vague path leads to a wall-junction and a stile (grid ref 518499). The main route now continues alongside the wall, rising gradually to the last top of Garnedd-goch, an undistinguished top.

From here, descend northwards down grassy slopes leading towards a ridge which in its upper part forms the retaining edge of Cwm Silyn itself. On the way down, you should get fine views across the cwm of the two llynnau and of the steep buttresses of Craig yr Ogof, with the Great Slab (looking vertical from here) being the obvious one furthest away. At the end of the descent, you will reach a gate in the transverse wall where it is pierced by the track running into the cwm. Turn left here down the track and, with luck, your transport will be waiting a little nearer to the road-end.

### 4.3(b) Rhyd-Ddu to Garnedd-goch and return to Rhyd-Ddu
*10¹/₂ miles/16.9km        6–7 hours*

The double traverse of the Nantlle Ridge is not as arduous as may be imagined, being only 3¹/₂ miles/5.6km longer and gaining only another 1000ft/305m of height than on the single traverse. You'll probably be a bit slower on the return leg, so I've allowed an additional 2¹/₂ hours for the double journey. I am not generally in favour of 'there and back' walks but this is such a varied journey that I can recommend it.

Having walked the route from Rhyd-Ddu already (*see* **4.2** and **4.3(a)** above) there should be no problems in finding it on the return from Garnedd-goch as it follows the main ridge line. Only on the descent from the top of Craig Cwm Silyn is a little extra care perhaps needed, where the path leads to the top of the steep buttress above the Bwlch Dros-bern. Here, keep on until the wall blocking the edge of the crags comes into view just below and then veer very sharply back, leftwards, to outflank the steep drop. Thereafter it is a reversal of the outward route precisely, although it can be surprising how different the same mountain scenery looks when you are going in the opposite direction.

### 4.3(c) The Round: start and finish in Cwm Pennant
*10¹/₂ miles/16.9km        6 hours*

A good round or circular walk of the Nantlle Ridge, starting and finishing at the same place in Cwm Pennant, rather than linear walks from Rhyd-Ddu as described above in **4.3a** and **4.3b**, is in fact possible without access problems because of the helpful attitude of the owner and farmer of the land in Cwm Ciprwth

which is crossed on the descent. I would suggest that the best place to start the walk is at Plas-y-pennant (grid ref 529464) where there is a tea-shop. This is one of the very few places available to park anywhere in Cwm Pennant, apart from the valley-head, but you must ask for permission. This is not likely to be refused but it is a courtesy that anyone can appreciate.

From here, it is easiest to simply walk up the very quiet road of this delightful valley to the end of the tarmac at the head of the valley. Here there is an open space and a couple of barns. The way up onto the northern end of the Nantlle Ridge from here is to reach the Bwlch-y-Ddwy-elor (pass of the two biers) which was presumably an old corpse road. Use the ladder-stile over the little stream next to the parking area and then follow the path to the north-east and which can be seen going up a bracken-covered hillside towards a roofless ruined building about 200ft/61m higher. Cross the ladder-stile at the right-hand (south) end of the ruin and follow the path round a little knoll beyond it to a substantial roofless building beside a stream draining Cwm Trwsgl, at the head of which were former slate quarries. Arrow signs lead through this ruin and then north-east up Cwm Trwsgl on the west side of a little reservoir, then steady climbing leads through the derelict works and onto the broad col of the Bwlch-y-Ddwy-elor.

The main path leads down the other side into the forest and to Rhyd-Ddu but turn north-west up a grassy ridge, with the forest on your right-hand side. The ridge soon sharpens and curves up to the summit of Trum y Ddysgl. To collect the summits of Mynydd Drws-y-coed and Y Garn you will need to turn now to the north-east, returning to Trum y Ddysgl when you have done so. If you haven't been over them before this visit, then you should not omit them now as it is only a short descent then re-ascent to the first and the little scramble down to the second, Y Garn, and then back up again is most enjoyable.

From Trum y Ddysgl you now turn south-west and continue

to the obelisk on Mynydd Tal-y-mignedd and to Craig Cwm
Silyn and Garnedd-goch, as already described in 4.3(b) above.
To return to the valley of Cwm Pennant the logical way is down
Cwm Ciprwth. Fortunately the farmer and landowner of Cwm
Ciprwth, at Gilfach Farm, is sympathetic towards reasonable
and considerate walkers and with his permission I can describe
a most delightful and interesting descent, with a minor varia-
tion, to reach the public paths in the valley-bottom.

Strike down to the SSE of Garnedd-goch to reach the head of
Cwm Ciprwth as soon as possible. You will be descending rocky
but easy angled heather slopes and, half way down the cwm, will
reach a solid wall and ladder-stile next to the stream, the
Ceunant Ciprwth, (grid ref 522481) which is easily seen from
above. Follow the line of the stream now, through bracken, to
where it goes through a little ravine. Just beyond and below this
is the extraordinary sight of a huge black iron water-wheel
beside the stream, together with the remains of some old buildings. This is the site of the old Gilfach copper-mine and the
wheel, together with the leat which fed water from the stream to
the wheel enabling it to pump water from the nearby shafts, is
in process of being restored by the Snowdonia National Park
Authority. You can easily go over to it for a look.

Leaving the mine, keep on the left bank of the stream,
descending through a gap for sheep in a transverse wall and
towards some sheepfolds (grid ref 528478) where the stream is
forced to swing sharply right (south) by a rise in the land ahead.
If you continue going east, over the rise, you will find yourself
descending steeply past some old mine spoil-heaps just above
some woods. This is conservation woodland, fenced to keep out
the sheep, and you will soon reach the wire fence. There are
signs directing you to a stile over this and you may then

The water-wheel at the old Gilfach copper mine in Cwm Ciprwth.

descend down the old mine path towards the road in the valley bottom. It is, however, a scenically prettier way, much less steep and avoids the woods completely if, instead of going straight ahead from the sheepfolds, you swing south and follow sheep-tracks down the left bank of the stream. This soon reaches a wooded gully and turns east to reach the valley below. Just before reaching the gully, turn left (east) yourself and follow a narrow path through bracken, and through gaps in two transverse walls. Immediately after going through the second wall, swing right and descend to the wire fence enclosing the woodland directly ahead, then follow it for a few yards to the right to a gate across the break between two enclosed areas of woodland. Descend the break, wire-fenced on each side, which leads quickly to the bottom of the wooded gully and the stream again; here are ladder-stiles over the fence on each side and you have reached the public footpath that will quickly lead you back to the start. Take the stile on the right, cross the footbridge immediately beyond and you reach the ruins of the old farm called Ciprwth. From here a series of posts and signs guide you along the path and track to Gilfach Farm and the farm track beyond soon leads to the road again. Turn right along this, and the car and welcome tea-room are only a short distance away.

## 4.4. Moel Lefn and Moel yr Ogof from Cwm Pennant
*6½ miles/10.5km        4½ hours*

This very good, fairly short and little-used walk enables you to visit the lovely Cwm Pennant and traverse two of the fine hills on its eastern flank. The return is simple and avoids all the potential problems of navigation in the Beddgelert Forest.

Cwm Pennant is drained by the meandering Afon Dwyfor and the narrow, single-track road, signed off the A487 Caernarfon-Porthmadog road, crosses and re-crosses the river several times as it leads up the almost level valley. Passing-places are few and far between and parking spots even more rare, but on this occasion it is perfectly simple: just drive to the head of the valley, putting your 50p (in 1991) parking-fee in the box on the second of the two gates across the road on either side of Braichydinas Farm (grid ref 534485). The parking area is a little way further on, where the metalled track ends at an open space which has a couple of barns (grid ref 540493).

The lowest notch seen to the north-east on the skyline of the cirque of fine peaks which now enfold you is the Bwlch-y-Ddwy-elor; this is the direction to take. Use the ladder-stile next to the parking spot, cross the little stream immediately beyond it and then follow the path heading north-east, which can be seen going up a bracken-covered hillside towards a roofless ruined building about 200ft/61m higher. Cross the ladder-stile at the right-hand (south) end of the ruin and follow the path round a little knoll beyond it to a substantial roofless building beside a stream. (Curiously, this is not shown on the 1:50,000 map although the smaller ruin is.)

This stream drains Cwm Trwsgl, at the head of which were substantial slate quarries, and the path is signed (arrows) through this large ruin which must have been some sort of warehouse for dressed slate. The path leads towards the impressive cliffs of Moel Lefn and you may either follow it round to where it goes alongside the west side of a little reservoir, or walk up an old incline and then the footpath beyond, heading directly for the former quarries. Another incline, in the same direction, leads up a series of terraces cut across quarry spoil. Both paths join about here and to keep going uphill leads to the Bwlch-y-Ddwy-elor, but the pass you need is the Bwlch Cwm-trwsgl which is to the east and at a lower altitude. So turn east (right) here, when on the level of the third terrace, and you'll find a faint path over very stony ground leads towards and then alongside a stone wall. At the lowest point on the col (grid ref

553496) there is a break in the wall and, just beyond the break, a wire fence encloses the Beddgelert Forest. Do not take the path which leads over a stile at the fence and heads eastwards down into the forest to return to Beddgelert; instead keep outside and alongside the wall, heading south. A faint path now starts to climb the broad ridge rising towards Moel Lefn, staying alongside the forest for a short way but soon leaving it behind and climbing steadily. About 600ft/183m above the bwlch, the path skirts to the right below a crag of easy-angled rock ribs and grooves, then curves up a stony gully to easier ground, reaching a cairn on a good viewpoint just below the highest rocks on Moel Lefn itself.

From Moel Lefn, a straightforward short descent and slightly longer climb leads to the rocky top of Moel yr Ogof, another good viewpoint, with the southern flank of Snowdon and the Moelwyn filling most of the eastern skyline. Immediately to the south-east are the steep slopes leading up to the top of Moel Hebog.

Moel yr Ogof, Hill of the Cave, gets its name from the cave which was used as a hiding place by Owain Glyndwr after the failure to seize Caernarfon Castle in 1404, when a garrison of only twenty eight men withstood the last gallant attempt to re-establish an independent Welsh kingdom. A fairly short day such as this is a good opportunity to seek the cave, but it is elusive. One way to find it with certainty is to descend the rock-filled gully to the broad Bwlch Meillionen and then descend just a little further towards the edge of the Beddgelert Forest. Now curve round to the left (north) immediately below the steep and vegetated crags, pass the bottom of one smallish gully and then scramble up the next major gully. Not until you are half way up it will the cave be visible, but then it is unmistakable. It is about 5ft 6in/1.7m high at the mouth and 10ft/3m across, with a level floor extending backwards for about 30ft/9m into the cliff and clearly it could have formed a hiding-place for some period of time, if somewhat damp. When I visited the cave, the only occupants were spiders which scuttled away into dark corners. The view from the mouth is to Moel Hebog.

Returning to the lowest point on Bwlch Meillionen, a ladder-stile will be found in the wall-corner on the Moel yr Ogof side of the pass. Beyond it, the vague path to the south-west down Cwm Llefrith soon disappears but the easiest going is well up on the right (north) side of the wide cwm and, at about the 450m contour, you should pick up a track where, via a gate and ladder-stile, it crosses a sound wall and then the collapsed remains of a second. This track now continues, none too clearly, towards the middle of the cwm and reaches another gate and stile just to the north (right) of a little stand of conifers. Just 200yds/183m down the field beyond the stile, still going south-west and immediately before reaching a transverse wall, you will find the unmistakable narrow and grassed-over embankment of the discontinued narrow-gauge railway (grid ref 544466). Turn north now and enjoy delightful walking along its course. There are several ladder-stiles along the way and it almost disappears at one point as it curves round a wide grassy bay, but it contours gently along the hillside, giving fine views of the head of Cwm Pennant. Rounding a bend, two half-dismantled pillars come into sight and it soon reaches the stream and derelict slate warehouse seen on the outward journey. Cross the stream and make a last easy descent down the brackeny hillside, with warm western light bathing the slopes above, to reach the parking spot and the end of a delightful day.

## 4.5 The Round of Cwm Pennant
*13½ miles/21.7km          7–8 hours*

There are several excellent views of the Cwm Pennant skyline from the A487 main road between Porthmadog and Caernarfon; every peak and pass is clearly seen and the challenge to walk the crest immediately recognisable by committed mountain-walkers. In the valley itself, there is plenty of evidence of past human endeavour. The map shows many indications of occupation by Iron Age and Bronze Age peoples: enclosures, house platforms and settlements, although these are not easily seen on the ground. That copper and slate miners sweated and toiled here will become much more obvious as you descend to Bwlch Cwm-trwsgl from Moel Lefn in a few hours' time – and the final descent has a real surprise. But the valley itself, facing the western seaboard and therefore lit by the setting sun, is tranquil and almost secret now, home only to a few scattered farms and their inevitable sheep.

The road up the almost level valley is single-track with passing-places and, as already mentioned in **4.4** above, parking is very limited. I would like to start the round in an anti-clockwise direction by gaining the slopes south of Moel Hebog from the tempting lane and path starting from the chapel and phone box at grid ref 532454, but walkers doing this in the past have caused obstruction since there is only room for one car and then nobody else can use the phone or the chapel, so you might find a tyre let down. Even if you risk parking here, once you head up the slopes to the north-east towards Moel Hebog, it is not possible to proceed without climbing some walls, to the irritation of the farmers who have to rebuild them. I therefore propose a different solution to make this fine round possible, solving both parking and access problems.

Drive up the single-track road up Cwm Pennant as far as Plas-y-pennant Farm at grid ref 529464. Here there is a tea-shop and, even if it is closed, there is room to park a few cars so long as you ask permission. This is unlikely to be refused, but it is simply courtesy to ask.

The first objective on the circuit is Moel Hebog and you can see it clearly enough on the skyline. A right-of-way path goes up Cwm Llefrith to the Bwlch Meillionen, between Moel Hebog and Moel yr Ogof and I suggest that you reach the bwlch and go up and down Moel Hebog first, then continue the circuit anti-clockwise along the crest, the Cwm Pennant skyline. So start from Plas-y-pennant and walk north up the valley for about 100yds/91m to a cattle-grid. Immediately beyond this take the small stile over the wire fence (next to a metal gate) and cross the field eastwards to find the stepping-stones across the Afon Dwyfor. From the stile over the wire fence on the other bank, look south-south-east (150° magnetic) to see a metal gate in a wall about 200yds/183m away. The gate gives onto a metalled road leading up to the farm at Brithdir-mawr and you need to reach the road. There is a nasty wire fence in the direct line however, so you should walk in a left-curving arc, going just left of a couple of oak trees, to find an almost hidden stile over the fence at the side of a little brook. Now you can reach the gate. (Strictly according to the map, the path goes up the field beyond but, at the time of writing, a new fence is in the course of being erected alongside the metalled road and at present there is no stile over this, although I am told that there will be; obviously if you can see one you will not need to go to the gate.)

Reaching the gate, turn left (north) up the road for 130 paces, just where the road goes into some trees, and you'll spot another small stile on the right. (If you reach a gate across the road itself you have gone about 100yds/91m too far.) Beyond this stile, walk up the field, to the east, through scattered trees, keeping just to the right of a large conifer on the near skyline, to find a large ladder-stile over a wall. Keep on up the field to a second ladder-stile onto a track. Turn left and follow the track, curving to the right and over a little rise, to reach the farm of Cwrt Isaf on the bank of the Afon Cwm-llefrith. Go through the farmyard ahead and turn left just beyond the highest barns to find a ladder-stile beside the track. This track leads up the left bank (as you look up it) of the Afon Cwm-llefrith and the way should now be clear.

The crags of Moel Lefn and the old mine-workings of Cwm Trwsgl.

After a couple of gates, the track fizzles out but continue just a little further in the same direction and you will intersect with the dismantled railway line (grid ref 544466, see Walk 4.4) from the old slate quarries in Cwm Trwsgl at the head of the valley. Cross the grassy embankment and continue north-east to see a ladder-stile about 200yds/183m ahead to the left of a small clump of conifers. Once over this stile, simply continue up the grassy slopes ahead; the path (such as it is) keeps to the left of the stream and the terrain becomes rougher and rockier as you climb, to reach a ladder-stile in a wall corner on the wide Bwlch Meillionen.

From here, the path beside the wall climbs straight to the summit of Moel Hebog, a tough but fairly short climb (about 750ft/229m) and you are, at last!, on the first and highest of the day's peaks. Return to Bwlch Meillionen and then clamber up the Moel yr Ogof to the north-west and when you have reached the top, you will have gained half the day's altitude total. Continue to Moel Llefn and descend to Bwlch Cwm-trwsgl as in Walk 4.1. where, instead of turning east into the forest, follow the wall where it curves to the north-east round the prominent small hill of Y Gyrn towards the extensive workings of the old quarries. A path leads across one of the terraces of the old workings and then joins the main path climbing the last short slopes towards the wide and boggy Bwlch-y-Ddwy-elor.

Here turn off the main path which heads for the forest and Rhyd-Ddu to the north-east and instead strike up the broad ridge to the north-west. The ridge sharpens as it climbs higher above the forest in Cwm Du and you get splendid views down Cwm Pennant on the left hand and over to Snowdon on the right of the slope. A final sharp grassy ridge curves up to the summit of Trum y Ddysgl and a fine view over the other side to the Nantlle valley. It is only a short descent, then climb, to reach the summit of Mynydd Drws-y-coed less than 1/4mile/0.4km away to the north-east and you can do it easily. Purists may well now continue northwards and make the scramble-descent to Y Garn, the last peak on the northern end of the ridge, and then return. If it is your first visit to this fine chain of peaks, I would certainly recommend it because the little scramble down and up again is easy and most enjoyable, but if you have already done that section you probably won't bother on this occasion; I wouldn't myself.

Now, from Trum y Ddysgl, the main line of the ridge ahead should be clear and is already described in **4.3(a)**, going beyond the fine obelisk on Mynydd Tal-y-mignedd and continuing over the stony top of Craig Cwm Silyn and on to the last top of Garnedd-goch, an exhilarating tramp.

There is no public right-of-way down Cwm Ciprwth and yet it is the logical way to complete the round. Fortunately for walkers, the landowner and farmer of Cwm Ciprwth, Mr Nigel Warren of Gilfach Farm, has done plenty of hill-walking himself and is sympathetic towards considerate walkers. With his permission, I can describe a most delightful and interesting descent, with a variation, to reach the public paths in the valley bottom.

The descent is down Cwm Ciprwth, to reach the stile over the wall next to the stream at grid ref 522481, which should be easily seen from above. Follow the stream, Ceunant Ciprwth, down the cwm until you pass the restored iron water-wheel by the site of the old Gilfach copper-mine. Continue downhill to some sheep-folds where the stream turns sharply south and stay on its east bank until just before it reaches a wooded gully or ravine down which it turns to descend to the valley below. Here, as described in detail in Walk **4.3(c)**, follow paths down to Gilfach Farm and so back to Plas-y-pennant.

## 4.6 A Round over Moel Hebog from Cwm Pennant
*8 miles/12.8km        4–5 hours*

For an interesting round, as opposed to a straight up and down ascent/descent of Moel Hebog on its own, it is worthwhile starting from Cwm Pennant even though I am afraid that you will need two maps at either the 1:50,000 or 1:25,000 scale to show the whole route (i.e. at 1:50,000, sheet 124 (Dolgellau) is needed in addition to 115 (Snowdon); at 1:25,000, sheet 18 (Harlech and Bala) is needed as well as 17 (Snowdon)).

Park, with permission, at Plas-y-pennant (grid ref 529464) in Cwm Pennant, where there is a tea-shop attached to the farm. Then, following the detailed way described in **4.5**, cross the stepping-stones over the Afon Dwyfor and pick up the path that leads up the fields to Cwrt Isaf and then up Cwm Llefrith as far as the Bwlch Meillionen. Then follow the path beside the wall climbing up to the top of Moel Hebog.

From the cairn and trig point on the summit head south along the edge of the crumbling buttresses that support the summit plateau. Descend the broad ridge to the SSW, trending just left (south) of the strict ridge-line for about half a mile/0.8km to spot a ladder-stile over the first wall reached. Four more follow in the same direction, towards Llyn Cwmystradllyn, the last one

The hills of the Nantlle Ridge seen from Snowdon's south ridge.

being at the junction with a metalled track. Follow this, passing the hamlet of Tyddyn Mawr, and in a further 400yds/366m you will reach the dismantled railway where it swings sharply from east-west to north-south. Leave the road here, going west along the railway and follow it as it contours back gently to the point where you crossed it on the outward journey at the end of Cwm Llefrith. From here you turn down the fields again to the farm buildings at Cwrt Isaf and reverse the route back to Plas-y-pennant and the car.

## 4.7 Mynydd Mawr from Rhyd-Ddu
*6 miles/9.7km        3–4 hours*

Mynydd Mawr is an attractive, isolated mountain with a deep rocky cwm, Cwm Du, on its northern flank and a fine scarp of dramatic rock buttresses and pinnacles, Craig y Bera, on its southern one. (Craig y Bera gives a superb scrambling route in the sunshine, *see* **4.8**.) The best, the most scenic ascent, is by its east ridge, from Rhyd-Ddu, which is the way described, because although there are right-of-way paths from the southern end of Llyn Cwellyn at Planwydd Farm, there is nowhere to park there. A traverse of the mountain is perfectly feasible, say from Rhyd-Ddu over the mountain to Betws Garmon, but there would be transport problems and so the route described is a there-and-back one. It is very suitable for a short day and is a good viewpoint to Snowdon and to the peaks of the Nantlle Ridge, although you will generally only see the latter in silhouette against the light.

Mynydd Mawr and Llyn Cwellyn from the western slopes of Snowdon.

You can park on the SNP car park at Rhyd-Ddu (grid ref 571527) and then walk north along the main road through the village to the sharp-angled junction where the road turns off for Nantlle (grid ref 569530). Turn towards Nantlle and then take the forestry track on the right hand side, just beyond the few houses beside the road (grid ref 568529). (If you are lucky you may be able to park a couple of cars at the very end of the track before the gate is reached.) After about a quarter of an hour's easy walking along the good and level forestry track heading NNW, it becomes a single path running along a terrace for 100yds/91m, then a narrow path picking a way through brush-wood for another 100yds/91m. The shelf of the forestry track now re-appears but there is little sign that it is used and you leave it anyway for a path slanting up to the left through a for-est-break, heading WSW. This quickly reaches the edge of the forest at a ladder-stile over the forest fence and with a good view of Mynydd Mawr directly ahead. Turn uphill now alongside the forest edge, crossing two more stiles, to reach the top edge of the forest (grid ref 553543). Here a traversing path leads off round the hillside towards Craig y Bera (see **4.8**) and the east ridge path continues straight up the slope. It is an easy, though fairly steep climb up a grassy slope, crossing a broken wall, to reach a shoulder, Foel Rudd, after which easier angled walking on a good path winds round the head of the cwm drained by the Afon Goch, to reach the rounded summit with its cairn. Return the same way.

From Mynydd Mawr towards Glyder Fawr and Moel Cynghorion.

## 4.8 Scramble on Sentries' Ridge, Craig y Bera

SUMMARY: 499ft/152m of Grade 2 scrambling, south-facing; 6 miles/9.6km; 4–4¹/₂ hours. Once located, this slender and multi-pinnacled ridge gives superb scrambling on good holds and mostly good rock. The route splits naturally into two sections after about 200ft/60m; the direct start is best avoided on the right.

Craig y Bera has a reputation for loose rock, but I haven't really found it to be justified so far as Sentries' Ridge is concerned, and I have been there at least three times myself. Perhaps there has been enough traffic to remove most of the former loose rock. There definitely is still some rock which needs to be avoid-ed, but it is obvious enough and easy enough to avoid it. What is left gives a superb scramble of about 500ft/152m fairly low in difficulty and frequently (unlike anything in Cwm Du on the northern flank of the mountain) warm in the sunshine.

*See* 4.7 above for the details of access to the point where the traversing path leaves the east ridge route, and then follow a path towards the crags to a ladder-stile over a wire fence on the edge of a scree-field just before reaching them. It should take an hour and a quarter or so to reach this point.

From here the left-hand skyline is dominated by a big rock buttress with a prominent notch about a quarter of the way up it. To the right of this, nearer to you, is a wide scree gully bounded on its right by a broad-based buttress which has a great deal of heather in its middle section. Sentries' Ridge is a comparatively slender ridge of rock going directly up the centre of the wide scree gully although, from your viewpoint by the ladder-stile, you can only see some of the upper pinnacles; the lower ones are hidden from sight until you approach nearer. The lowest rocks are only 20ft/6.1m above the path but look steep and awkward and are avoided by going up scree to their right-hand corner, then a scramble on good holds up the rocks above for about 40ft/12.2m leads to a little neck. About 100ft/30.5m of easier heathery scrambling follows, to reach the base of some much steeper rock and what looks like the ridge proper. The direct approach looks very intimidating and is best avoided by simply going about 8ft/2.4m to the right and then upwards on good holds and at an easier angle, to reach the crest about 50ft/15.2m higher. A spiky bit of rock and a gendarme (or rock pinnacle), turned on the left, now follow. A sharp bit of rocky crest is next, for about 40ft/12.2m, leading to a little gap;

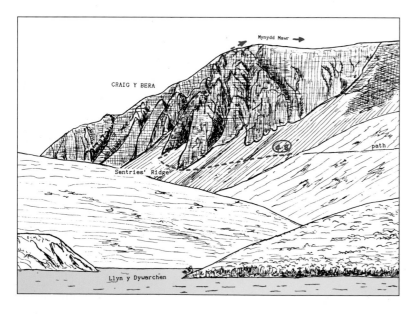

Craig y Bera and Mynydd Mawr seen from Llyn y Dywarchen.

this is followed by a slab of rock taken directly and leading towards the point of another pinnacle about 20ft/6.1m higher. You can scramble about half way up this and then step easily to the right to another little notch, followed by another little pinnacle. Immediately beyond is a broad, grassy col. You have gained about 200ft/61m of height and are at the end of the first obvious section.

Ahead a faint path runs up a heather runnel with rock on both sides. To the right, the rock is steep and bounds a scree gully; to the left, it does the same but is not so steep, is more broken generally and looks like the obvious line to take. In fact, the rocks just left of the heather runnel do give delightful scrambling on the lower section and then it is pleasanter to move right nearer the top. After about 100ft/30.5m you can step

Looking west along the upper cliffs of Craig y Bera.

across the face of a last gendarme to reach a rocky col and another natural pause.

Above now is about 30ft/9.1m of steeper but good rock and good holds and then a 20ft/6m stretch of heathery ridge. The heather continues up the groove beyond but you can now find good holds, this time on the rocks on the right-hand side of the heather-filled groove, until you reach easier ground below three final rock gendarmes. The rock on the first two looks loose and unsafe so they are best and easily turned on the left. The rock on the third is much better and can be scrambled over directly, to a final bit of rock and a grassy col. It is the end of a splendid route.

The fantastic array of pinnacles on the rest of the crag are now on your left hand as you almost immediately join the east ridge path to the top; your descent will be made memorable by fine views to Snowdon's Cwm Clogwyn and Moel Cynghorion.

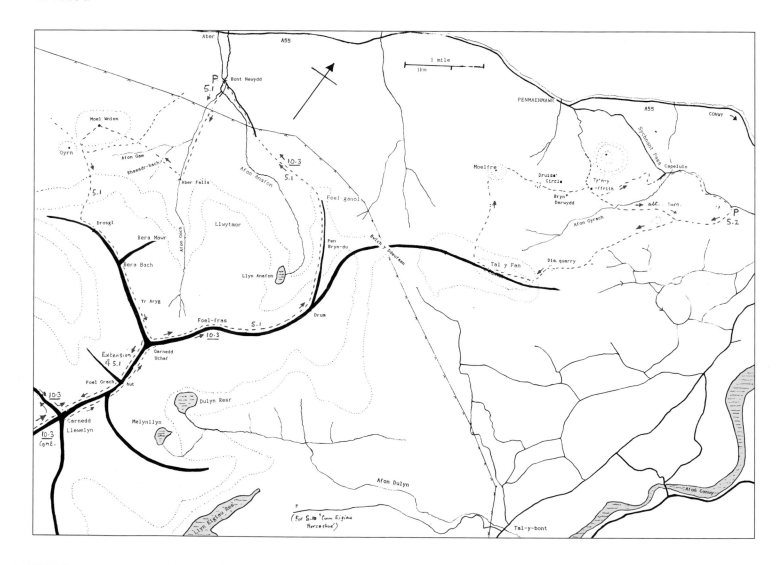

# 5: The Carneddau

## Part 1: Northern Carneddau

| | |
|---|---|
| BEST MAPS: | OS 1:50,000 Landranger 115 Snowdon & surrounding area<br>At the 1:25,000 scale, both maps, Outdoor Leisure 16 Snowdonia: Conwy Valley area and Outdoor Leisure 17 Snowdonia:<br>Snowdon area, are needed for Walk 5.1. For Walk 5.2, the 1:25,000 map is very confusing and is best avoided: stick to the 1:50,000. |

| Approx Distance | Approx Time | Highest Elevation Reached | Height Gained | Star Rating | Scramble Difficulty Grade | Scramble Height Gain |
|---|---|---|---|---|---|---|
| **5.1 Aber Falls and the Northern Circuit** | | | | | | |
| 11 miles/17.7km | 6–7 hours | 3038ft/926m | 3281ft/1000m | *** | — | — |
| **5.2 Tal y Fan and the Standing Stones** | | | | | | |
| 8½ miles/13.7km | 4–4½ hours | 2001ft/610m | 1499ft/457m | ** | — | — |

The northern part of the Carneddau feels more remote and is less popular than the southern, but the lonely summits above deep cwms give splendid walking when there is fine visibility. The two walks described below should give a good idea of its attractions.

### 5.1 Aber Falls and the Northern Circuit
*11 miles/17.7km        6–7 hours*

This wild and desolate area of high, wide plateaux, sprinkled with stony outcrops and cut by deep glaciated cwms, gives wonderful walking. Less frequented than the other parts of the massif, it should be treated with even more caution than is always needed on the Carneddau in unfavourable weather conditions. The walk described is a natural horseshoe-shaped circuit of the high hills whose streams drain to Conwy Bay just north of the famous Aber Falls. Don't go on a misty day; apart from problems of navigation you'll miss some glorious views over the Menai Straits to Anglesey and Puffin Island.

There is a small car park at Bont Newydd at grid ref 664720, just before the road crosses the Afon Aber and then, crossing the bridge and turning right, a twenty-minute walk south up the wooded tourist track leads to the superb Aber Falls. Here the white waters of the Afon Goch leap and twist down black crags in a tremendous cascade and at the foot of the falls you must

find enough dry boulders for a crossing to the other side. It's an easy matter when the water level is low but a different proposition in winter if they are glazed with ice. On the other bank, a stile leads to a path that contours to the smaller falls of the Rhaeadr-bach and continues westwards beyond them to cross the stream of the Afon Gam. A climb up the grassy slopes beyond crosses a track slanting round the shoulder of Moel Wnion and leads to the trig point on its top.

A short descent to the south now leads to some spoil-heaps and stone shelters beside the little pimple of Gyrn and then a path is joined which climbs steadily up the grassy hillside and so to the stony top of Drosgl. You've gained most of the height when you get here, a fine viewpoint, with splendid views to the south to Carnedd Dafydd, and the seamed face of the Ysgolion Duon (Black Ladders) seen over the long ridge thrown down to the north-west from the outlying summit of Yr Elen. Beyond are all the peaks of the Ogwen skyline and on a clear day even the knife edge of Yr Eifl on the distant Lleyn Peninsula cuts the skyline.

Press on to Bera Bach, the 'little hayrick', a heap of boulders and spiky rocks. To the north-east is Bera Mawr which, despite the fact that the Mawr in its name suggests that it is higher or larger than Bera Bach, is lower and smaller. It does, however, have an unusual pair of vertical spikes of rock which, seen from the west side, are curiously reminiscent of the similar spikes of Adam and Eve on Tryfan. Back in a south-easterly direction is Yr Aryg, a smaller outcrop of rocky spikes and boulders in a grassy expanse. Then a gentle climb in the same direction leads to the rocky eminence of Garnedd Uchaf.

*Left:* The Aber Falls in winter.

*Opposite:* Looking south-west towards Bethesda over Drosgl from Bera Bach.

Here you join the main highway across the Carneddau and, given sufficient energy and time, may choose to continue a little further before turning for home. If you do continue, to the south a well-marked path descends to a broad saddle and rises beyond it to Foel Grach, where there is a new mountain refuge. Like many others, in my time I huddled inside the old one, out of the wind, devouring my sandwiches and Mars bars, before either heading back to Ogwen or tackling the last remaining miles of the 'Welsh Threes' to Aber, but too many walkers started to rely on it, staying overnight in the squalor, waking to mist or white-out the next day, and then got into trouble. There were serious thoughts given to demolishing it altogether but the new hut is the best answer.

*Above:* Carnedd Llewelyn and Yr Elen seen from near Garnedd Uchaf.

*Opposite:* The ridge from Carnedd Dafydd rising to Carnedd Llewelyn.

Beyond Foel Grach, still heading south down a little descent followed by a steady climb, is the highest summit of the Carneddau, Carnedd Llewelyn (3491ft/1064m). To go there from Garnedd Uchaf and back will add just over 3 miles/4.8km, 557ft/170m and about an hour and a half to your day's efforts; a straightforward but rewarding climb, with magnificent views round the cirque of the Afon Llafar. On the return, a peep over the shoulder on the descent towards Foel Grach will disclose the superb ridge snaking up from Pen Llithrig-y-wrach to Penyrhelgi-du and Carnedd Llewelyn (see **5.10**). Whether you continue and return, or do not go on to Carnedd Llewelyn at all, the way is now north-east. Foel-fras is higher than Garnedd Uchaf, the last of the Welsh three-thousanders in this direction, and it has a beautifully made stone wall, visible for miles, on its summit. This wall, shortly transformed into a fence, curves down long convex slopes trending towards the reservoir of Llyn Anafon. These pass almost unnoticed in summer but under winter ice and wind I have found myself struggling to avoid slithering at ever-increasing speed downhill and was glad of my crampons.

A short rise leads to the summit of Drum, where there is a little stone windbreak, and then a jeep track continues north for a short distance to where a cairn marks the junction with a path leading north-east to the road (and those awful electricity pylons) at Bwlch y Ddeufaen. The jeep track continues and is still useful until, after about half a mile/0.8km, it swings round the side of the prominent little hill of Pen Bryn-du, when it is left for a faint path over the stony top of the hill itself. This is followed by a second stony top, Yr Orsedd, which switchbacks to the north then west again, before leading to the final rocky little top of Foel-ganol. This little ridge is a splendid conclusion to a grand day and shouldn't be missed.

The descent from Foel-ganol is to the west, steeply down a shaly slope to reach a track which, with one kink at the bottom, leads to a gate and the tarmac road-head. All that remains to complete a great day is about a mile/1.6km of easy walking downhill on the road to Bont Newydd and the car.

## 5.2 Tal y Fan and the Standing Stones
*8½ miles/13.7km        4–4½ hours*

You can stand on the ramparts of the magnificent ruins of Conwy Castle and see the crinkly little ridge of Tal y Fan, the most northerly mountain of the Carneddau, on the skyline. Leave the town behind, take the car to the Sychnant Pass, linking Conwy and Penmaenmawr, then take to your feet and within minutes you'll be well on your way towards it. This walk visits some of the standing stones and circles which perch inscrutably in great profusion in the northern Carneddau, then curves back to visit a particularly striking prehistoric stone circle high above Penmaenmawr. The walking is easy and delightful and gives a good short day almost any time, even though the higher hills may be shrouded in mist.

Approaching from Conwy, you pass through a little pine wood just before the road suddenly descends from the top of the Sychnant Pass. There is a little parking place right at the top of the pass itself but it is much better to park on a large open area to the left of the road immediately before it enters the wood (grid ref 754769) where there is a track heading up a little valley (signed 'not for motors') and a footpath sign.

Walk south-east along the track, past some little pools on the right and then, just before reaching a small house ahead, swing right, south-west, and follow the path leading well below the crest of a broad ridge crowned with a large monumental cairn on its northernmost eminence. After a mile/1.6km, by which time the path has become a broad grassy track, you reach the

The Druids Circle near Tal y Fan.

first of the stone circles; there are only about seven fairly small stones, but they are unmistakable. (The stone circle is clearly shown on the 1:50,000 map (grid ref 745753) which is much the better for this particular walk anyway, but not shown at all on the OS 1:25,000 map.) Apparently the Welsh thought at one time that these standing stones were symbols of idolatry and so lit fires next to them, then poured water over them to try to crack them into pieces. They don't appear to have had a lot of success.

Keep on to the south-west along this pleasant grassy track beside the wall, passing close by the end of a tarmac road where there are a group of sheepfolds, and staying on it as it becomes rougher underfoot and starts to climb to the west. After passing a large and solitary standing stone, this track shortly bends south and trends uphill to end at a disused quarry. Climb pathless and rough pasture behind the quarry to the south-west to reach the end of the Tal y Fan ridge when a path will be found shadowing a wall up to the fine rocky top some distance along the ridge, where there is a trig point just over the wall.

Downhill to the north-west, across rough open moorland grazed by wild ponies sheltering in little hollows, is the prominent hillock of Moelfre. There is little sign on the ground of the path on the map, and there is a skirt of gorse to avoid on the lower slope of Moelfre, but once you have climbed to its grassy windswept summit, the reward is a superb view. Don't descend to the path that runs below Moelfre on its northern side; instead stay on the broad grassy ridge heading ENE and ahead you'll soon see a very fine stone circle, approximately thirty yards/27m in diameter, with five big stones standing and others on the ground. This is the Druids Circle (grid ref 723746). It's a wonderful site, backed by wild mountains and overlooking the sea.

From here a good grassy track leads east, keeping on the east side of the knobbly little ridge, turning down through a gateway to pass in front of the house of Bryn Derwydd, recognisable by the half-dozen straggly pines near it. The same track continues to a junction near Ty'n-y-ffrith Farm. A left turn here (north-west) will take you quickly and steeply down Mountain Lane to Penmaenmawr and should be avoided; instead follow the signs round the farm to the north-east. You then have a choice of continuing in that direction and along the left (west) edge of a wooded valley down which flows the Afon Gyrach: if you go this way, you will follow a track that winds down to a promontory, then doubles back into the valley bottom before completing its descent to the little village of Capelulo. It is straightforward and the only snag is that you will then have to walk back up the steep bit of the Sychnant Pass road. Alternatively, if you head due east from Ty'n-y-ffrith, a faint path crosses the Afon Gyrach well above the wooded valley below and while it is still a small stream, enables you to cross over the end of the broad ridge ahead, connect with your outward path and so return to the car park without much loss of height.

# Part 2: Southern Carneddau

| BEST MAPS: | OS 1:50,000 Landranger 115 Snowdon & surrounding area<br>OS 1:25,000 Outdoor Leisure 16 Snowdonia: Conwy Valley area<br>and Outdoor Leisure 17 Snowdonia: Snowdon area |

| Approx Distance | Approx Time | Highest Elevation Reached | Height Gained | Star Rating | Scramble Difficulty Grade | Scramble Height Gain |
|---|---|---|---|---|---|---|
| **5.3 The Cwm Llafar Horseshoe** | | | | | | |
| 9 miles/14.5km | 5–6 hours | 3491ft/1064m | 3176ft/968m | **/*** | — | — |
| **5.4 Scramble to Carnedd Dafydd by the Llech Ddu Ridge** | | | | | | |
| 6 miles/9.6km | 5 hours | 3491ft/1064m | 2703ft/824m | ** | 1 | 650ft/198m |
| **5.5 Cregiau Gleision, Llyn Cowlyd and Pen Llithrig** | | | | | | |
| 10 miles/16.1km | 6 hours | 2621ft/799m | 3156ft/962m | ** | — | — |
| **5.6 Penyrhelgi-du and Pen Llithrig-y-wrach from the A5** | | | | | | |
| 7 miles/11.3km | 4–5 hours | 2733ft/833m | 2598ft/792m | ** | — | — |
| **5.7 Pen yr Ole Wen and the Carneddau from Llyn Ogwen** | | | | | | |
| 9 miles/14.5km | 5–6 hours | 3491ft/1064m | 2651ft/808m | **/*** | — | — |
| **5.7(a) Carnedd Dafydd from Ffynnon Llugwy** | | | | | | |
| 7½ miles/12km | 4 hours | 3425ft/1044m | 2500ft/762m | * | — | — |
| **5.7(b) Carnedd Dafydd via Cwm Lloer** | | | | | | |
| 6 miles/9.7km | 4 hours | 3425ft/1044m | 2451ft/747m | * | — | — |

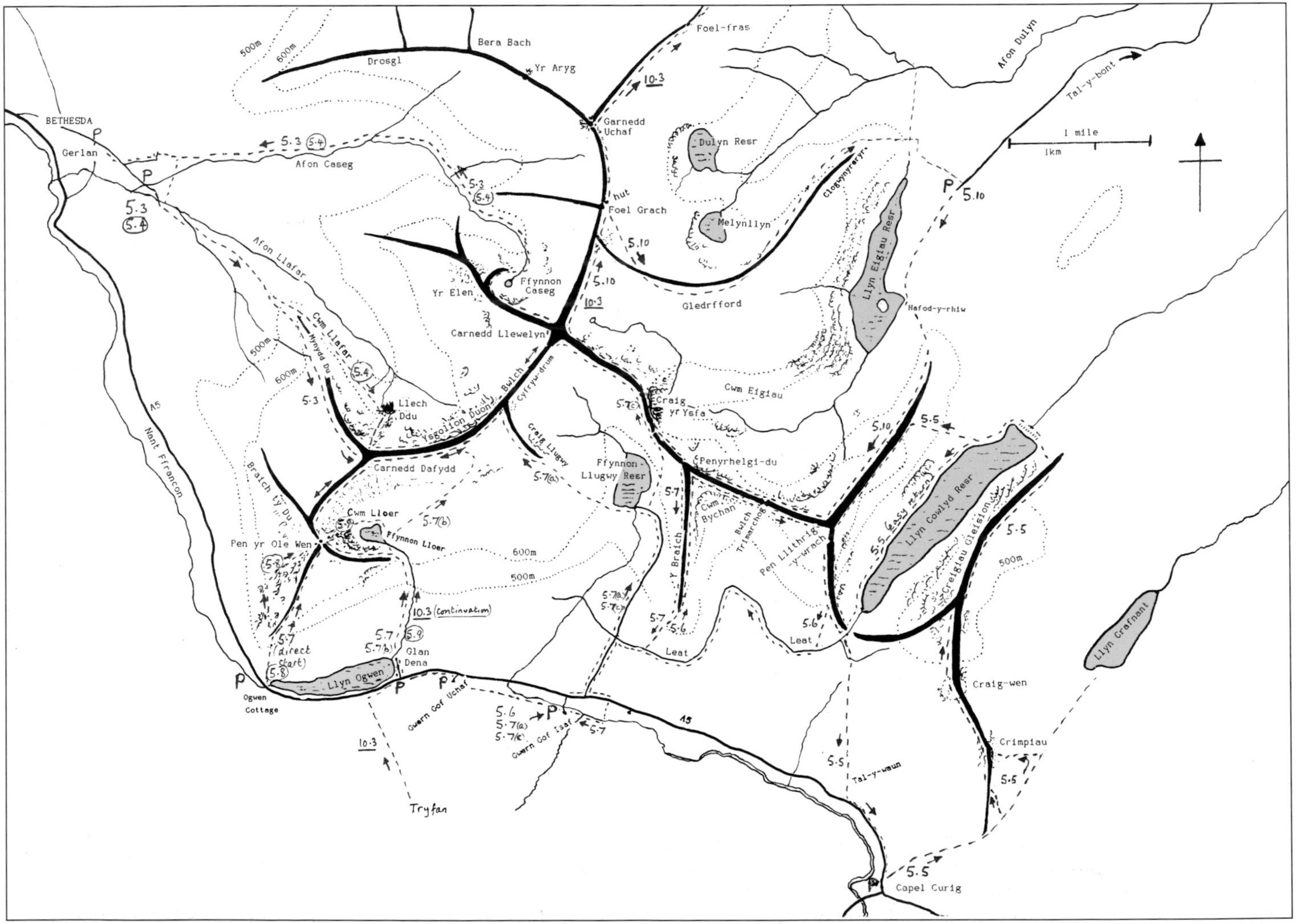

Bera Bach
Drosgl
Yr Aryg
Foel-fras
Afon Dulyn
Tal-y-bont
BETHESDA
Gerlan
Afon Caseg
Garnedd Uchaf
Dulyn Resr
1 mile
1km
hut
Foel Grach
Melynllyn
Cloqwynyrarar
Llyn Eigiau Resr
Afon Llafar
Ffynnon Caseg
Yr Elen
Gledrffford
Hafod-y-rhiw
Carnedd Llewelyn
Cwm Llafar
Mynydd Du
Llech Ddu
Bwlch Cyfryw-drum
Ysgolion Duon
Craig yr Ysfa
Cwm Eigiau
Craig Llugwy
Ffynnon Llugwy Resr
Penyrhelgi-du
Carnedd Dafydd
A5
Nant Ffrancon
Braich ty Du
Cwm Lloer
Ffynnon Lloer
Cwm Bychan
Bwlch Tryfan
Y Braich
Pen Llithrig y-wrach
Llyn Cowlyd Resr
Creigiau Gleision
Pen yr Ole Wen
600m
500m
Leat
Glan Dena
Llyn Ogwen
Llyn Crafnant
Craig-wen
Ogwen Cottage
Gwern Gof Uchaf
Gwern Gof Isaf
Crimpiau
Tal-y-waun
Tryfan
Capel Curig
10.3 (continuation)
5.5 (easy return)
5.7 (direct start)

The landscape of the southern part of the Carneddau, like the northern, is one of high plateaux with generally rounded summits, but it has been even more carved by ice and erosion, creating crags and wild cwms in the process. It contains the highest tops, and access is generally easy especially from the Ogwen valley. It is consequently more popular and the range of walks and scrambles I have chosen reflects this.

### 5.3 The Cwm Llafar Horseshoe
*9 miles/14.5km       5–6 hours*

This fine circuit of the skyline of the Afon Llafar takes in the two highest peaks of the Carneddau, with a trip out to and descent from the delightful outlying summit of Yr Elen. When you are doing the 'Welsh Threes', the turn off the main Carneddau ridge to take in Yr Elen usually seems more of an irritation than a pleasure, but this walk will enable it to be seen in its true light. Don't choose a misty day.

The start is actually in Gerlan, rather than Bethesda and parking is very limited, being possible for a couple of cars on a junction at grid ref 634663 or, if you are lucky, on a bend just by the bridge over the Afon Llafar at the south end of the village (grid ref 638660). This is just below the Welsh Water Authority's Gerlan Water Treatment Works and you need to walk up the road towards this and climb a ladder-stile just to the right of the Water Works gate. Go up the field beside the slate and wire fence, over a second stile towards the Afon Llafar and, in 200 yds/183m beyond the works, a track winds south-east through sheepfolds and old buildings to reach a bridge over a subsidiary stream. The track leads to another stile, then to more open country and a final stile over a wire fence, often enclosing ponies. The rather vague track beside the Afon Llafar now climbs gently over open moor although it improves dramatically once it starts to descend slightly into Cwm Llafar itself.

The great cirque of Cwm Llafar, showing the Llech Ddu ridge.

Before it does, you pass some sheepfolds on the left of the track and turn off here to climb the shapely, grass-covered ridge of Mynydd Du. There is only a faint path but the direction is obvious enough, with good views into the cwm of Afon Llafar below, where wild ponies are commonly seen grazing the hillside. The ridge leads to a grassy col and then the main bulk of Carnedd Dafydd rears up ahead. The ascent is now over a mixture of grass, stony ground and, in places, jumbled blocks, although these give way to smaller scree the higher you climb. The summit is crowned by a heap of stones and a three-sided windbreak in a stony wilderness but the descent westwards over rocky ground leads to grassier walking on the rim of the cirque of Afon Llafar. Long scree slopes fall to the south to the Ffynnon Lloer but to the north the crags of Ysgolion Duon (the Black Ladders) plunge impressively into the depths of the cwm, giving dramatic views across the gleaming Lavan Sands to Anglesey.

As it swings to the north-east, the ridge leads across the Bwlch Cyfryw-drum, becoming much narrower and more exposed and curving up towards Carnedd Llewelyn. (An escape would be possible from the ridge, and desirable if cloud or mist seriously reduce visibility at this point (or when on Carnedd Llewelyn) by turning down slopes to the north-west, skirting below the crags of Ysgolion Duon to reach the shelter of Cwm Llafar, and the excellent path down to it.) A last rocky slope leads to the summit, with a large cairn and fine retrospective views back to Carnedd Dafydd.

The stony ground has sprouted many cairns here but ensure any that you use as indicators now head WNW, slightly downhill initially and then out to a narrow rocky and exposed ridge which leads all too quickly to the usually peaceful rocky summit of Yr Elen. The tiny llyn of Ffynnon Caseg sparkles just below on the east side of Yr Elen and a delightful little ridge curves round the northern edge of its sheltering cwm, giving a little bit of a scramble but generally easy descent to its shore.

There is no such luxury as a path from here on the first part of the descent, following the line of the infant Afon Caseg, but you'll soon find a path at a sheepfold on the north bank (grid ref 673663) which will lead you along the north bank of the stream towards Bethesda. Where you were able to park in Gerlan or Bethesda will influence your choice for the last bit of the return. If parked near the Water Works, once you reach a disused quarry and spoil tips, turn south, cross the Afon Caseg and contour round the slope outside the enclosing fence to pick up the route of ascent just above the Water Works. If parked in Bethesda, continue going west and tracks and lanes will return you more directly.

## 5.4 Scramble to Carnedd Dafydd by the Llech Ddu Ridge

SUMMARY: 650ft/198m of Grade 1 scrambling, north-facing; 6 miles/9.6km, 5 hours. A ridge with several towers links the cliff of Llech Ddu to the upper slopes of Carnedd Dafydd. Its crest, attained by a slanting traverse from the broad gully at the right side of the cliff, gives an easy but exhilarating scramble.

This very good and easy scramble in a splendid position offers a most interesting approach to Carnedd Dafydd, in many ways much better than the walk just described. The start is exactly the same, from Gerlan (grid ref 638660) but don't turn up the ridge of Mynydd Du. Instead, continue south-east over just a slight rise into a long level valley which clearly at one time held a lake. An excellent grassy path leads towards the cwm until a little turn on a bend by a ruined sheepfold discloses a view ahead of the big crag of Llech Ddu, stretching apparently from bottom left to top right and backed by the deep gullies and vegetated buttresses of Ysgolion Duon. From being a lazy meandering stream, the Afon Llafar now becomes turbulent and the rising path deteriorates to fade out in a maze of boulders on the 500m contour directly below Llech Ddu. This is now seen as a huge black triangular-shaped crag, with its apex at the top. From the apex of the triangle, an elegant ridge or spur curves up almost to the summit of Carnedd Dafydd and this is the line of the scramble.

You could go to either side of the triangle of Llech Ddu's crags to find a way to the apex, but it is slightly shorter and more interesting to go to the right of the cliff. Make your way easily up to a sheepfold beside some huge boulders at the base of the crags and then up a vague path between the cliff and a water-slide to its right. Rocks and scree lead up the wide gully to a point where you can make use of a sheep-track to curl back left and so (just below the 800m contour) reach the grassy apex of the triangle of steep crags below: a superb eyrie.

Easy-angled rocks above now lead via ledges and grooves to where the actual crest of the ridge itself is reached. This is fairly narrow and furnished with several small rock towers, then a bigger one and then one which looks smaller. The small towers are taken direct, scrambling up little walls and level ledges on delightful rock at an overall easy angle. The bigger tower goes in the same fashion; then more little walls and ledges and a few grooves. It's most entertaining scrambling in a spectacular but not particularly exposed position. To be on the safe side, on a winter's day visit I made with Victoria Coghlan, we each eased one of my little dogs into our rucksacks, with their heads peeping out, but we didn't need to take any other safeguards.

The big tower ends at a neck with what is now seen to be a broader and steeper buttress ahead. This can also be tackled head-on although it is easier to traverse just a little left and ascend easier-angled rocks to the point where the ridge quite suddenly merges with the hillside. The summit is now just a few minutes away up easy ground to the south-east, where the main ridge path from Carnedd Dafydd to Carnedd Llewelyn is joined and the walk continued as in **5.3** above.

## 5.5 Cregiau Gleision, Llyn Cowlyd and Pen Llithrig
*10 miles/16.1km        6 hours*
*(Best map: 1:25,000 sheet 16 Conwy Valley area)*

This walk is an undulating traverse over a series of interesting rocky tops thrust up rather haphazardly from a surrounding grassy moorland. The terrain on the approach is not unlike that of the Moelwyn round Cnicht and Moel Meirch: rocky steps and knolls, grassy hollows and surprise views. An easier return than proposed would avoid the climb up Pen Llithrig-y-wrach and use the lakeside path alongside Llyn Cowlyd for the return.

There is a signed car park behind the shops in Capel Curig (grid ref 720581), then cross the road opposite the post office/store and take a signed path just to the left of the church. This leads up a field just left of and below the prominent rock knoll of The Pinnacles (used by students training at the nearby Plas Y Brenin mountain activities centre), then continues, swinging east and leading eventually to Llyn Crafnant. Our objective is the intriguing skyline of rocky outcrops up to the left and there are various well-concealed stiles to escape the enclosing walls, but it is simpler to head east, swinging to north-east, towards Crafnant on this path, round the toe of the ridge, into a wide basin drained by the Nant y Geuallt. At a junction with another path, which is also where the Nant y Geuallt stream is crossed, turn NNW and climb on a much sketchier track to a solid ladder-stile over a fence. You are now on open fell and an uphill climb to the north may leave you wondering where on earth you are exactly until you spot the little Llyn y Coryn, backed by a view of the crags of Craig-wen to the north, seen across an intervening depression. Nearer and to the north-east is the rocky little ridge of Crimpiau and you may go either over it or skirt round its north-west (left) flank by a well-defined path. If this approach to Crimpiau via Llyn y Coryn sounds confusing, or seems so when you are on the ground, simply stay on the very obvious path towards Crafnant until it reaches a col with a clear view down to the Llyn Crafnant Reservoir (grid ref 738596). From this col, a narrow path cuts back to the south-west and soon climbs up to Crimpiau.

From here a path continues towards the rock tiers of Craig-wen, the final one being inclined at an easy angle so that its upper surface gives enjoyable easy scrambling to the summit cairn. This is an even better viewpoint, especially along the wide valley towards Ogwen and Tryfan. Heading north, more rocky summits beckon. First a short descent to the flat boggy area of Bwlch Mignog, then a wide grassy gully leads you left of the broken rocks of Moel Defaid to its top, distinguished by two cairns. Craiglwyn follows, then an easier stretch to gain, at last, the ridge of the Creigiau Gleision and a first view of the reservoir of Llyn Cowlyd in a long glacial valley below.

Beyond the first summit cairn, the broad heathery ridge leads past an unusually large outcrop of brilliant white quartz to a second summit cairn, a little lower, but it is not until you get this far that you get any idea of the steepness of the crags that buttress the valley side above the lake. An attempt at too sudden a descent towards the dam would soon lead into difficulties and it is advisable to follow the ridge path through the heather even when it appears to be swinging away east towards Crafnant. When a junction of wire fences is reached, leave the main path and swing north along the line of the other fence until that also starts to take too steep a line. Then, grassy runnels lead more easily down to very rough and bouldery ground along the water's edge near the dam. Here a stile leads over the wall so that you can cross easily behind the dam.

A relatively painless return is possible now by simply following the good path which skirts the north-eastern shore of the lake and there is only a slight rise to overcome at Bwlch Cowlyd, which closes off the end of the lake, before it is downhill all the way back to Capel Curig. However, the great hunched shape of Pen Llithrig-y-wrach and its long north-eastern spur, which will have been well seen from Creigiau Gleision, will pose a challenge as well as a tougher way home.

To take this, the lakeside path helps for a little way before a slanting line leads to grassy rakes above a derelict farmhouse and its enclosed land. Keeping a course due west, you soon gain height but it is trackless ground and there's not much of a path even when you reach the broad top of the ridge. This is perhaps a little surprising in view of the fact that it forms one of the arms of the great Cwm Eigiau Horseshoe (*see* **5.10**) although

Craig-wen, near Crimpiau, seen from the tiny Llyn Coryn.

one develops on the steady rising tramp leading to a wide grassy plateau followed by the last pull up to the grassy summit crowned with a pile of stones. To the north-west, the eye is drawn almost irresistibly to the great cirque around the head of Cwm Eigiau: Penyrhelgi-du, the great cliffs of Craig yr Ysfa and, behind and beyond, Carnedd Llewelyn.

The south ridge from Pen Llithrig is quite well-defined to start but then becomes broad and shapeless; it's a much better descent than ascent for that reason. A conduit runs around the fellside on the south side of Llyn Cowlyd, which could be awkward to cross but there are bridges which enable you to pick up the well-marked path, with occasional ancient guide-posts, which now leads south across the wide moorland towards Capel Curig. As the road comes nearer you cross a stile and then bear left round the back of Tal-y-Waun Farm, after which very pleasant walking through greener fields and little clumps of trees leads to the road. About ten minutes later, you will be back in Capel Curig.

### 5.6 Penyrhelgi-du and Pen Llithrig-y-wrach from the A5
*7 miles/11.3km        4–5 hours*

The water authority's access road to Ffynnon Llugwy Reservoir, while being an eyesore visually, has made rapid access to the central part of the southern Carneddau really very easy for walkers and climbers, although cars are not allowed to use it. However, two or three can park with care so as not to block the road at the point where it meets the A5 (at grid ref 687602). Alternatively, park at Gwern Gof Isaf 200yds/183m or so to the west. This then makes possible a satisfying round of both Penyrhelgi-du and Pen Llithrig-y-wrach, which has good views into Cwm Eigiau and also to Snowdonia's deepest lake, Llyn Cowlyd.

Walk up the access road to the concrete bridge crossing the leat or water conduit (grid ref 691609), turn right (east) along this for a long ¼ mile/0.4km to where it is crossed by a footbridge. Now follow the path slanting up the slope to the right and the gap in the transverse wall and follow the path up the grassy ridge of Y Braich to the cairn on the broad top of Penyrhelgi-du. Now swing south-east, contouring round the rim of Cwm Bychan and make the fairly steep and roughish descent of about 600ft/183m to the col of Bwlch Trimarchog. A steady re-ascent leads to the grassy top of Pen Llithrig-y-wrach. This is an unremarkable summit in itself, but the descent of its south ridge (*see* **5.5**) gives good views of the deep dark waters of Llyn Cowlyd. (As an ascent it is a horror.) On the last bit of the descent, trend right to reach the conduit and then follow its path, contouring and curving into Cwm Tal-y-braich and then round to the south end of the Y Braich ridge to meet up with the outward route.

### 5.7 Pen yr Ole Wen and the Carneddau from Llyn Ogwen
*9 miles/14.5km        5–6 hours*

This fine clockwise horseshoe round of the highest summits of the Carneddau is best achieved by starting from the east end of Llyn Ogwen. Park on the verge of the A5 between Gwern Gof Uchaf Farm and Glan Dena (about grid ref 668606), then cross the bridge past Glan Dena towards the farm at Tal y Llyn Ogwen. Just before the farm, turn right beside the wall, go over the ladder-stile and, on an occasionally boggy and disappearing path, follow the line of the stream northwards and upwards towards Cwm Lloer. After a ladder-stile, the path is more obvious for a way but then fades again near the lip of the cwm, about 1100ft/335m above the road. The little lake of Ffynnon Lloer is a little way back from the lip and not seen until you have gained some height. The start up the broad end of the east ridge is not always immediately obvious but you will soon find yourself working up a short gully with some very easy scrambly

From Penyrhelgi-du looking over The Saddle to Craig yr Ysfa.

bits and then later up a path winding up the crest of the ridge, with a fine view of the little Ffynnon Lloer in the cwm below. Unlike the flog up the south ridge, where you reach endless tops masquerading as the summit before you reach the real one, this route finishes as near to the real top as makes no difference, though the cairn is not as impressive as the one slightly lower down, which commands better views over the Nant Ffrancon.

The fastest way of reaching this same point, from Ogwen Cottage and then up the brutally steep and shaly south ridge of Pen yr Ole Wen is also used by many walkers. It does allow grand views across the valley to Tryfan and the great cwms of the Glyders, but the unremitting slog of 2215ft/675m is hard going. If you still feel it is the way for you, start from Ogwen Cottage (grid ref 651603), walk a few paces down the A5 to where the road bridge crosses the Afon Ogwen just above the falls, then use the stile on the north side of the road. (If you peep below the modern road bridge, you'll see the little pack-horse bridge beneath it.) Paths now either lead to the right to avoid the first rock outcrop, or climb over it, but they quickly join and then zigzag up grass slopes which soon turn into rough and shaly ones of interminable length. Scramblers will be interested to know that there is a very good alternative up this south side of the mountain, not avoiding all the scree but adding a great deal to the interest (see **5.8**).

From Pen yr Ole Wen, heading along the main ridge, slightly east of north towards Carnedd Dafydd, the path passes over Carnedd Fach where there is a huge mound of stones, almost too big to be man-made yet not looking natural either. There is a wind-break hollowed out on top and a little further on there is another but smaller wind-break of the same kind. A steady rise of about 250ft/76m now leads to a three-chambered wind-break and a collapsed cairn on the stony top of Carnedd Dafydd. Initially, the gentle descent to the east around the head of Cwm Llafar is quite rocky but soon becomes easy and grassy in contrast to the steep crags of Ysgolion Duon, which tumble away on the left hand. Their steep gullies catch and hold snow and ice, giving good though serious winter sport for climbers but a glance backwards across the great face shows quite clearly the easy angle of the Llech Ddu ridge, once above its initial precipice (see **5.4** above). Across Cwm Llafar can also be seen the outlying peak of Yr Elen, disliked by many a 'Welsh Threes' walker, but a gem for all that.

Just before the ridge reaches its lowest point, at Bwlch Cyfryw-drum, where it becomes noticeably sharper, it also becomes much stonier. It is perhaps worth mentioning that a comparatively easy descent down an ill-defined broad spur to the south-east is possible from here to reach the reservoir of Ffynnon Llugwy and its metalled access road. This would give a useful escape in the event of bad weather although crags just above the lake need to be avoided.

A steady trudge over stony ground now leads uphill for nearly 450ft/137m to the wind-breaks and cairns on the mighty Carnedd Llewelyn. From this highest point of the Carneddau, the distant views are wide ranging, with a fine one back towards Carnedd Dafydd, but its domed plateau makes it difficult to be certain of the precise direction you will need next and it is advisable, in anything other than clear conditions, to rely on a compass bearing to the south-east before moving off the summit. A single marker cairn then indicates the top of the path, firstly down scree to a rockier section on the edge of the upper rim of Cwm Eigiau and then just below and to the right of the edge. As height is lost and the ridge temporarily broadens, the path itself becomes much less visible as it threads amongst the rocks and stones on the approach to Craig yr Ysfa. The presence of this dramatic cliff is only half-suspected; even when you've seen it many times before and know it is there, it still comes as something of a shock to look down from the rim of the tremendous amphitheatre dropping away with such dramatic suddenness into Cwm Eigiau.

After reaching Craig yr Ysfa the terrain changes completely as you make a descent of about 60ft/18m down to the grassy but narrow and exposed col before the climb on the other side to Penyrhelgi-du. This descent is down broken rocks and for about 30ft/9.1m these are well polished and need great care in wet, windy or winter conditions especially, as a slip could lead to an uncontrolled descent to the left into Cwm Eigiau or to the right towards the dark waters of the Ffynnon Llugwy Reservoir which are now almost directly below. The narrow ridge of the col itself, while easy enough in summer, needs great care in high wind.

The cairn at the lowest point is a place for changing your mind, if any is needed, for you have a choice of ways. A steep path, down very shaly ground (although pieces of rock have been bundled in plastic netting to consolidate the path in places) descends from here to the south for about 400ft/122m towards the shore of Ffynnon Llugwy, from where the metalled access road leads swiftly to the A5. If you resist this temptation and complete the slight ascent (about 150ft/46m) up to the broad and rather featureless summit of Penyrhelgi-du, the rock is shaly and a bit loose in places; adverse conditions could make it quite tricky in either direction. Going this way, however, does enable you to keep more to the spirit of this grand walk, enjoy a delightful descent ridge and avoid some tarmac.

So from the summit, head due south on a path along the broad and grassy ridge of Y Braich, gradually descending, until you reach a gap in a transverse wall. A conduit or leat contours at 1312ft/400m in two big loops, collecting water across these southern slopes of the Carneddau from the Afon Llugwy to Llyn Cowlyd (and beyond). The ground that it crosses is boggy and well-furnished with the sort of clumpy grass tussocks that are purgatory for walking through, especially towards the end of a day. On the other hand, the immediate banks of the conduit give firm, grassy and fast walking, and unerringly lead to various footbridges by which it may also be crossed. So from the gap in the wall, first contour to the right and then pass right down a grassy slope to where one of these footbridges enables you to cross to the south side of the conduit. The path alongside this goes west quickly and leads to the metalled access road at a concrete bridge and you can then soon reach the A5.

I'm afraid just over a mile/1.6km of road-walking is almost unavoidable now to return to the car. If, however, you are prepared to turn east along the A5 towards Helyg for just a short way, you'll be able to take the footpath signed across the fields to connect with the track of the old road. This will lead much more pleasantly to Gwern Gof Uchaf Farm and the main road again, but now with only a few paces of tarmac.

It is not worthwhile trying to cut directly across the moorland to Glan Dena from the Ffynnon Llugwy Reservoir, although it may look tempting. The way soon becomes exceptionally boggy and you get snarled up in the fences surrounding Glan Dena. It is much better to use the way described above.

### 5.7a Carnedd Dafydd from Ffynnon Llugwy
*7½ miles/12.1km*      *4 hours*

As already mentioned above, the spur running south-east from the point where the Carnedd Dafydd-Carnedd Llewelyn ridge becomes rocky (Bwlch Cyfryw-drum) can be used as a means of escape down to Ffynnon Llugwy. It is clear that this same ridge is being used as a means of ascent to, as well as descent from, Carnedd Dafydd, as there is now a sketchy path in places.

Park at Gwern Gof Isaf (grid ref 685601), walk back to the A5 and turn right (east) for 250 yds/230m to the end of the metalled reservoir road (no vehicular access) at grid ref 687602. Walk up this to its end, then head north-east up the spur, curving west when you reach the main ridge above the cliffs of Ysgolion Duon and so reach Carnedd Dafydd. The logical continuation is then over to Pen yr Ole Wen, with a descent down its east ridge, and so to reach the A5 at Glan Dena (**5.7** in reverse). Now the old road between Gwern Gof Uchaf and Gwern Gof Isaf gives a much pleasanter return to the start than the A5.

### 5.7b Carnedd Dafydd via Cwm Lloer
*6 miles/9.7km*      *4 hours*

This even shorter mini horseshoe completely avoids all tarmac bashing. The walk goes from Glan Dena into Cwm Lloer as far as the outflow from the lake, then climbs easy (though tedious) grass slopes to the north-east for 1000ft/305m towards Craig Llugwy and then, reaching the main ridge, turns uphill along it to Carnedd Dafydd. A traverse from there to Pen yr Ole Wen and a descent down its east ridge lead back to Cwm Lloer and an easy return to the car.

| Approx Distance | Approx Time | Highest Elevation Reached | Height Gained | Star Rating | Scramble Difficulty Grade | Scramble Height Gain |
|---|---|---|---|---|---|---|
| **5.7(c) Carnedd Llewelyn and Carnedd Dafydd from Ffynnon Llugwy** | | | | | | |
| 9 miles/14.5km | 6 hours | 3491ft/1064m | 3018ft/920m | *** | — | — |
| **5.8 Scramble on west face of Pen yr Ole Wen by the Horned Ridge** | | | | | | |
| 3½ miles/5.6km | 4 hours | 3209ft/978m | 2215ft/675m | ** | 2/3 | 751ft/229m |
| **5.9 Scramble in Cwm Lloer** | | | | | | |
| 5½ miles/8.9km | 5 hours | 3425ft/1044m | 2461ft/750m | */** | 2 | 298ft/91m |
| **5.10 Cwm Eigiau Horseshoe** | | | | | | |
| 10½ miles/16.9km | 6–8 hours | 3425ft/1044m | 3120ft/951m | *** | — | — |

### 5.7c Carnedd Llewelyn and Carnedd Dafydd from Ffynnon Llugwy
*9 miles/14.5km       6 hours*

The unsightly but useful access road (no vehicular traffic) to Ffynnon Llugwy Reservoir from the A5 speeds the approach to the two highest mountains of the Carneddau. The start is as for **5.7a** above, parking at Gwern Gof Isaf and walking up the access road to the reservoir. From here an obvious path starts across the hillside and then zigzags up to the bwlch between Penyrhelgi-du and Craig yr Ysfa. The potentially tricky although short scramble up to the latter is followed by the ascent of the long ridge on the southern rim of Cwm Eigiau to the summit of Carnedd Llewelyn and the traverse of the ridge curving south-west and up to the top of Carnedd Dafydd. The traverse continues to Pen yr Ole Wen with a descent down to Glan Dena via the east ridge. Return as detailed in **5.7a**, using the old road rather than the A5 to reach Gwern Gof Isaf.

Wild pony on the slopes of Carnedd Llewelyn above Ffynnon Llugwy.

## 5.8 Scramble on west face of Pen yr Ole Wen by the Horned Ridge

*3¹/₂ miles/5.6km        4 hours*

SUMMARY: Approx 750ft/229m of Grade 2/3 scrambling, south-facing; 3¹/₂ miles/5.6km, 4 hours. A short lower section on some easily identifiable pinnacles just above the A5 (marked Clogwyn Llys on the 1:25,000 map) followed by 800ft/244m of walking up scree leads to a very spiky but continuous spur (not too easy to locate) leading through the upper crags.

The one drawback to this otherwise splendid scramble is that there is about 800ft/244m of uninteresting ground between the two halves. Having said that, the lower section gives about 150ft/46m of very good scrambling and the upper section about 600ft/183m of similar quality so it is definitely worth making the effort to link the two. The upper section shows very little sign of use; it deserves to be much better known.

From 'the horns' on the west face of Pen yr Ole Wen, above Ogwen.

The start is as for the south ridge (*see* **5.7**). Follow the path slightly left and up the rock staircase to the top of the first rise, where three circular stone windbreaks look down the Nant Ffrancon like gun emplacements or lookouts. When the path begins to zigzag up grassy slopes beyond them, traverse left instead below several rock buttresses towards a longer and more continuous ridge which has a steep buttress just above the road, then an easier angled vegetated section and finally a steeper rocky section topped by two very distinctive pinnacles looking just like a pair of horns. Cross a collapsing wall about half way towards this ridge then slant up towards the shoulder below the horns. The broad gully to the right of our ridge has a wall built across its width about 50ft/15m or so above the point where you can easily step onto the ridge below the steeper rock.

From the bottom of the crags, go round left to where a much easier spiky rib with plenty of heather leads upwards on excellent holds for about 120ft/37m to a little platform immediately below and to the left of the horns. Climbing up onto a big flaky spike round on their left side enables you to step into a gap between another bigger spike and the first horn and so onto a ledge on the south face, looking towards Ogwen Cottage. Traverse right on big holds, continuing the traverse across the Ogwen face of the second horn to another gap and then a final bit of rocky ridge leads to a heathery shoulder. It's delightful, airy scrambling; what a pity it isn't longer.

Now a faint path leads to a grassy gully between a small buttress on the left and a bigger one on the right and by the time you're at its top, you've gained about 350ft/107m. The skyline directly ahead is a mass of pinnacles, but if you ignore the lowest slightly detached section on the very left, the remainder of the rock on the left-hand skyline looks as though it forms a continuous ridge made up of rock spikes and towers, and it does. To get there, requires an ascent of another 450ft/137m thrashing up stony runnels between heather and bilberry. Now you can

step onto good rock again, up little ramps and ledges and, trending across to the right hand side when it becomes too steep, you gradually gain about 250ft/76m of height without any particular difficulty, reach the top of a first coherent group of pinnacles. Now there is an angled slab to cross, to reach an easier little groove on its right and this leads across the left side of a large tower. Above again is another tower with a harder-looking groove up its face, but once more you can take an easier grassy groove to the right to avoid it. Finally, you can pull onto the almost level crest of the ridge, quite sharp and delightful, which all too soon runs into a grassy ridge. It's almost all over now: just one easy-angled stretch of rock and you reach the path at an altitude of about 2725ft/831m. I wish I'd known about it years ago.

A pleasant return route from here would be to continue to the top of Pen yr Ole Wen and descend the east ridge to the outflow from Ffynnon Llugwy. From there descend to the farm at Tal y Llyn Ogwen and then follow a path along its north shore back to Ogwen Cottage. This will enable you to avoid a road walk.

### 5.9 Scramble in Cwm Lloer
*5¹/₂ miles/8.9km      5 hours*

SUMMARY: Approx 300ft/91m of Grade 2 scrambling, east-facing; 5¹/₂ miles/8.9km, 5 hours. This takes the easiest line up the left-hand edge of the most prominent buttress in the cwm, traverses right at half-height at the foot of an obvious slab to an airy perch and then goes upwards to the finish. Some tedious scree leads to the summit of Pen yr Ole Wen.

Apart from being a better way onto the Carneddau than the direct ascent of the south ridge of Pen yr Ole Wen, which is steep, loose and tedious, the approach by way of its east ridge also gives the opportunity for this short but good scramble on excellent rock. Cwm Lloer itself is a delightful, secluded place and well worthy of a visit in its own right.

Park on the side of the A5 near Glan Dena (grid ref 668606) and then (as in Walk **5.7**) follow the line of the stream northwards and into Cwm Lloer. Apart from the path using the east ridge of Pen yr Ole Wen, a second, less-used path circles the small lake of Ffynnon Lloer and then scrabbles up a rather tiresome scree slope to reach the ridge connecting Pen yr Ole Wen with Carnedd Dafydd. On the far (west) side of the lake this path almost touches the lowest rocks of what is by far the most prominent rocky buttress in the cwm. This forms a distinct nose at the end of the broken ridge projecting into the upper part of the cwm from Pen yr Ole Wen and is separated from three other bands of vegetated rocks to the left by an easy-angled gully with a scree fan at its base.

As you ramble round the shore of the lake, with trout leaping and plopping from the tranquil waters, the buttress can be seen to consist of a series of steep rock ribs separated by grassy gullies which taper towards the top. There are rock climbs on all the steeper rock but the left-hand edge of the buttress looks as though it has the easiest angle with a continuous line, until it reaches a prominent inclined slab of pale rock about two-thirds of the way up. The scramble goes to the foot of this slab and then traverses across its foot before going upwards again.

Follow the path round the shore and then uphill to the point where it is almost level with the base of the rocks on the right-hand edge of the buttress. Then traverse left below the crag and, passing a grassy bay almost overhung by steeper rock, reach the right-hand edge of the main, wide gully. Here a narrow ridge is found, starting with some tilted blocks. The blocks themselves are too awkward but a sloping slab just to their right has enough holds to gain 20ft/6m, then gain the ridge itself for some easier scrambling for a further 40ft/12m or so. You'll reach a large

block split by a 10ft/3m crack, which can be avoided by going left, although there are good holds up the right-hand edge of it. An easy bit of the ridge follows, leading to a broken heathery ledge at the foot of the prominent inclined slab seen so well from below. There is an obvious escape into the continuation of the gully on the left from here, but at considerable loss of the quality of the route, for the best bit now follows.

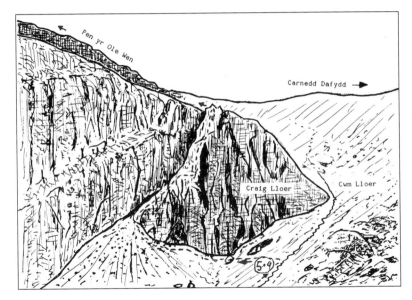

A grassy ledge at the foot of the slabs runs out to the right for about 20ft/6m giving easy progress, then a further 10ft/3m on good rock holds leads to a breath-taking position in a notch on the skyline overlooking a steep groove on the right, with the sweep of the big slab on the left; it's a wonderful place to be for a

few moments. Happily, immediately above the notch, good holds lead to more ledges with short walls between them and easy progress is made to reach some very knobbly rocks just before a gap. This is quickly crossed to reach the next section, which is rather like scrambling over blocks of aggregate with embedded quartz pebbles. A steeper, but easy 15ft/4.6m chimney finally leads to easy ground, about 300ft/91m from the start, at a neck where the buttress is joined to the rest of the hillside.

It is now a straightforward walk up an easy, stony slope for a further 250ft/76m or so to reach a steeper band of broken and vegetated rocks penetrated by an easy gully bridged at one point by a large rock flake. Scramble-walking in the steps of the sheep who also use this route soon leads to the final easy slopes and the cairn on the summit at 3209ft/978m.

Unless you are descending to the valley, the logical continuation now is to Carnedd Dafydd, then out along the ridge above the cliffs of Ysgolion Duon to a point before it narrows onto Bwlch Cyfryw-drum. Turn back sharply to the south-west and you can descend the shaly then grassy slopes back to Ffynnon Lloer to rejoin the route of ascent.

## 5.10 Cwm Eigiau Horseshoe
*10½ miles/16.9km        6–8 hours*

The north-eastern slopes of the Carneddau are wild, remote and magnificent, with a quietness and solitude rarely found. Paths are not particularly well marked on the ground except in the middle section and so it is not a walk for a day of uncertain visibility. Fortunately, the road to the reservoir of Llyn Eigiau makes it possible to drive almost into the heart of this superb mountainscape and to begin this classic Welsh circuit at just

Ffynnon Lloer and Cwm Lloer on Pen yr Ole Wen.

over 1200ft/366m above sea-level. The narrow road starts from Tal-y-bont (grid ref 767688) in the Conwy valley, and climbs steeply to the road-head at a gate at grid ref 732663. (Take care not to take the road to Llanbedr-y-cennin which is signed and has a pub on the corner. If going north down the Conwy valley, the road you seek is 50yds/46m before this one, immediately before crossing the Afon Dulyn, and is unsigned.) At the end of the metalled section, there is a good parking area beside the gate (no access for cars beyond), just by a ladder-stile and a rough track which leads to the reservoir of Melynllyn; this track will be used on the return.

Head south-west now along the track, over a couple of ladder-stiles on the way, towards the dam wall of Llyn Eigiau. You shortly pass a breach in the wall at its highest point (about 15ft/4.5m), which is presumably where it failed in the disaster of 1925 when sixteen people were drowned as a result. The prospect ahead is of a long line of crags and very steep ground on the right hand, while the skyline shows the notch of the Bwlch Trimarchog and the rise up to the dark silhouette of Pen Llithrig-y-wrach, the first main objective. Reaching another break in the dam wall, the main track continues up the valley floor, swinging to the north-west and enabling you to reach Carnedd Llewelyn or Foel Grach very directly on some other occasion. This time, however, turn left (south-east) on the other track towards the house of Hafod-y-rhiw sheltering in some trees. Just before passing it, turn off up grass slopes behind and to the east of the house to get onto the broad north-east ridge of Pen Llithrig. The grass soon gives way to dense heather and the odd sheep track is only of marginal help as you gain height over heather and rock to about 2000ft/610m, when a splendid view of the tremendous crag of Craig yr Ysfa, hidden until now, appears illuminated in morning light. The initial struggle is now over and a path develops as you cross a broad and sometimes boggy hause, pass over a broad hump and then tackle the last slope up to Pen Llithwrig. The actual grassy summit is about 100yds/91m away from the top of the path, to the east and a little bit higher, but it is the splendid ridge to the north-west, dominated by Craig yr Ysfa, which commands your attention now.

The near-500ft/152m descent to the wire fence and ladder-stile on the Bwlch Trimarchog is simple and straightforward, as is the 600ft/183m ascent beyond to the cairn on the stony top of the next summit Penyrhelgi-du, although, rather curiously, there is a grassy hump a little beyond, but definitely higher, on which there is no cairn. This will be of academic interest only, however, once you are just beyond this point, for the ridge ahead suddenly sharpens noticeably and drops away at your feet, with Craig yr Ysfa directly ahead and the black waters of Ffynnon Llugwy below on the left hand.

The descent to the bwlch beyond follows. It is only about 150ft/46m but it is steep and shaly and some of the rock is loose, so care is needed, particularly in the wet or wind. Unlike the Bwlch Trimarchog earlier, this one is not just a V-shaped notch, for it undulates over a length of perhaps 400yds/366m; a cairn marks the spot at the far end where the path begins the descent to Ffynnon Llugwy. Almost immediately the path starts to climb and in two minutes your nose will be up against a little section of rock slabs, easy-angled and only about 50ft/15.2m in height but polished with use. Hands will only be needed for keeping you balanced if it is dry, but in wet or windy conditions they will certainly be needed for assistance. At just below 3000ft/914m you will be on top of Craig yr Ysfa and peering down the Amphitheatre Gully to the old ruined buildings seen way below in Cwm Eigiau.

Take care when leaving Craig yr Ysfa not to wander onto a lower curving path that heads off towards Bwlch Cyfryw-drum and Carnedd Dafydd, avoiding Carnedd Llewelyn. The path to the latter which you need is not cairned, keeps initially just below the edge of Cwm Eigiau but then joins the edge at a point where it becomes noticeably rocky and where you can peer over to see two tiny llyns at the head of the cwm below. The last bit is simply a plod, with a single marker cairn only, just south-east of the summit. Apart from the views along the ridge snaking back to Carnedd Dafydd and over to Cwm Llafar, this is not a great viewpoint but it is the high point. It should have taken you about four hours to get here.

Foel Grach is about a mile/1.6km away to the NNE, a cairned descent of about 400ft/122m over rough and stony ground which terminates at a couple of prominent and spiky rock castles, after which the path runs out onto a wide grassy col. Yr Elen and the little edge curving down from its summit, hidden from almost all other angles, is seen from here as the path very gently climbs up the last 150ft/46m to the stony top of Foel Grach. Almost hidden amongst the rocks just north-east of the summit is the specially reconstructed refuge hut. I have memories of the older one; what a grotty place that was. When I popped into the new one, one mid-December, I was intrigued to find half a dozen inflated balloons and some shiny red tinsel decorating the interior; I am happy to report I didn't find any empties.

This is the turning-point. To return, the first objective is to get onto the broad ridge which curves in a big arc to the south of Melynllyn and to the north-west of Llyn Eigiau Reservoir (marked 'Gledrfford' on both 1:50,000 and 1:25,000 maps). This is quite straightforward in clear weather, simply descending the slopes to the SSE from Foel Grach onto a wide and gently sloping plateau distinguished by some large boulders. You may pick up the path shown on the maps climbing out of Cwm Eigiau, but it is not very clear on the ground. If you do find and use it, ensure you leave it when on the plateau and turn east, swinging to north-east, along a tractor-track and heading for a spot-height (2390ft/735m) at grid ref 713655, a rocky outcrop on the edge of the crags overlooking Llyn Eigiau. This is marvellous striding-out country and the sense of remoteness is at its greatest here.

The Pen Llithrig-to-Penyrhelgi-du Ridge seen from Foel Grach

The steep slabs dropping into the waters of Melynllyn remain out of sight until you have lost some height and without a glance at the map, only the steep crags below the distant summit of Foel-fras would make you suspect the hidden presence of the Dulyn Reservoir, for this is hidden completely until you reach the area of the spot-height.

The tractor-track now starts to descend more steeply and, although you may think of slightly more direct ways back to the car, it is easiest to simply walk downhill with it. It turns east when just north of the craggy ground of Clogwynyreryr, crosses the tunnel (for the water flowing from Llyn Eigiau Reservoir) and quickly leads you back to the ladder-stile next to the car park area.

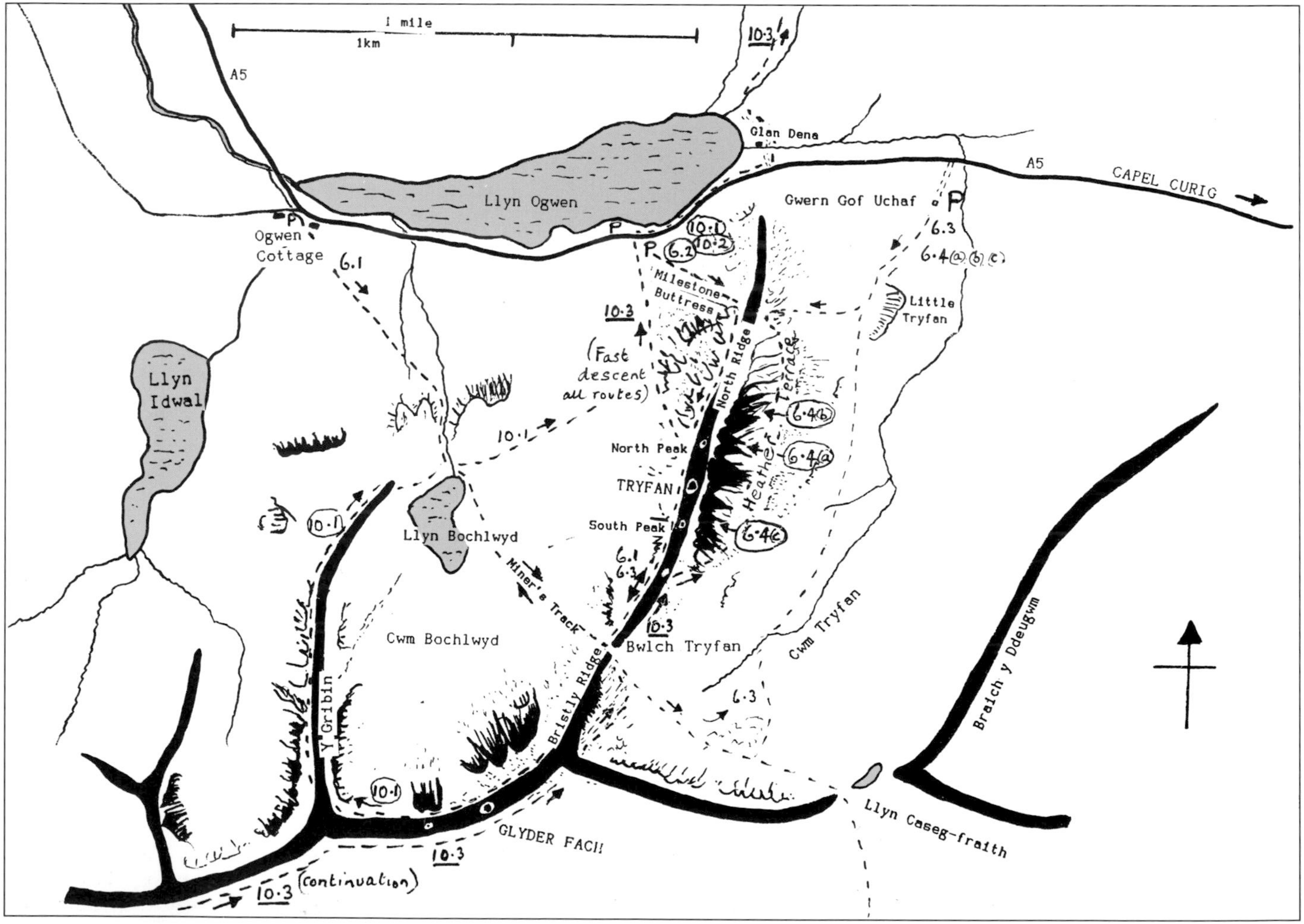
1 mile
1km
A5
10·3
Glan Dena
A5
CAPEL CURIG
Llyn Ogwen
Gwern Gof Uchaf
P
6.3
6·4 ⓐ ⓑ ⓒ
Ogwen Cottage
6.1
10·1
10·2
6.2
Milestone Buttress
Little Tryfan
10·3
(Fast descent all routes)
North Ridge
Heather Terrace
Llyn Idwal
10·1
6·4ⓑ
6·4ⓐ
North Peak
TRYFAN
South Peak
6·4ⓒ
Llyn Bochlwyd
Miner's Track
6.1
6.3
10·3
Bwlch Tryfan
Cwm Tryfan
Cwm Bochlwyd
Bristly Ridge
Y Gribin
6.3
Braich y Ddeugwm
10·1
GLYDER FACH
10·3
Llyn Caseg-fraith
10·3 (continuation)

# 6: Tryfan

| | | | | | | |
|---|---|---|---|---|---|---|
| BEST MAPS: | OS 1:50,000 Landranger 115 Snowdon & surrounding area | | | | | |
| | OS 1:25,000 Outdoor Leisure 17 Snowdonia: Snowdon area | | | | | |

| Approx Distance | Approx Time | Highest Elevation Reached | Height Gained | Star Rating | Scramble Difficulty Grade | Scramble Height Gain |
|---|---|---|---|---|---|---|
| **6.1 Tryfan by the South Ridge from Bwlch Tryfan** | | | | | | |
| 3¹/₂ miles/5.6km | 4 hours | 3002ft/915m | 2018ft/615m | * | — | — |
| **6.2 Tryfan by the North Ridge, descent by the Heather Terrace** | | | | | | |
| 2¹/₂ miles/4km | 3–5 hours | 3002ft/915m | 2018ft/615m | *** | Grade 1 by the easiest route; Grade 2 by the most direct | 499ft/152m |
| **6.3 Tryfan by the Heather Terrace and the South Ridge** | | | | | | |
| 2¹/₂ miles/4km | 3–4 hours | 3002ft/915m | 2018ft/615m | * | — | — |
| **6.4 Scrambles from the Heather Terrace** **6.4(a) The central route by Little Gully** | | | | | | |
| 2¹/₂ miles/4km | 3–4 hours | 3002ft/915m | 2018ft/615m | ** | 1 | 650ft/198m |
| **6.4(b) The north buttress route** | | | | | | |
| 2¹/₂ miles/4km | 3–4 hours | 3002ft/915m | 2018ft/615m | * | 1–2 | 551ft/168m |
| **6.4(c) The south rib route** | | | | | | |
| 2¹/₂ miles/4km | 4 hours | 3002ft/915m | 2018ft/615m | */** | 3 | 499ft/152m |

The view of the east face of Tryfan, seen from the A5 going from Capel Curig towards Llyn Ogwen, is one of the unforgettable sights of the Welsh mountains. It looks such a *real* mountain: a classic shape with three fine rocky summits, a long craggy north ridge, its east face seamed by four deep gullies separating soaring buttresses; all tell of the grinding ice of the glaciers and of standing proud against fierce winters since the ice departed. It is a sight to make any mountain-lover's heart beat a little faster in anticipation. It doesn't look an easy mountain to scale; even the easiest routes need some simple scrambling, but the sense of achievement is that much greater as a result of literally getting to grips with the rock. Its popularity, at all seasons, is as great as ever and deservedly so, but in icy winter conditions all its routes can become major expeditions requiring not just the right equipment but the ability to use it properly. As well as the detailed sketch map, I have also included a sketch of the East Face of the mountain where the bulk of the scrambles are found, and readers should check this for further clarification (*see* Walk **6.4**).

### 6.1 Tryfan by the South Ridge from Bwlch Tryfan
*3½ miles/5.6km        4 hours*

This is the easiest of the ways up Tryfan, requires very little use of hands and is normally therefore the safest and pleasantest for those who just want to get to the top. It is worth mentioning that it also takes the full force of the normal south-westerly winds and weather, more so even than the North Ridge and certainly more than the East Face routes.

The start is the Miner's Track from Ogwen Cottage (grid ref 651603) at the west end of Llyn Ogwen; there is plenty of parking there or in laybys along the edge of the A5. Follow the track signed for Idwal round the newish buildings near the Youth Hostel and then, having crossed the river and reached the point where the main Idwal track turns sharp right (south-west), keep straight on instead, heading for the outflow from the unseen Llyn Bochlwyd. After reaching the lake, bear left round its perimeter and head for the lowest notch on the skyline ahead, Bwlch Tryfan, with the profile of Glyder Fach's Bristly Ridge on the right-hand skyline above the bwlch (not marked on OS maps; *see* sketch map). The path is well-marked and obvious enough, arriving at the wall on the col itself. (The Miner's Track continues in the same line beyond, across the rough screes of Cwm Tryfan to a second col where Llyn Caseg-fraith lies, before descending to the main A4086 at Pen-y-Gwyrd.) The wall climbs uphill from the col to the south to merge with the impressive rocks of the Bristly Ridge and in the opposite direction starts to climb Tryfan's south ridge.

A true ascent of the South Ridge will follow the side of the wall until it ends at the steeper rocks which lead up to a subsidiary top on the ridge, the Far South Peak, keeping just left of the crest and scrambling up in a fairly direct line. Few parties do this, however, most preferring to take a well-marked path trending initially north to skirt round to the left of Far South Peak before climbing in a more direct line and at a steeper angle over rough and rocky ground up the broad ridge of the South Peak itself. The way is well-marked with numerous variations and leads to a large platform on the south summit. Here timorous parties munch sandwiches, admire the tremendous view to Glyder Fach and look over the eastern void of Cwm Tryfan. The more adventurous continue the extra little distance on polished rocks round the edge of a slightly more exposed rock cirque, gaining a few more feet in height and reaching the two rock monoliths of Adam and Eve crowning the main summit.

Various descent routes are possible. The quickest is probably to head for the North Peak, seen just beyond Adam and Eve, making a curving descent leftwards into a shallow rock bay, then going down a shaly, easy-angled gully to the west (left) before reaching North Peak. This soon reaches much easier ground and a very steep, shaly path heads down north towards the A5. Once you have spotted the line to take, it is very obvious, but it is steep and confidence is needed to deal with it.

The west face of Tryfan seen from Pen yr Ole Wen.

Many walkers will prefer to return to the South Peak and will then be tempted by a line of cairns leading off down the west flank towards Llyn Bochlwyd. This also fairly quickly gets off the rocks onto easier ground but it is not particularly easy to follow and involves much stepping from big blocks tilted at odd angles to other big blocks also tilted, and if they are wet care is needed to negotiate them: boots slipping off opposite sides of a sharp block can have disastrous consequences . . .

If you have any doubts about the descent down the gully between the north and main peaks mentioned above, it is probably better to reverse the route of ascent up the South Ridge, although some of the ledges that were scrambled up with ease will look a little more intimidating on the way down, so do not be surprised that it may take almost as long to return to Bwlch Tryfan as it did to reach the top from it.

## 6.2 Tryfan by the North Ridge, descent by the Heather Terrace

SUMMARY: About 500ft/152m of actual scrambling, Grade 1 by the easiest route but Grade 2 on the direct sections, north-facing: 2½ miles/4km, 3–5 hours. The direct approach from below the Milestone Buttress is up a wide gully to a broad shoulder. Easy scrambling and scramble-walking leads to a white quartz ledge and the distinctive rock 'Cannon'. The 'direct' way goes straight up keeping to the crest of the ridge as far as possible to a definite 'notch' at the top of Nor' Nor' Gully. It then goes round the right side of the tower above to reach the North Peak on its top. Easier variations go left from the Cannon, except near the top when the 'notch' is reached. From here the 'path' leading across the East Face is best avoided in favour of a rightward traverse from the 'notch' when a path leads round to the right of the final tower of the North Peak. Easy scrambling now leads to the Main Peak.

The North Ridge of Tryfan is one of the best-known and most exhilarating ascents in Wales. It is rightly a classic, not so exposed anywhere as the traverse of the Crib Goch Ridge on Snowdon and more easy to escape from than the latter, but still having the feel of being on a great mountain, particularly under anything other than perfect conditions.

At its base, it is much more a broad shoulder than a ridge, but it narrows as it gains height and becomes more interesting. Seen in profile from near Ogwen Cottage at the west end of Llyn Ogwen, the outline is of two convex curves leading to a little notch at what looks like about half height. Pointing out of this notch at about 45° and clearly visible from Ogwen is a rock looking like the barrel of a gun and known as 'The Cannon'. In fact, this is about 1350ft/411m above the road and there are then about another 675ft/206m of height to gain beyond it to the summit, so it is well over half way up. Most of the interest of the ascent is in the section beyond 'The Cannon' but there are easier ways to dodge the most direct route. The 'direct' is unquestionably the best way (best line, best rock, best views, best sense of achievement and most exhilarating) but it is as well to know about the easier ways in case of need or choice, so I will try to deal with both.

Although it is simple enough to approach the North Ridge from Gwern Gof Uchaf Farm I will deal with that approach in the section on the Heather Terrace routes (see 6.4a–6.4c) because the most straightforward way is to start from the laybys at the bottom of the ridge itself, by the Milestone Buttress (grid ref 663603). A wall runs to the base of the Milestone Buttress and a new kissing-gate enables you to go up an obvious track with steps towards a wide gully slanting back left from the base of the Buttress. After about 700ft/213m of ascent from the road, the various paths up this bouldery gully run out onto a heather shoulder. Veer a little to the right here up the continuation of the gully, with big boulders on the left and heather below steep rocks on the right. The path goes up a lighter-coloured scree fan leading to the rocks.

The first scrambling, as opposed to simple walking, starts here, using big holds up a short rock gully. This leads to easier ground and then the continuation of the gully snakes upwards for some distance, ending with a short flight of rocky steps leading to a broad, level ledge with a huge cairn (about 300ft/91m from the start of the scrambling). Easier ground follows, the way upwards being well cairned to reach a large ledge or plateau covered in white quartz and with the distinctive rock of 'The Cannon' on its far side. Reckon on about an hour to here from the road.

Avoid the steep rocks behind 'The Cannon' by going left and back right onto level ground again above them, from where the first view is obtained of the rest of the ridge, now looking like one for the first time since stepping onto the mountain, rising ahead across a stretch of heather and rocky ground. A walk across this leads to interesting scrambling up well-scratched rocks onto another shoulder; for those who want to avoid the scrambling, a path leads round to the left and then onto the same shoulder, where there is another cairn. Now the ridge rises again in a broad pyramid shape, with two rocks sticking out of a pile of blocks at its base, like a smaller, double-barrelled version of 'The Cannon', 300ft/91m below. Let's call it 'the shotgun'.

The first really continuous scrambling starts here. Begin by climbing up some big blocks well left of 'The Cannon' and then straight up the front of the ridge; it is delightful work up well-scratched cracks and grooves at a fairly easy angle of about 45°, although fairly exposed. It is however less affected by the winds of the prevailing westerlies than might have been expected. In about 200ft/61m, you reach the top and descend carefully into a little notch (at the top of Nor' Nor' Gully) after which a much shorter rise takes you onto another flat top. Yet another tower rises ahead, the steepest rock so far. A possible direct route

On the North Ridge of Tryfan, above the 'Cannon'.

straight up the front doesn't look marked at all, but there is a square-cut gully just to the right of the centre which has big holds and gives good scrambling, continuing on good spikes and blocks to emerge onto the top of the tower; this is the North Peak. Adam, the largest of the two summit blocks on Main Peak (Eve is out of sight behind him), is visible beyond the rim of rocks that curves the short distance across to it and it is now an easy scramble across to complete the ascent.

For those for whom the scrambling sections looked too intimidating or for whatever reason wished to avoid them, the alternatives are fairly straightforward. From my observation over the years, everybody gets easily enough to 'The Cannon' and also just beyond it, to the point where the ridge rises ahead noticeably. Now, where the direct line goes straight up, a path goes round the step sections to the left. It avoids the steep rock above 'the shotgun' by keeping left and going up to a notch overlooking a gully (Nor' Nor' Gully). Here it is advisable to scramble up the jammed blocks in the gully and rejoin the direct route at the top of this gully because the final tower (the North Peak) can be avoided by going out well to the right (not the left this time) on a well-marked path leading to the summit rocks. If you don't rejoin the main ridge from the notch, you can continue traversing on a good path on the left (east) side across a cirque below the North Peak. The path continues to reach a second notch, beyond which it continues contouring across another cirque or amphitheatre below the rocks of the Main Peak. This is straightforward enough, but there is a little vertical step to ascend on the path across the second cirque and there is a steep little wall, about 15ft/4.6m high although with good holds, to climb at the other side of the cirque. Climbing this little wall lands you amidst a jumble of huge blocks and wondering where the main summit is. You can, however, see across another little cirque to the South Peak and so will realise that you have slightly overshot the main summit and must trend back

right over the big blocks and then up a well-scratched and inclined slab to emerge right next to the twin vertical blocks of Adam and Eve. These are, even in thick mist, unmistakable.

It all sounds very complicated, much more so than it is, but it is just too easy to say 'Follow your nose, the rocks are all well-scratched', because, under unfavourable conditions, we all need the easiest way, not the hardest. The point I am labouring is that the 'path' which looks as if it is going to skirt all problems by going left onto the east face all the time has in fact two tricky bits at its very end and it is better to rejoin the North Ridge at the top of Nor' Nor' Gully to avoid them.

As a fitting return to the bottom of the Milestone Buttress, assuming that you are not continuing to the Glyders, may I suggest the Heather Terrace. For this, you will need to continue the little distance over to the South Peak, then descend the South Ridge keeping near to the edge overlooking Cwm Tryfan, until you reach the little wall between South Peak and Far South Peak, which is about 300ft/91m lower than the latter. Here a ladder-stile leads over the wall and the path leads onto the Heather Terrace which can be used to return to the shoulder at the beginning of the North Ridge.

It may be worth mentioning that an alternative scrambling start to the North Ridge is possible up, or rather across, Milestone Buttress but the chances of getting snarled up with rock-climbers and their ropes are fairly high and the rock is very polished and so can be very tricky in the wet.

### 6.3 Tryfan by the Heather Terrace and the South Ridge
*2¹/₂ miles/4km        3–4 hours*

Seen from a distance, the Heather Terrace shows as an obvious slanting ramp line rising across the buttresses and gullies of the east face and giving access to them, but its start is rather indefinite. Fortunately, it is well-marked and gives an interesting

Tryfan seen from Llyn Caseg-fraith.

alternative approach to the South Ridge. There are no more difficulties on the Terrace than there are on the South Ridge but, because of its indistinct start, it is as well to have a careful look at the mountain from somewhere near Gwern Gof Uchaf Farm (grid ref 673603) where there is parking, or along the laybys beside the A5 going west. A prominent tongue of pale scree will be seen cutting through the heather and issuing from a short gully above; the two possible paths both make for this. From opposite Glan Dena, the path goes more directly; from Gwern Gof Uchaf, the path goes below the slabs of Little Tryfan (*see* sketch map) to a grassy hollow then strikes right to the scree gully. (If in any doubt, take any path slanting to the right just before reaching a wire fence.) From the road to the top of the gully, it takes about half an hour and has a height gain of almost 800ft/244m; there is a large cairn at its top.

Immediately you reach the well-defined top of the gully, turn sharp left on a path which slants steadily up through boulders, heather and bilberry for another fifteen minutes or so. It becomes more apparent as you gain height that you are on the Terrace and then there is no doubt as you find yourself at the foot of the first unmistakable gully, between rocky walls and running straight up to a notch on the skyline of the North Ridge. This is Bastow Gully, its foot about 1200ft/366m above the road. It would give a very boring ascent under reasonable conditions but can also give an easy descent, with care on one slightly tricky bit near the top.

Continuing beyond Bastow Gully, the next one is Nor' Nor' Gully, similar to Bastow, with a clear line to a notch on the north ridge. Immediately to the left of the next gully, the letters 'GA' (standing for 'Grooved Arête', a popular rock-climb), about a foot high, are marked on a rock wall and serve to identify Green Gully which is easy-angled, has plenty of grass in it and defines the right side of the North Peak. Continuing fifty yards/46m along the Heather Terrace beyond Green Gully is the first and deepest of several runnels and then comes the very obvious North Gully. It is deep, clearly splits the north and central buttresses, has a black cave in its bed just above the level of the Terrace and the path along the Terrace itself is partially blocked by a large, free-standing rock just beyond it (the first such rock on the Terrace). The path goes either side of this and in about 150 paces passes the foot of South Gully which clearly defines South Peak from Main Peak. Just beyond South Gully, the path is almost level for a little way until it reaches a large cairn where it divides; the downward one heads into Cwm Tryfan, the upward one shortly crosses an inclined grooved slab and then soon reaches the col between Far South Peak and South Peak at a ladder-stile over a short stretch of wall. Here

you are now on the South Ridge and can thus easily reach the triple summits. Descent by the South Ridge to Bwlch Tryfan is probably still the best way off at a similar standard of difficulty, although to return to Gwern Gof Uchaf it will obviously be worth descending to the path running down Cwm Tryfan.

### 6.4 Scrambles from the Heather Terrace
*2¹/₂ miles/4km          3–4 hours*

The East Face of Tryfan is particularly suited to scrambling and the following routes are by no means all there are. These are chosen because their starts can be identified fairly easily and then follow the easiest lines of resistance. The rock is generally very good, rough and with good holds. The main gullies are feasible but, as always, can be very wet and greasy and therefore unpleasant so I would generally advise avoiding them as scrambles. To back up this view, I tried Nor' Nor' Gully after rain, largely because the entertaining Patrick Monkhouse guide-book of the thirties doesn't hesitate in recommending it to walkers with some scrambling experience. I found that, when wet, overcoming the first difficulty – a large flat-faced boulder somewhat discouragingly known as The Tombstone – was 'entertaining' (a euphemism in climbing guides for making you tremble a bit). A blunt rock nose above this was passed easily enough by a groove on its right but the third tricky bit, another jammed boulder, was a different story. Maybe I should have gone right instead of left, maybe rock-falls have changed things a little, but in the wet I found the exit over the boulder to be very precarious. My dogs, left at the foot of the gully, began howling which didn't help, and I had to reverse about 25ft/7.6m and then avoid the bad bit altogether by a diversion to make use of some huge rock flakes well out on the right wall. The following scrambles therefore avoid the direct line of the main gullies.

Looking down the North Ridge of Tryfan from the North Peak.

The fastest descent to the road at the foot of the Milestone Buttress is by the path from the North Peak (*see* sketch map). To return to Gwern Gof Uchaf, either descend the North Ridge (*see* **6.2**) or descend to the South Peak and return down Cwm Tryfan (*see* **6.3**). To do another scramble, descend the South Ridge to the stile on the little col between South Peak and Far South Peak and thus get back onto the Heather Terrace. Or, alternatively, descend as described in Walk **6.4(a)**.

### 6.4(a) The central route by Little Gully

SUMMARY: 650ft/198m of Grade 1 scrambling, east-facing; 2¹/₂ miles/4km, 3–4 hours. A huge boulder blocks Heather Terrace just beyond North Gully and the route outflanks the steep lower part of this on its immediate left by way of a very much less defined one (Little Gully). Easy scrambling on good holds leads to the 'path' in the cirque or depression between the North Peak and Main Peak, and so to the top.

The first scramble is chosen because it is the easiest climb and the easiest to locate.

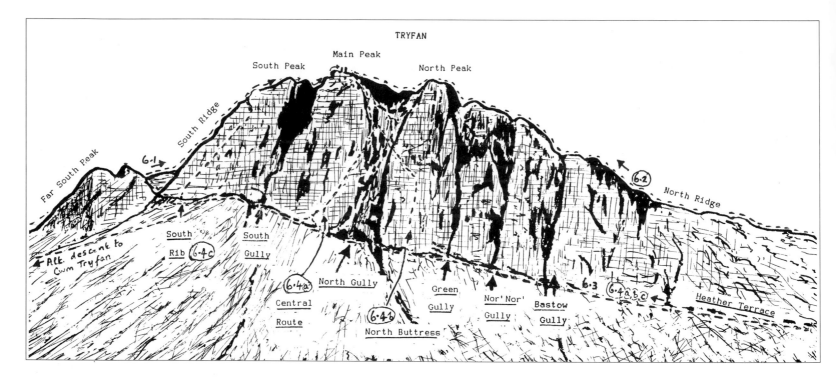

TRYFAN

The North Ridge of Tryfan is justly famous as one of the most exhilarating mountain scrambles in North Wales, but it is much less well-known that there is a scramble of a different kind which passes through some dramatic scenery, is probably easier than the North Ridge, is certainly less exposed and is a very direct way to the main peak. Once located, it is very obvious.

The route uses Little Gully, which is more of a groove slanting in from the left towards the upper part of the North Gully, and so avoids the obvious difficulties in its (North Gully's) lower part. It reaches the amphitheatre between the north and central buttresses, then goes easily up to the path just below the North Ridge. Once ascended, so that you know the line, it gives a useful descent route as well and shows signs of fairly frequent usage. The North Gully is very recognisable from the Heather Terrace as the fourth deep-cut one from the northern end of it, separates the north from the central buttress, has a black cave in its bed just above the path and, if still in any doubt, a large boulder blocks the Heather Terrace path just beyond it. (*See also* **6.3** to refresh your memory on the features of Heather Terrace.)

To outflank the lower part of North Gully walk just past the boulder blocking the path, slant up a little scree path which goes first left (facing the cliffs) for only ten paces or so and then up sharp right, below steep rocks, to reach a little square cut gully (Little Gully). Scramble easily up solid flakes on the left side of this and then up the bed of the dry groove/gully itself, snaking up little rock steps in a delightful and easy way until, about 150ft/46m above the path, a grassy neck almost connects it to North Gully. Keep going left up the groove on good flake holds until you can step onto a little path which zigzags across grassy ledges towards North Gully again, although a final rise of the groove on more flakes of rock leads to a pull over a jammed block to join the upper part of North Gully at last. You'll be about 350ft/107m above the path now. The next 150ft/46m or so is generally up the upper part of North Gully but the wet and mossy bits can be nicely avoided by ledges on the right until you can return to the main bed again and gain the 'footpath' running up the east side of the North Ridge and here traversing the cirque or depression between north and central buttresses. I say 'footpath' with reservations, because as soon as you turn left along it there is a little vertical step to climb and then further up there is a little vertical wall, albeit with big holds, which are both just as hard or easy – depending on your point of view – as anything on the North Ridge route. Above the little wall is the area of jumbled blocks immediately below the main summit; the rocks are well scratched leading round onto the sloping slab and the last few feet to Adam and Eve. From reaching the path to the top is a further 150ft/46m. I may add that my two little dogs, Henry and Freddie, accompanied me up this route, with some helpful shoves from behind and pulls on their leads from in front when necessary. But it is certainly a good job they are only little dogs.

## 6.4(b) The north buttress route

SUMMARY: 550ft/168m of Grade 1/2 scrambling, east-facing; 2½ miles/4km, 3–4 hours. Ascends to the central depression, but from the Heather Terrace *before* reaching North Gully, at a little cave formed by a rock-flake. A grassy runnel, followed by a ramp off to the left leads to ledges below a shallow rock bay. Trending left, further ledges lead to the central depression above North Gully and so to the 'path' there and the top.

This route uses the easy lower part of the North Buttress rock-climb but then goes left into the central depression instead of going right along the airy traverse at the top of Terrace Wall. It is about 350ft/107m to the bottom of the central depression and then a further 300ft/91m of easier ground to the Main Peak.

To find the start from the Heather Terrace, locate North Gully (the obvious one with the large boulder blocking the path just beyond it) and then, coming downhill on the Terrace, find Green Gully (the one with the letters 'GA' just to its left). Fifty yards/46m from the bottom of Green Gully going upslope towards North Gully is the first and deepest of several rock runnels. This is V-shaped, has white scree at its foot and a large rock-flake forming a little cave on its immediate right.

The first 40ft/12m uses nice rock steps up the runnel followed by grassier ground leading to an easy pull over a little chockstone. Above, the bed of the runnel is grassier still but gives an obvious line for a further 50ft/15m or so (although a little step out to the right onto a broken rock rib and a step back into the runnel a little higher up avoids some of the grass). Just before this runnel runs into a very steep rocky groove above, a slanting ramp leads off to the left for about 20yds/18m (gaining about 40ft/12m in height) to reach a large grass ledge immediately below a shallow rock bay. One delicate step up here leads to good holds and you can now gain a further 50ft/15m by just stepping onto more grassy ledges on which you curve round to

the left and onto a large and gently sloping area of heather below a wide, rather broken and generally triangular-shaped rock wall. (Higher above is the much steeper and compact Terrace Wall.) From here, head well left towards North Gully, surmount a short corner (6ft/1.8m), go right and then back left up a series of easy steps on a rock ramp until it runs out onto a path on easy ground just below the steep rocks of Terrace Wall now directly above. (If you walk right, you may well see climbers on Grooved Arête.)

The path leads left to a little rock ledge and a continuation with the Central Route (see **6.4a**). Finally, 300ft/91m of easier ground follows to the summit.

### 6.4(c) The south rib route

SUMMARY: 500ft/512m of Grade 3 scrambling, east-facing; 2½ miles/4km, 4 hours. Reaches a shoulder just below the South Peak by some quite exposed but enjoyable scrambling, with diversions to avoid harder sections, ending with a short traverse to the left on a ledge below the final wall.

This route takes the general line of the climb of the same name in the rock-climbing guides but skirts several of the harder sections of that route. It is fairly exposed in places but gives an enjoyable scramble at the higher end of the difficulty range.

Progressing along the Heather Terrace past the South Gully, which is wide and grassy and defines South Peak from Main Peak, the path is almost level until it reaches the cairn, where it forks. (An alternative descent to Cwm Tryfan goes to the left here.) Sixty paces beyond the cairn on the upslope fork of the path, it crosses an inclined grooved slab with a bay formed by two broken ribs of rock. These merge about 30ft/9m higher and the ribs of rock beyond, plus subsequent ones, give a scramble of about 500ft/152m overall to the South Peak.

Delightful climbing up big spiky holds on the left of the bay for about 100ft/30m ends at some huge blocks. The higher and slightly longer of two slanting gangways now leads out to the right from here, slanting up towards the crest of the next rock rib. Go up this and then up a little 6ft/1.8m chimney just before reaching the actual edge of the rib, then continue up the superb, though rather exposed edge beyond for about 20ft/6m to reach a notch. A further rock rib just beyond needs a long reach; it is too hard to start and too difficult to classify as scrambling. Those competent to tackle it anyway will no doubt do so; the rest of us will find it better to traverse left on a grassy ledge for about 40ft/12m until an easy-angled chimney with piled blocks enables its right-hand (outside) edge to be reached and then a step made to easy ground above the awkward rib. Five paces further right is another rock rib consisting of spiky blocks and you can either clamber over these or walk up grassy grooves to their left, gaining another 50ft/15m or so.

Here now are more grass ledges, bounded on the right by another rock rib, which is really the right edge of a fairly wide wall crowned by what looks like a pillar of steep rock. Climb the right edge on good holds by the easiest line to reach a grassy ledge and just below the 'pillar' which is now seen to be more like a large upstanding flake, with a little chimney round to its right-hand side. The little chimney leads to a large circular flake jammed in a gap and just beyond that the continuation of the rock rib leads easily to a large ledge below a steep final wall. The wall can be climbed directly by a little groove but it is much pleasanter to escape to easy ground by moving left along a two-tier ledge below the wall. Easy rocks and a very short final ascent lead to the South Peak.

The East Face of Tryfan seen from the ridge of Braich y Ddeugwm.

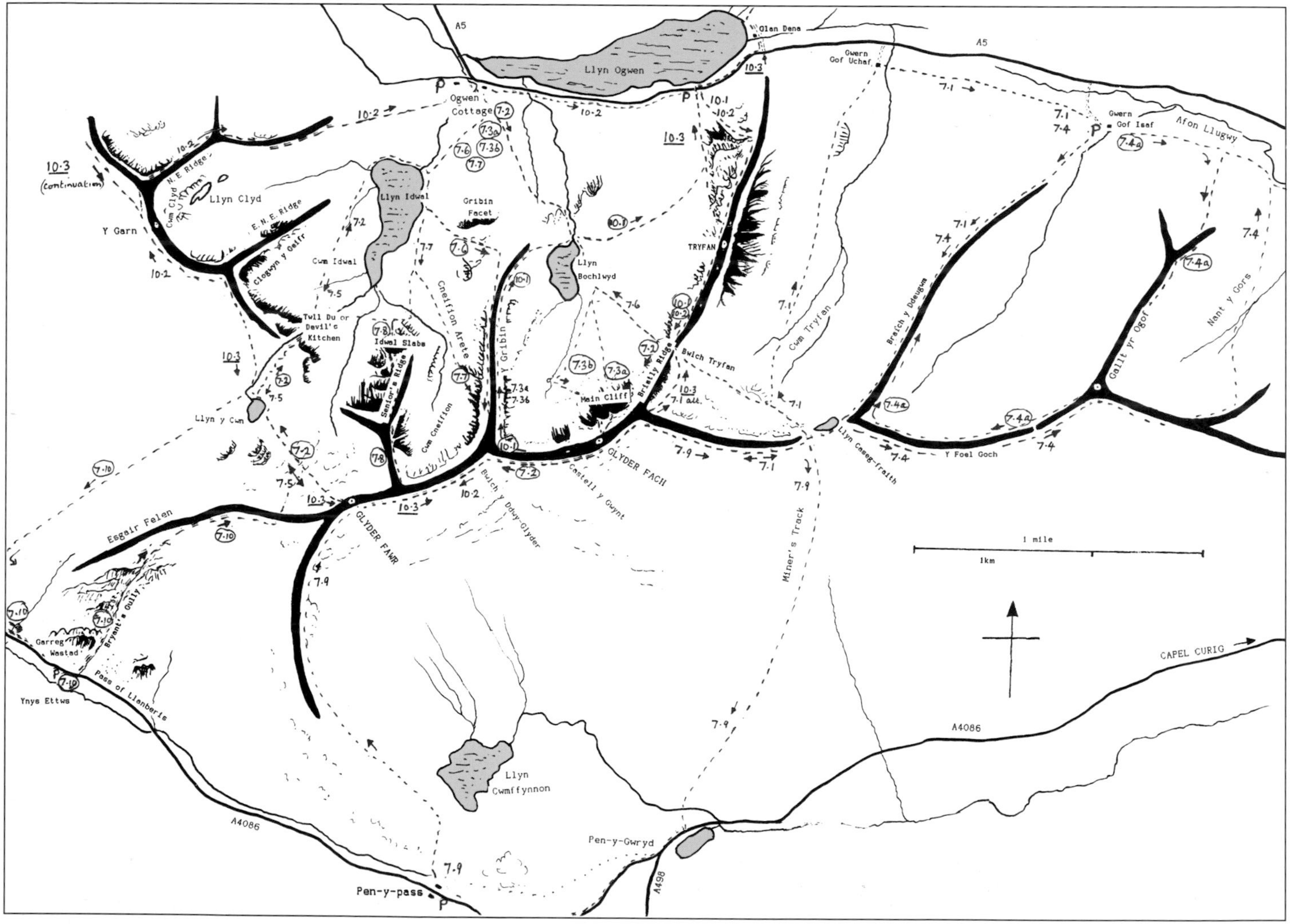
A5
Llyn Ogwen
Glan Dena
Gwern Gof Uchaf
Gwern Gof Isaf
Afon Llugwy
Ogwen Cottage
Llyn Clyd
Cwm Clyd
N.E. Ridge
E.N.E. Ridge
Y Garn
Clogwyn y Geifr
Cwm Idwal
Llyn Idwal
Gribin Facet
Twll Du or Devil's Kitchen
Idwal Slabs
Seniors Ridge
Cneifion Arete
Cwm Cneifion
Y Gribin
Llyn Bochlwyd
Main Cliff
Bristly Ridge
Bwlch Tryfan
TRYFAN
Cwm Tryfan
Bre'ch y Ddeugwm
Gallt yr Ogof
Nant y Gors
Llyn Caseg-fraith
Y Foel Goch
GLYDER FACH
Castell y Gwynt
Bwlch y Ddwy-Glyder
GLYDER FAWR
Llyn y Cwn
Esgair Felen
Miner's Track
1 mile
1km
Garreg Wastad
Bryant's Gully
Ynys Ettws
Pass of Llanberis
A4086
Llyn Cwmffynnon
Pen-y-Gwryd
Pen-y-pass
A498
CAPEL CURIG
10·3 (continuation)

# 7: The Glyders and Gallt yr Ogof

| | | | | | | |
|---|---|---|---|---|---|---|
| BEST MAPS: OS 1:50,000 Landranger 115 Snowdon & surrounding area<br>OS 1:25,000 Outdoor Leisure 17 Snowdonia: Snowdon area | | | | | | |
| *Approx Distance* | *Approx Time* | *Highest Elevation Reached* | *Height Gained* | *Star Rating* | *Scramble Difficulty Grade* | *Scramble Height Gain* |
| **7.1 Glyder Fach: from the north by the east ridge** | | | | | | |
| 6 miles/9.7km | 4–5 hours | 3261ft/994m | 2333ft/711m | */** | — | — |
| **7.2 Bristly Ridge and the Devil's Kitchen** | | | | | | |
| 5 miles/8km | 4–5 hours | 3278ft/999m | 2500ft/762m | *** | 1 | 449ft/137m |
| **7.3 Scrambles on Glyder Fach**<br>**7.3(a) Glyder Fach Main Cliff: scramble on East Gully Ridge** | | | | | | |
| 4 miles/6.4km | 4–5 hours | 3261ft/994m | 2333ft/711m | ** | 2 | 751ft/229m |
| **7.3(b) Glyder Fach Main Cliff: scramble on Dolmen Ridge** | | | | | | |
| 4 miles/6.4km | 4–5 hours | 3261ft/994m | 2333ft/711m | *** | 2 | 751ft/229m |
| **7.4 Gallt yr Ogof from Ogwen Valley** | | | | | | |
| 5½ miles/8.8km | 3–4 hours | 2641ft/805m | 1722ft/525m | * | — | — |
| **7.4(a) Scramble on Gallt yr Ogof** | | | | | | |
| 5½ miles/8.8km | 4 hours | 2641ft/805m | 1722ft/525m | * | 2 | 200ft/61m |
| **7.5 Glyder Fawr via Twll Du (Devil's Kitchen) and Llyn y Cwn** | | | | | | |
| 5 miles/8km | 4 hours | 3277ft/999m | 2333ft/711m | ** | — | — |

| Approx Distance | Approx Time | Highest Elevation Reached | Height Gained | Star Rating | Scramble Difficulty Grade | Scramble Height Gain |
|---|---|---|---|---|---|---|
| **7.6 The Glyders via the Gribin Ridge (Y Gribin)** | | | | | | |
| 3³/₄ miles/6km | 3–4 hours | 3261ft/994m | 2267ft/691m | */** | 1 | 200ft/61m |
| **7.7 The Glyders via scramble on the Cneifion Arête** | | | | | | |
| 4¹/₂ miles/7.2km | 4 hours | 3277ft/999m | 2333ft/711m | *** | 2/3 | 449ft/137m |
| **7.8 Glyder Fawr via scramble on north-west face and Senior's Ridge** | | | | | | |
| 4¹/₂ miles/7.2km | 4–5 hours | 3277ft/999m | 2333ft/711m | ** | 2 | 800ft/244m |
| **7.9 The Glyders from Pen-y-pass** | | | | | | |
| 6¹/₂ miles/10.5km | 4–5 hours | 3277ft/999m | 2503ft/763m | */** | — | — |
| **7.10 Glyder Fawr via scramble in Bryant's Gully** | | | | | | |
| 4¹/₂ miles/7.2km | 5 hours | 3277ft/999m | 2867ft/874m | *** | 2 | 1675ft/511m |

Although the southern slopes of the Glyders are not so lacking in interest as a first casual glance might suggest, the great delight of walking and scrambling up to and on the superb ridge of the Glyders is that the northern slopes are superbly rough and craggy, with deep cwms and dramatic ridges leading to jumbles of rough boulders and spiky rocks on the highest ground, particularly on Glyder Fach. There is very little 'easy' walking here.

### 7.1 Glyder Fach from the north by the east ridge
*6 miles/9.7km      4–5 hours*

Glyder Fach by its east ridge is probably as easy as it is possible to get from the north side and gives a good introduction to the area. The route described also allows some good, but optional, scrambling on the low-angled rock rib of Braich y Ddeugwm. The views of Tryfan are outstanding.

Park east of Lyn Ogwen at the farm of Gwern Gof Isaf (grid ref 685601; small fee for parking, and good camping). A stile over the wall to the right of the farmhouse leads directly to a path heading south-west beside a short rounded and fairly smooth rock rib, which gives delightful scrambling if you choose to ascend it. A second and third rib follow immediately, the

Looking over Llyn Caseg-fraith from the slopes of Glyder Fach.

ascent of the third being slightly harder, like walking up a whale's back. The rest of the ridge remains interesting, although the rock is more broken, allowing very easy scrambling; or just follow the faint path between the rocky bits. After about 1500feet/457m of ascent, during which time the splendid east face of Tryfan comes increasingly into view, a more open shoulder is reached. Also now seen is the jagged profile of Glyder Fach's Bristly Ridge, not named on the OS maps, but leading from Glyder Fach down to the col of Bwlch Tryfan (*see* map). Bristly Ridge incidentally gives a popular scramble (Walk **7.2**). There are several tiny tarns round here and the shallow Llyn Caseg-fraith; the broad hump of Y Foel Goch is just to the east. The Miner's Track crosses the ridge just west of the llyn although, for a path which was so well-used in the past, it can be somewhat difficult to detect from above in less than perfect visibility.

The first part of the continuation up the broad east ridge of Glyder Fach is by means of a well-cairned path and over stony scree although, as height is gained, it winds and twists through bigger blocks before emerging onto the summit plateau. Here a pile of narrow, sharp-edged blocks, tumbled and tossed about, has the well-known Cantilever Rock balanced on top; it is estimated to weigh about 70 tons and it is almost a tradition to walk along it, as if you were 'walking the plank'. Less than a hundred paces away and only slightly higher, the summit itself consists of an even bigger heap of faceted, sharp-edged blocks piled up in strange abandon. It takes a little scrambling to get to the top and although the OS map shows a trig point I've never yet found one, despite looking for it.

Although you have now reached the summit, it is well worth continuing just a little further to visit the Castell y Gwynt (Castle of the Winds), an array of fantastic pinnacles which are all that remains of a minor summit at the head of Cwm Bochlwyd. Continue westwards on a rather vague path over the

The Cantilever on Glyder Fach.

rocky ground, which goes to the right (north) of the summit rocks and then descends slightly. About 300yds/274m further, the pinnacles apparently block the way, with one sharp needle on the left-hand skyline being particularly striking.

There are two good options for the return, both obvious enough in clear conditions, but it is a confusing terrain in mist. For either, you must return to the summit area. Then, heading ENE with the pile of rocks containing the Cantilever on your right hand and continuing in that direction gently downhill, you will quickly reach the level jumble of rocks which define the top of the Bristly Ridge. To its immediate right is a light-coloured scree slope in a very wide gully and this gives a rapid descent down to Bwlch Tryfan, below the fantastic towers on the east side of Bristly Ridge. Under icy conditions, it can be as nasty as any other slope of this type. Reaching Bwlch Tryfan you would then pick up the Miner's Track to link up with the path descending Cwm Tryfan.

Alternatively, to return with certainty, veer right instead of descending the scree slope beside Bristly Ridge and reverse the cairned way of ascent down the easier-angled east ridge. At a point about two hundred yards/183m before reaching Llyn Caseg-fraith, look for the top of the Miner's Track. This slants down a ramp leading into a short gully and then contours across the head of Cwm Tryfan over rough scree slopes towards Bwlch Tryfan. Leave it before it starts to climb to slightly higher ground in the middle of the cwm and turn almost due north down Cwm Tryfan itself. The path picks a way between boulders and heather; it's rough, wild walking appropriate to the surroundings but gets easier as height is lost. Beyond a ladder-stile over a fence (shown as a wall on the 1:25,000 map) there is a steeper descent down a wide gully, towards Gwern Gof Uchaf Farm, passing alongside the smooth slab of the rock-climbing practice-ground of Little Tryfan; seen from one particular direction, its shape is a miniature of Tryfan itself. The track leads quickly to the main road (A5) but if you bear right (east) at the last stile beside the farm, you will join the pleasant grassy way of the old road and enjoy a traffic-free ramble back to Gwern Gof Isaf and the car.

## 7.2 Bristly Ridge and the Devil's Kitchen

SUMMARY: About 450ft/137m of Grade 1 scrambling, north-east facing; 5 miles/8km, 4–5 hours.

Starting up a gully just left of the lowest rocks to reach a shoulder on the crest of the ridge, the well-marked route climbs steeply to a first pinnacle, then traverses others to reach easy ground. The continuation walk suggested leads over the Glyders and descends by way of the Devil's Kitchen.

Bristly Ridge is not named on the OS maps but is the rocky spur leading towards Tryfan from Glyder Fach and ending at Bwlch Tryfan (see map). An intricate, although well-marked and popular scrambling route winds round and over the towers and slabs along its crest and provides a most interesting approach to Glyder Fach. The sense of exposure on the scramble is not at all high although the approach to it may appear intimidating; for those put off at the early stage, there is a purgatorial scree-slope which stretches all the way up the left (east) side of the ridge, thus avoiding the scramble altogether. This scree-slope is really much better used as a descent.

Looking towards Tryfan from the pinnacles of Bristly Ridge.

The most convenient start is the Miner's Track from Ogwen. Park near Ogwen Cottage (grid ref 651603), or nearby along the side of the A5, at the west end of Llyn Ogwen. The track towards Idwal is signed round newish buildings near the Youth Hostel, quickly crosses the river flowing from Llyn Idwal and heads south-east towards Tryfan before making a 90° turn to the south-west towards Idwal. Here take the Miner's Track which continues straight on from this point and can be seen ahead climbing more steeply towards the point where the stream flows out of Llyn Bochlwyd. Directly beyond, in the same line of sight, the western profile of the Bristly Ridge can be seen on the skyline. The path leads over a section which is being 'pitched' (over flat stones laid close together), then up beside the tumbling stream. The beautiful lake is soon reached, overlooked by the Gribin Ridge on the right hand, the main cliffs of Glyder Fach ahead and the steep slopes rising to Tryfan on the left. The path continues round the left edge of the lake, climbing gently through scattered rocks towards the lowest point on the skyline, where there is a wall and numerous ladder-stiles, so there are no excuses for knocking stones off the wall. This is Bwlch Tryfan.

From here the Bristly Ridge rises in a confusing mass of pinnacles and towers and it does not look at all obvious that there is a way up. There are in fact several alternatives starting lower down than the one I will describe, but this one is the easiest to find for certain.

Looking at the ridge from Bwlch Tryfan, the wall runs firstly straight towards it then curves to the right as it approaches the steeper rocks where it ends; a ladder-stile crosses it just here. (Ignore the steep gullies to the right and lower down.) Beyond and above the wall can be seen a crescent-shaped scree-slope curving clockwise towards the base of another gully. Go right or left of the wall to reach the top of this scree slope just beyond the point where the wall ends. The bottom of the gully just beyond is the start; it is full of stones and rubble, but there are plenty of ledges and it gives quite easy scrambling, by-passing a jammed chock-stone about 60ft/18m or halfway up it. The gully continues a little further, leading to a little groove with big spikes at its top which are easily climbed onto the open shoulder of the ridge itself.

From the shoulder, the well-marked way leads initially to the right, slanting across an angled slab and then going back to the crest again, giving easy and very attractive scrambling on superb rock at an easy angle. Now it rears up ahead, steeper but with big solid holds until you reach a point where you realise that this is just the first of several big pinnacles, as you can see more beyond and above. A slight descent follows round the left side of this first pinnacle into a deep gap. From here, you wind up to the right round an isolated pinnacle into a gully behind it, then wind round to the left of the next tower into another notch at the base of yet another. This can be climbed on either side to a ledge from where there are superb views looking back down the ridge. A series of small spikes follows, now on the continuous crest again (or dodge them round to the right) as the angle eases and the ridge fizzles out in a jumble of blocks and spikes on the edge of the summit plateau. The whole ascent gains about 450feet/137m from the bottom of the gully to the top rocks and is a delightful and entertaining scramble, well deserving its popularity.

There is a rapid descent down a scree-slope immediately to the left of the top of the ridge as you leave it which would quickly get you back to Bwlch Tryfan, but most parties will wish to continue over the Glyders before descending. A cairned path goes south-west over rocky ground, passing between two jumbles of spiky rocks, the left hand one having the Cantilever Rock on top, skirts the even bigger jumble of spikes and blocks of the summit area and gently descends to wind to the left (south) of the spiky Castell y Gwynt (see **7.1**). The col of Bwlch y Ddwy-Glyder is just beyond and from here the main path slants up towards Glyder Fawr. In an emergency, an escape could be made from the col down the scree-slopes at the head of Cwm Bochlwyd.

The path to Glyder Fawr is broad and obvious and not as rocky as on Glyder Fach except when you approach the summit area, where there are numerous rocky castles; the summit one is only a whisker higher than several rivals. In clear weather, there's a grand view to the Snowdon massif. From here a path descends over rocks to the south-west, passing another group of rock spikes looking like lobster claws. Emerging quite suddenly from that stony wilderness onto much flatter, grassier ground, now follow a line of cairns heading north-west downhill towards Llyn y Cwn. It is a gentle descent at first, down shaly ground, but then it seems to almost drop off the edge of the mountain while somehow remaining still on gravelly scree. Progress down a series of runnels in this and then down either of two rubble-strewn grooves or trenches beside a steeper gully above Llyn y Cwn; it feels a long way even going downhill and the same distance going up these tedious slopes feels a lot further. Llyn y Cwn is on a rock shelf at the top of the belt of cliffs split by the great gash of Twll Du, the Devil's Kitchen, although that isn't yet visible from here.

The descent is towards the right-hand (south) end of the Devil's Kitchen cliffs as you stand above them. Don't cross the stream which flows from the north edge of the llyn and tumbles shortly down the Kitchen, but stay with the path heading NNE. This quickly starts to wind down very rough ground at the top of the cliffs, but can be seen to be slanting back left towards the bottom of the great slit of the Kitchen itself. The path is obvious and there should be no difficulties in normal summer conditions, but it is a dramatic situation, especially if a wind is blowing the spray from the waterfalls in curtains across the lower parts of the path. Under icy conditions, this simple path can of course become a major hazard requiring ice-axe and crampons.

The return to the valley is now straightforward and is well-marked on a partly-stepped path to the outlet at the north end of Llyn Idwal, and then by the obvious track back to Ogwen. I say 'straightforward' but a long-time and very experienced friend of mine once cut a corner when the llyn was iced-over one winter; the ice broke and he went in, not just over his head but also under the ice. He can't swim a stroke and thought his last hour had come. Fortunately, as he came up he managed to smash enough ice to get his head out and his climbing companion pulled him to shivering safety.

### 7.3 Scrambles on Glyder Fach

The Main Cliff of Glyder Fach, lying very high above Llyn Bochlwyd (see map), is well known to rock-climbers but also yields several scrambles, of which I have chosen the two I consider the best. The approach to both is as for Bristly Ridge (see **7.2**) from Ogwen Cottage as far as Llyn Bochlwyd, when part of the main cliff can be seen. (The whole area of the crags curves round into the upper part of Cwm Bochlwyd and so is not seen in its entirety except from the ridge of Y Gribin, known generally as the Gribin Ridge, which forms the western arm of Cwm Bochlwyd.)

From Llyn Bochlwyd the first impression is simply of a great mass of broken rocks; closer inspection reveals much more detail and many definite features. It is worth remembering that the crags are north-facing and very high on the mountain and thus more likely to be wetter and therefore greasier than in sunnier places, particularly in gullies. The two scrambles chosen, however, apart from their easy starts, both use rock ridges and should give few problems.

Leaving the path at Llyn Bochlwyd and walking up the cwm, it will be seen that there is a triangular-shaped band of slabs at the base of the face; these, named after the rock-climbing routes ascending them, are known as the Alphabet Slabs, where the first scramble starts. On their left side, they are defined by Main Gully, which converges with another gully on the other (west) side of the Alphabet Slabs and which is East Gully. Further along to the right (west) and hidden round the bend in the upper cwm is the West Gully, the start of the second of the scrambles. The main rock-climbing area is the East Buttress, which is just to the left of Main Gully. This is made up of beautiful grey rock towers and walls, split by clean cracks which, although inconspicuous from a distance, are very apparent indeed as you get closer to them. Both scrambling routes finish on or very near to the summit of Glyder Fach and returns could be made to the valley by descending Bristly Ridge (*see* **7.2** above) or the Gribin Ridge (*see* **7.6**). In deteriorating conditions, the scree slope on the Cwm Tryfan side of Bristly Ridge will be the fastest way down, followed by a reversal of the Miner's Track to Ogwen Cottage (*see* map).

### 7.3(a) Glyder Fach Main Cliff: scramble on East Gully Ridge

SUMMARY: 751ft/229m of Grade 2 scrambling, north-facing; 4 miles/6.4km, 4–5 hours. Starting at an altitude of almost 2500ft/762m and finishing on the summit, this very fine route gains the top of the Alphabet Slabs from the left, traverses right from a quartz ledge for 30yds/27m to a rock rib, then upwards, trending right into East Gully when it becomes harder. The finish is up the left-hand bounding ridge of the amphitheatre above.

Start up Main Gully (*see* drawing) to the immediate left of the Alphabet Slabs, on loose but very easy rock for about 100ft/30m to reach the quartz-speckled ledge at their top. Don't be tempted to continue up Main Gully: although there is an easy, but

greasy, rock staircase leading up there, it quickly tapers to a constriction with a jammed spike below a chock-stone and needs a precarious and strenuous struggle that has no place on a scramble and which you would not enjoy. The other temptation to be avoided is the rock ridge directly above the quartz ledge at the top of the Alphabet Slabs. This is graded 'Moderate' in the rock-climbing guide but its start is much harder.

The solution is to traverse to the right for about thirty yards/27m, on a path from the quartz ledge at the top of the Alphabet Slabs. This leads round a little quartz-speckled bulge and into a grassy bay with an impending block, peppered with

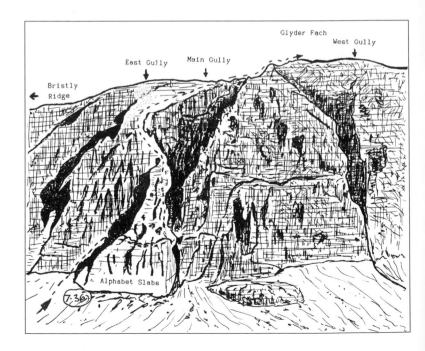

quartz, above. Good holds on the easy-angled rock rib to the immediate right of the bay then enable you to climb about 50ft/15m up to a gap behind the block, directly behind which are two more ribs of rock separated by a grassy chimney. Excellent, slightly scratched holds up the left-hand rib now take you up this, alongside East Gully, over a mass of more jumbled spikes and blocks for about 100ft/30m to where the rib becomes much steeper, split by a hand-crack below a smooth bulge. This is obviously rock-climbing territory, not scrambling. Here traverse right for about 20 feet/6m towards the East Gully. A broken line of slabs forms a ramp, above the bed of the gully but below the crest of the ridge you were on; you can use the cracks here to make an energetic pull onto a point just below the crest of the ridge again. Youngsters will swarm up with ease; older and stiffer joints will find this move a bit strenuous. If necessary, it can be avoided completely by just going up the easy right side of East Gully and scrambling up to an amphitheatre. Assuming you do return to the ridge you will find easy rocks quickly lead you to the amphitheatre about 250ft/76m from the start.

Tryfan seen from the East Gully Ridge of Glyder Fach.

It looks as though the natural line and the most interesting scrambling above will be curving up from the left-hand side of this amphitheatre and so it proves. Easy and delightful progress is now made up the remainder of this quite broad ridge, clambering over lots of piled blocks, with views across to the profile of Bristly Ridge. There is a steeper little nose to surmount, or avoid if you prefer, at about halfway but otherwise it is remarkably consistent, to emerge beside one of the groups of spiky rocks on the summit plateau, about 150feet/46m above the amphitheatre. The group of rocks containing the Cantilever Rock is just beyond and the summit just a little further.

### 7.3(b) Glyder Fach Main Cliff: scramble on Dolmen Ridge

SUMMARY: 751ft/229m of Grade 2 scrambling, north-facing but getting afternoon sunshine; 4 miles/6.4km, 4–5 hours. Straightforward scrambling to the right of West Gully, trending into it at the side of the vertical wall of Dolmen Buttress. A ramp leads back left to the crest, then upward progress leads to the neck at the head of West Gully and the broad ridge beyond, finishing almost at the summit.

Making your way towards the upper part of Cwm Bochlwyd, you will find a tiny llyn not shown on the maps but at about the point where the cliffs curve to the west. Seen from here (and see sketch), the great mass of broken rocks are defined on the left by the West Gully. About half way up the left-hand side of this gully is a compact buttress of steep rock, Dolmen Buttress, which has a sloping ledge of grass and quartz called 'The Courtyard' at its foot. This part of Glyder Fach gets afternoon sunshine and scrambling here can be a delightful experience.

The main interest of the route starts when you get to Dolmen Buttress itself, which you can do by going directly up West Gully to its foot (damp and loose) or, much better and almost as directly, by the rocks just to its right. Start about 10ft/3m just to the right of the very foot of the gully, crossing a broad belt of quartz immediately after the start. After 20ft/6m up an easy groove, trend right up and across some quartz ledges and then up the right edge of a large quartz-faced sloping slab. About half way up this slab, scramble onto steeper rocks on the right and then gain more height up several easy grass ledges towards Dolmen Buttress, visible higher up. Two easy rock steps and a few more greasy ramps lead up the right edge of the gully to a point just above the top edge of 'The Courtyard' and about 250ft/76m above the start. There is a chockstone in the gully bed and the vertical wall of Dolmen Buttress towers above to the left.

Feral goats high on the Dolmen Ridge of Glyder Fach.

Go up the easy bed of the gully for about 40ft/12m and an obvious ramp will then be seen going back left across the face of the Dolmen Buttress to its edge. That's the way to go; traverse along this ramp, which is quite broad, and leads to a steep groove at its end. Excellent holds lead up the groove and after about 20ft/6m (halfway) you can either continue up it by stepping slightly right and then back higher up or, make a step out left on very good holds to a sensational position on the very edge of the buttress. What a wonderful place to be in sunshine, perched like an eagle, with warm rough friendly rock to hand and only the odd croak of a raven and the tinkle of the stream below to break the silence of the hills.

Happily, easy holds above follow to where the angle eases and then easy scrambling over big blocks follows for about 60ft/18m to where the ridge rears up again. This time, a wide groove choked with blocks leads straightforwardly to a point where you can peer over the dramatic drop into the West Gully, followed by traversing steps past a little plaque screwed to the rock in memory of one Ian Richards, who died in 1986. There is no indication of how he died, but I noticed my own grip on the rock tightened a little as I passed by. I then walked carefully along a short quartz-capped neck of rock which was followed by more delightful scrambling, curving round to a second neck at the head of West Gully. Just before reaching this, and certainly above 3000ft/914m, I heard unusual noises and was amazed to see three wild goats also scrambling up rock ledges, on a parallel course to mine. I have seen a small herd several times high up in Cwm Cneifion but this was a delightful surprise.

Good scrambling over big spikes and blocks continues to a point where you could go left, leave the rocks and just walk easily to the top, but to do so will miss out a final 40ft/12m scramble up superb blocks, to end directly on the summit plateau only 50 paces from the summit rock pile. An excellent route.

## 7.4 Gallt yr Ogof from Ogwen Valley
*5¹/₂ miles/8.8km      3–4 hours*
*Best map: 1:50,000/115*

Gallt yr Ogof, Cliff of the Cave (the cave being visible on the main crag), is really the blunt nose at the end of a ridge that is ³/₄ mile/1.2km long and is connected to the Glyders, but the name is also used for the highest point on the ridge. Although comparatively neglected in comparison with its better-known neighbours to the west, Tryfan and the Glyders, it is the last peak in an attractive traverse from Pen-y-pass to Capel Curig. More conveniently, since no special transport arrangements are needed, it can be the objective for a good short round from Gwern Gof Isaf in the Ogwen Valley.

For the walk, start at Gwern Gof Isaf Farm (grid ref 685601, small parking fee and good camping) and then climb the ladder-stile just to the right of the farm buildings and go south-west-wards up the gently-angled rock and grass ridge of Braich y Ddeugwm. This has some lovely ice-smoothed rock ribs low down which give a few short stretches of optional pleasant scrambling. The views towards Tryfan across Cwm Tryfan become increasingly good as height is gained and the ridge leads naturally to the boggy plateau near Llyn Caseg-fraith (*see* **7.1**). From here head west, gently uphill again and on a fair path, to what I always knew in the past as 'The Nameless Peak' but which the OS maps now name as Y Foel Goch. This is, in fact, the highest point of the round for a gentle descent follows to the north-east to a grassy col, then a gentle climb to the largest of several cairns on the Gallt yr Ogof ridge.

Gallt yr Ogof seen from the A5.

There is a rim of steep little crags around the head of the valley of Nant y Gors, as well as some awkward and unsuspected slabs lower down, so it is advisable to go east along the main line of the ridge towards Capel Curig for about a mile/1.6km to a broad col before slanting down north (traces of path) to pick up the old road. This links Capel Curig with Gwern Gof Isaf and gives an easy and almost level (if boggy in places) stroll back to the start.

### 7.4(a) Scramble on Gallt yr Ogof

SUMMARY: 200ft/61m of Grade 2 scrambling, north-facing; 5½ miles/8.8km, 4 hours; note that the 1:50,000 map/115 is best. This short scramble uses the upper part of an obvious ridge where the rock is not smothered by heather and gives an alternative approach to the ascent.

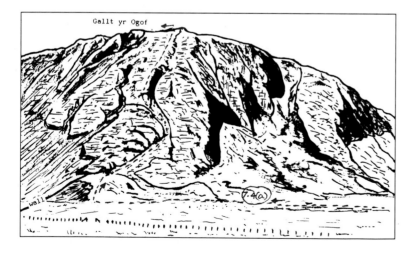

Every rock-climber who has ever attempted any of the routes on Gallt yr Ogof will tell you that it is over-run with heather, and it is. Nevertheless, I kept looking at one particular ridge-line which I felt sure would repay exploration and, although I must have reservations about the lower part because of the heather, the upper part is quite independent and gives a good route with no problems of a vegetated nature. The actual scrambling (hands as well as feet) is restricted to about 200ft/61m but the continuation of the ridge beyond gains a lot more height. Anyone who can find a better route than mine on the lower slabs will be able to add another 250ft/76m or more, but the lower slabs are very overgrown with heather and will therefore stay wet for a long time after rain.

Start as for 7.4 above, from Gwern Gof Isaf but follow the line of the old road towards Capel Curig until you reach a gate and ladder-stile in about ⅔ mile/1km, then turn up the hillside. The ridge which gives the line of the scramble is now very visible on the left-hand skyline and is in fact made up of a number of buttresses linked together by heather terraces. A wide and easy-angled gully defines the right-hand side of the ridge and a wall, the only wall to do so, runs from the almost level moor to the lowest buttress. This lowest buttress looks too steep for scrambling so it can be by-passed to where a second bit of wall reaches the foot of the second buttress. If you continue further still up the gully (very easy) you will be able to curve back left, to reach a broad heather shoulder above which the ridge rises again in a broad pyramid, defended by a fairly steep nose of rock.

The rest of the ridge can be seen now, rising beyond a broad pyramid ending in the steep little rock nose mentioned above. The nose can be turned by an open groove on its right and then climb up the short wall beyond on lovely sharp holds to reach a long section of easy-angled rock ribs, perfect rock with good holds. These lead you to another steep wall with a square-edged flake sticking straight out of its middle. Go left a bit here along a slanting ledge and then back up right through a weakness above; it's still steep but quite easy. You'll find yourself at a place where you can walk across a narrow neck to connect with the rest of the mountain, with an unsuspected vertical drop off to the left.

There is still about 400ft/122m of vertical height to gain to the top but it is only walking now and the line of an old wire fence shows the way up easy-angled rock ribs sticking out of the heather. Higher up, the broad shoulder narrows and almost becomes a ridge where it reaches an overhanging compact buttress overlooking Nant y Gors. The summit is still further on, hiding behind two other false tops, but there is no mistaking the big cairn on the main top. Now reverse 7.4 for a pleasant return to the start.

## 7.5 Glyder Fawr

As Glyder Fach has the wild and beautiful Cwm Bochlwyd carved from its northern flank, so Glyder Fawr is gouged by both the Nameless Cwm (otherwise known as Cwm Cneifion) and Cwm Idwal; the latter is so distinctive that it is a designated Nature Reserve. You might reasonably expect such superb terrain to yield some exciting walking and scrambling of great interest, and indeed it does.

Unfortunately the normal direct 'tourist route' from the north side to the top of Glyder Fawr on its own, the only one not requiring the use of hands as well as feet, is very tedious and exhausting in its upper half, although it certainly qualifies for 'great interest' in its lower half, as far as Llyn y Cwn. For a 'good' tourist route you would need to traverse over Glyder Fach first, via the Miner's Track, to Llyn Caseg-fraith, carry on to Glyder Fawr and then descend via the cliffs beside the Devil's Kitchen. Done this way, because you descend quickly, the tedium of the upper slopes of the Fawr in ascent is not noticed so much.

Looking down the cleft of Twll Du, the Devil's Kitchen.

However, there are times when tedium may be preferable to excitement so I will briefly describe this 'direct tourist route' before moving on to the other alternatives.

### 7.5(a) Glyder Fawr via Twll Du (Devil's Kitchen) and Llyn y Cwn
*5 miles/8km      4 hours*

The two-star rating given for this route in the specifications at the beginning of the chapter is for the splendid scenery around the area of the Devil's Kitchen; the route from there to the summit above isn't worth any.

The start is from Ogwen Cottage (grid ref 651603) and the track to Llyn Idwal is signed round the buildings near the Youth Hostel, heading south-east, crossing the river from the lake and then swinging south-west to reach the kissing-gate near the outflow. The main track continues round the east side of the lake, towards the splendid and unmistakable sweep of the Idwal Slabs at its southern end (not on OS; *see* sketch map) or you may cross the footbridge and head west round the north end of the lake. It doesn't really matter for the initial objective is well in view, the point where the stream from Llyn y Cwn (unseen on a ledge on the cliffs above) has cut a deep black gash into the vertical cliffs to the right (north-west) of the Idwal Slabs. Well-named the 'Devil's Kitchen', no doubt from the way the spray from the waterfall can be blown like smoke around some demonic cauldron, a distant view of it is one of my own earliest memories: from Anglesey, I had it pointed out to me by my father.

The path beyond the Idwal Slabs rises in steps, then picks a line through a great downfall of boulders and scree, climbing steeply towards the base of the cliffs and the point where the waterfall emerges from the depths behind. From this point, breaking away to the left and directly below the black and vegetated cliffs, the path clambers over more scree, rock slabs and boulders, wending a tortuous way up a wide gully defining the left-hand end of the cliffs as you look at them. Cairns mark the way and it is all easy enough in summer conditions, emerging onto easy-angled ground on a broad shelf, where Llyn y Cwn lies below steeper terrain.

Just before reaching the little lake, the path turns up a slanting rubble-strewn runnel leading through fairly steep and rocky ground and to the left of a steeper gully; this degenerates into a dreary tramp up a worn path of loose scree and soil, of the 'two steps forward and one step back' variety which, when frozen, can require crampons or at least an ice-axe and the ability to use it to arrest a fall if necessary. When wet it turns into a sort of mud-slide and when dry is still like trying to slither up a slope of ball bearings. Then the angle eases, the ground is not so unstable and the line of cairns leads steadily to the rock 'castles' on the summit of Glyder Fawr.

The obvious choices to return are threefold: carry on over Glyder Fach and descend its East Ridge (*see* **7.1**) which will add quite a bit to the distance; return by the route of ascent (which is what I have assumed in the distance/time given); or, more adventurously, descend by the easy scramble down the Gribin Ridge (Y Gribin on the OS maps) which separates Cwm Cneifion, the Nameless Cwm, from Cwm Bochlwyd. This latter is much the same in distance but could take a little longer in time because more care will be needed to complete the easy scramble in descent. It is accomplished by going down rocky ground from Glyder Fawr to the north-east to reach a large, gently-sloping grass and earth plateau studded with flattish stones, at the edge of which a circular stone windbreak marks the beginning of the descent. Once started down it you will reach either Llyn Bochlwyd or Llyn Idwal and it is easy enough to reach Ogwen then from either.

On the summit plateau of Glyder Fawr looking to Glyder Fach.

## 7.6 The Glyders via the Gribin Ridge (Y Gribin)

SUMMARY: 200ft/61ft of Grade 1 scrambling, north-facing. 3¾ miles/6km, 3–4 hours. This easy and popular scramble simply picks the most interesting line up the ridge of Y Gribin between Llyn Idwal and Llyn Bochlwyd to reach Bwlch y Ddwy-Glyder.

Take the track from Ogwen beside the Youth Hostel (grid ref 651603), signed for Idwal. Initially the view ahead is of the west flank of Tryfan but then the track swings right (south-west) and the cliffs of the Devil's Kitchen dominate the view instead. Before Llyn Idwal comes into sight there is a large rock outcrop on the left of the track with some sloping slabs in its middle; this is Clogwyn y Tarw, the Gribin Facet, and it terminates the Gribin Ridge. Keep on the track to reach the gate at the fence near the outflow from Llyn Idwal. Here immediately turn left and climb uphill beside the fence to reach the bottom right hand side of the Gribin Facet. A broad gully with several tracks leads upwards now, the tracks converge into a recognisable path and emerge onto a shoulder well above the Gribin Facet at an altitude of about 2000feet/610m (about 1000 feet/305m higher than Ogwen). This same point could just as easily be reached by using the Miner's Track as far as Llyn Bochlwyd and then climbing only slightly to the west from its outflow. The Gribin Ridge path really begins from this shoulder, although purists might care to note that a clearly defined rock-studded ridge rises more directly from the shore of Llyn Bochlwyd itself to the upper rocks of the Gribin, and would give a variation on the usual route.

From the shoulder, the way is up a very easy grassy gully onto the broad crest of the ridge higher up, with dramatic views down to Llyn Idwal in particular, coming out onto a quartz-speckled grassy shoulder. The rocky part of the Gribin Ridge now rises up ahead and a path slants across towards it, although if you want to enjoy the scramble along the crest, it is better to take a higher slanting line, for the path picks the easiest possible route well below the crest on the west side. The direct route clambers up the very easy-angled edges of tilted slabs onto a fairly level section of rock spikes along the crest and then up and over big broken blocks; it is exhilarating, quite easy, but exposed on the edge itself, with splendid views into Cwm Bochlwyd, into which you could quite easily be blown in a high wind. The way taken by the path scrabbles rather than scrambles up rocky grooves and over easy ledges covered with rock debris, then over the big blocks higher up to reach a large cairn and, shortly above it, a circular stone windbreak. It is a pity that the rocky section is so comparatively short, gaining only a little over 200feet/61m in vertical height.

A good return would be over Glyder Fach and then descending Bristly Ridge or the scree path beside it to Bwlch Tryfan, returning to Ogwen by the Miner's Track.

## 7.7 The Glyders via scramble on Cneifion Arête

SUMMARY: 450ft/137m of Grade 2/3 scrambling, west-facing; 4½ miles/7.2km, 4 hours. The route takes a well-marked and direct line up the crest of an obvious, clean and slender ridge rising from the upper part of Cwm Cneifion. Starting just right of the toe of the ridge, the initial moves are steep and fairly polished on good holds, but the angle then eases and the route continues up the left edge of big rock flakes to the top.

Cwm Cneifion or the Nameless Cwm is a wild secluded place, sufficiently so to harbour a small herd of feral goats high above Cwm Idwal, with the Gribin Ridge on one flank and the Senior's Ridge of Glyder Fawr on the other. At its head, on the Glyder

Looking down the upper part of the Gribin Ridge to Ogwen.

Cwm Cneifion, with the Cneifion Arête, from Senior's Ridge.

Fawr side, is a ferociously steep and black crag, Clogwyn Du, which rarely sees the sun and causes travellers on the Glyders ridge to give it a wide berth. The other side of the cwm, above a protecting rock lip and below the crest of the Gribin Ridge, is favoured by afternoon sunshine and has several slanting rock ribs piercing through the predominating shale, one of which is outstandingly obvious and gives the line of this first-class route. (The 'Sub-Cneifion Rib' is shown on the 1:25,000 map but is well below the lip of the Nameless Cwm; the Cneifion Arête is at grid ref 648587, well above it.)

There is no obvious path into the Nameless Cwm but, starting from Ogwen (grid ref 651603) a walk up to Llyn Idwal gains about 330feet/100m and a tramp up grassy hillside for the same height gain to the immediate right of the Sub-Cneifion Rib (an obvious rib of beautifully ice-smoothed and rounded rocks east of the Idwal Slabs) brings you to a shallow rocky gully beside it. A scramble up this leads directly onto the path coming from the cwm above, the lip of which is now a further 500feet/152m high-er. Alternatively you could slant to the right (south) from the bottom of the Gribin Facet to reach the bottom of the Sub-Cneifion Rib.

Once in the cwm, the arête of steep, clean and well-scratched rock is unmistakable. The start is just to the right of the toe of the buttress and then good holds, excellent spikes that your fin-gers curl over, curve back left to the crest. It's a bit polished down at the beginning as the route is used as a mountaineering winter climb but as a summer scramble at the upper end of the scale I think it is perfectly justifiable as there are no strenuous pulls needed and the strata are all in your favour. About 100feet/30m above the start, there is a step left into a little chimney, on excellent holds, and then onto ledges and easier-angled rock above. About 50ft/15m of excellent scrambling on good holds on the crest is followed by 40ft/12m of easier ground, then it is out onto the edge again; delightful scrambling, mostly up the left side of big flakes of rock in a superb position. It's an almost Alpine experience and gains in total about 450ft/137m of height, reaching the almost level plateau at the top of the sec-ond shoulder on the Gribin Ridge and just below its final rock ridge. A continuation up this makes possible a round taking in Glyder Fawr with a descent down to Llyn y Cwn and then beside the Devil's Kitchen back to Ogwen.

### 7.8 Glyder Fawr via scramble on north-west face and Senior's Ridge

SUMMARY: 800ft/244m of Grade 2 scrambling, north-facing; 4$^1$/$_2$ miles/7.2km, 4–5 hours. This long route takes a groove up the obvious buttress just right of the Idwal Slabs to its top, then trends over easier ground towards slabs just right of a gully iden-tified by a notch on the skyline. Intricate route-finding up ledges and walls beyond these leads to a junction with Senior's Ridge from where a continuation can be made to the summit, or a descent into Cwm Cneifion.

Although not marked on the OS maps, the Idwal Slabs are an unmistakable feature of Cwm Idwal and are, along with the steeper rock walls above them, a major rock-climbing play-ground (see map). Seen on the approach from Ogwen Cottage, they look clean and smooth, sweeping down almost to the water's edge at the far end of the llyn. The left side of the slabs is terminated by the steep East Wall and a gully runs down the junction of this and the rocky hillside beyond. This gully is the route of descent for climbers descending from the very popular climbs on the Slabs and, although it ought to give a reasonable scramble, it is exceptionally polished and smooth on certain crucial sections, especially the groove from the top of the Slabs and a gully/groove lower down; a slip from either of these places could have serious consequences and I don't think it is justifi-able as a scramble.

The 'ordinary route' on the Slabs would probably also have been a good scramble years ago; now it has suffered the same fate as the descent route, i.e. it is very polished and also very frequently used. The easy-angled continuation of the rocks above the East Wall is known as Senior's Ridge, a series of short rock walls linked by grass terraces, probably best approached from Cwm Cneifion, but this is hardly worth calling a scramble on its own.

A good scramble can still be found, however, a route of great interest and, excluding a grassy section in the middle, on excel-lent rock, giving unusual views of the climbers on the main sweep of the Slabs nearby. Continued eventually by the upper part of Senior's Ridge it would give a route all the way from Llyn Idwal to the summit. If you don't wish to go all the way to the top, an easy descent can be made into Cwm Cneifion instead.

Because of the size of the face, it would not be a good route to seek in unclear conditions and since it is almost impossible to describe the full detail of the last bit of the route to the notch on Senior's Ridge, this route should only be used by experienced scramblers.

At the right hand side of the Idwal Slabs is a subsidiary buttress, separated from the Slabs by a deep, black and usually dripping cleft. The path leads under the Slabs on its way to the Devil's Kitchen cliffs and then almost touches the lowest rocks of this subsidiary buttress just before crossing a little stream (occasionally dry). Scrambling up quartz-faced slabs from this point (on the lowest rocks) quickly leads into a grassy bay at the foot of a rather vegetated groove or furrow. The groove, and then the rock rib on its right, lead pleasantly up good rock with good holds and at an easy angle. Pick the easiest line, which involves trending right a little at one point and then moving back to the main groove after it splits into two, until you reach the top of a gully dropping away to the right and can then quickly gain the top of the buttress, having ascended about 250ft/76m from the start.

Ahead is what looks like another short little buttress, though it proves in fact to be just the blunt end of a longer and easy-angled rock rib. Seen beyond the little buttress and to its left is an obvious wide notch on the skyline, with a rocky couloir or shallow gully descending from it and with white quartz bands on each side of it. The notch is actually a break in Senior's Ridge and is the next objective. So either climb up the little buttress (by a shallow groove) and ridge, or just walk up the very wide grass gully to the left of the ridge, gaining another 250ft/76m, to reach the bottom of the rocks just right of the foot of the couloir dropping from the notch. On the approach, these rocks look smooth and impregnable but on closer acquaintance prove to be well supplied with satisfying little ledges giving superb scrambling up this sweep of easy-angled rock, gaining a further

200ft/61m or so, to reach a large grassy ledge about 60ft/18m below the obvious quartz band that was so clearly seen from lower down. Now the notch is a little higher but well left; to the right are the steep upper cliffs of Glyder Fawr.

The rocks above the ledge are a little steeper than lower down and you may choose to trend right and then back left to get above the quartz band, or climb up more directly, on good holds and without difficulty in dry conditions, to reach the sloping grassy ledges above it. From the left-hand end of the biggest ledge, a short chimney (about 8ft/2.4m) leads up to another ledge, then moves up the rib of rock at the right-hand end of this lead to more ledges. Continue, quite easily now, trending left, along more ledges and up shorter walls, to reach easy grassy ground in the notch and the end of a full 1000 feet/305m of ascent, of which 800ft/244m has been good quality and very enjoyable scrambling.

The continuation, up the upper part of Senior's Ridge, is a matter of wide choice as it is broad and undefined, leading gradually up grassy slopes and runnels, ledges and rocky slopes for a further 700ft/213m to the summit of Glyder Fawr. The quickest descent would then be as in **7.2** down to Llyn y Cwn and then by way of the cliffs beside the Devil's Kitchen.

### 7.9 The Glyders from Pen-y-pass
*6½ miles/10.5km        4–5 hours*

The impression of the south side of the Glyders gained on the approach from Capel Curig is one of rather dreary boulder-studded grass slopes of little interest to a walker. Once you've turned down the deep defile of the Llanberis Pass, your attention is completely taken by the great roadside crags and steep scree slopes which appear to effectively block all access to them anyway. To realise that the south side of the Glyders isn't all boredom and monotony, you need to be looking across the Pass from high in Cwm Glas or on the North Ridge of Crib Goch; then you can see that there is a cwm facing east and sheltering Llyn Cwmffynnon. It curves round from Pen-y-pass (or Pen-y-Gwryd) up to Glyder Fawr and the edge of this cwm forms an easy-angled spur which gives a surprisingly more attractive route than you would think possible. It is not as well-defined as any of the cwms on the north side, the path is not well-marked on the ground and the line is therefore not so easy to follow in mist, but there is a path, marked more by red paint blobs on the rocks than by boots on the ground, which makes clever use of every fold and groove. It will be obvious that, given good visibility, the views to the peaks on the other side of the Llanberis Pass, particularly Crib Goch, are outstanding.

The best start is from the car park at Pen-y-pass (grid ref 647556). It is advisable to get there early to be certain of a parking place, but there are alternatives: first, by leaving the car at the large car park (free) in Nant Peris (grid ref 607583) from where a Sherpa bus is supposed to go up and down (mid-July until the beginning of September) at half-hourly intervals to Pen-y-pass. (I have never needed this myself so would suggest you check that it is operating on the day you need it by getting a leaflet from the National Park Information Centres or ringing their offices on 0766-770274.) Alternatively, drive down the road to Pen-y-Gwryd where there is free parking in laybys towards Capel Curig, then walk back up to Pen-y-pass. This will take about twenty minutes and it is a very busy road so I wouldn't be too keen myself. The third alternative, which is probably better than the second because of the traffic problem, is to park near Pen-y-Gwryd and start to walk back towards Pen-y-pass. Go just past the hotel and you will spot a ladder-stile leading you off the road. Go west up grassy slopes, keeping just to the right of the wall, up onto the little hillock of Moel Berfedd from where you will see Llyn Cwmffynnon and can pick up the path marked by red paint blobs leading to Glyder Fawr.

Assuming you park at Pen-y-pass, cross the road to a gate at the west end of the Youth Hostel, go over a ladder-stile at the other side of the memorial garden and then follow the paint blobs. These quickly slant uphill towards the end of the broad ridge coming down from Glyder Fawr, passing Llyn Cwmffynnon on the way. The ground is quite boggy low down but the footing becomes much drier as height is gained. The views to Crib Goch's east and north ridges are very fine and you will be able to peep into the upper part of Cwm Glas where the Clogwyn y Person Arête should be seen on a clear day. There are plenty of little rock outcrops and the path zigzags through them, going to the right side of some steeper cliffs at one point and finishing with some rough walking over boulders near the summit. It is a good route, not well known as yet.

The continuation is down the gentle but stony slope skirting the head of Cwm Cneifion to the Bwlch y Ddwy-Glyder, climbing towards and then skirting round the rock blades of the Castell y Gwynt and so on to Glyder Fach. In poor visibility, don't bother with the summit itself but stay on the path which skirts it on its north (Ogwen) side, where there are cairns. Under such conditions, take care also not to stray on paths leading into the wide couloir at the east (right hand) side of the Bristly Ridge but follow the cairns down the rocky East Ridge, the upper edge of Cwm Tryfan. As height is lost, the ground becomes grassier and in good time the boggy plateau near Llyn Caseg-fraith is reached. About 300 yards/274m before actually reaching the llyn, turn south and pick up the Miner's Track which initially climbs over gently rising ground before descending over grass, boulders and bogs to Pen-y-Gwyrd. If you parked here, it is the end of the walk; if you parked up at Pen-y-pass, you will need to walk up the road to complete the journey.

Llyn Cwmffynnon and the Glyders seen from the North Ridge of Crib Goch.

## 7.10 Glyder Fawr via scramble in Bryant's Gully

SUMMARY: 1675ft/511m of Grade 2/3 scrambling, south-facing; 4$\frac{1}{2}$ miles/7.2km, 5 hours. A superb, traditional gully scramble, although all difficulties can be turned, usually on the left lower down, and on the right higher up. The gully splits naturally into three sections of approximately 425ft/130m, 800ft/244m and 450ft/137m, trending rightwards in the upper half and emerging on the top of the Esgair Felen.

This magnificent scramble gives about 1700ft/518m of absorbing interest and is easily the longest continuous route in Snowdonia. It is in three well-defined stages, passes through some superb and dramatic gully scenery and has the great merit that the harder technical difficulties can all be by-passed with very little loss of overall interest. This is particularly useful since a great deal of water pouring down the gully can make these harder places either virtually impossible or mean that you will be in for a soaking, at best. The difficulty grading in the specifications at the start of the chapter is for dry conditions; in wet ones, a difficulty grade of 2/3 would be appropriate for the route as a whole, taking the easier alternatives where necessary. The whole face gets sunlight for much of the day.

Bryant's Gully is in the dramatic Pass of Llanberis, almost directly opposite the Climbers' Club hut of Ynys Ettws (grid ref 624567) and immediately to the right (south-east) of the rectangular-shaped crag of Garreg Wastad. It cuts a way through a triangular mass of rock which forms the end of the Esgair Felen, the stony spur thrown down to the south-west by Glyder Fawr.

The nearest parking will be found in either of the two laybys below Clogwyn y Grochan, the next crag down the Pass at grid ref 621572. From here, slant up very steep hillside for about 350ft/107m to the right of Garreg Wastad; then go 50yds/46m to the right of the top corner of the crag, to where the bottom of the gully is deep-cut and has several big trees in it.

The first section gains about 425ft/130m. Start directly and quite easily up the gully-bed and, at a point about 30ft/9.1m below the first big tree, reach the first problem, a constriction where the water pours down an inclined and completely smooth slab. Just a little lower down, an easy diversion can be made to the left, returning to the bed of the gully above the obstacle. The gully now widens, but is choked with boulders and the extent of your willingness to risk a wetting will determine whether you continue directly or, again, scramble up the left bank before returning to the gully-bed a little higher, about 200ft/61m above the start of scrambling.

A very big boulder now jams the gully. You could climb up either side of it, and get soaked in each case, or, as appears the most used way, go up a little chimney on the left wall of the gully and keep dry, returning to the gully bed above it. It is easier now for a little way, scrambling up waterworn runnels and leading towards a steeper section which is another obvious problem. If you take it directly, you will be glad of the handholds provided by a really useful young tree to pull up into a little bay and open hillside. You may pleasantly avoid this problem by climbing the rib of rock on the right.

The second section gains about 800ft/244m. To begin with, there is no gully as such and progress is made by scrambling up the thin groove of clean, waterworn rock cutting through the heather. It's delightful, but after a little less than 100ft/30m, the groove runs into a well-defined and V-shaped gully again, reaching a small amphitheatre with a mossy and rather greasy back wall; this is avoidable on the right if necessary. Only 50ft/15m or so higher, the heather comes to an end as the gully narrows and sheer rock walls rise on both sides and you reach a short rise of about 8ft/2.4m to a jammed chockstone. Awkward moves, and another soaking if you make them under wet conditions, lead over the chockstone and into a high-walled chamber like a narrow dungeon. The exit looks problematical, clearly involving moves on the right wall up to a scoop and then steeply upwards for a height gain of perhaps 20ft/6m. Under wet conditions, it looked altogether too exciting for me, so I retreated and scrambled up steep rock but on quite good holds on the right wall to get above the obstacle, then traversed back in again.

Immediately ahead is another little recess, its left wall made up of three bulges, one above the other and progress is only possible up the bed of the runnel, with more mossy and slithery rock beyond, so again the right-bounding rib of rock provides a drier, cleaner and more attractive way. Just 50ft/15.2m or so higher, another amphitheatre is reached, its left wall composed of square-cut black and overhanging rocks like rotten teeth; entry is easy enough but exit is to the right on very shaly rock that doesn't inspire confidence, but once more a rib of clean rock on the right is preferable, to reach a point immediately above this black chasm where the gully divides into two, the route continuing up the right-hand one.

Scrambling in Bryant's Gully, on the first section.

It's quite easy to go up the back wall, trending left initially, before stepping onto the rock rib separating the two gullies. Then the rib itself gives enjoyable scrambling until you can trend easily to the rubble-filled right-hand gully. A few steps up and out of this onto the rock rib on the right suddenly reveals, for the first time, a fine view of the outer world, overlooking the huge columnar crag of Dinas y Cromlech and across to Dinas Mot and Crib Goch on the other side of the Pass of Llanberis.

More delightful and easy scrambling on spiky rock up this rib soon leads to a grassy neck and a wide scree bowl. It is another fine viewpoint, with marvellous rock scenery and ends this long second section.

Ahead is still about 450ft/137m of most enjoyable open scrambling, either up rock-littered ledges and easy-angled short walls on the left, or, much better, up the rock rib on the right, composed of more columns of the square-cut rock typical of this hillside, until it runs up against vertical crags ahead. Here you can move easily into a final little scree-filled gully leading to the grassy platform and splendid viewpoint on the end of the Esgair Felen ridge itself, which is reached almost immediately.

An easy-angled broad ridge of small stones now rises gently towards the rock 'castles' on the summit of Glyder Fawr to the east, about half a mile/0.8km away and only 550ft/168m or so higher, so it is a pleasant stroll to continue to the top, leaving the small stones and crossing a wide grass plateau just before the last pull up. Alternatively, on reaching this plateau, traverse north-east, avoiding the summit, to pick up the cairned normal ascent/descent route to Llyn y Cwn on the shelf above the Devil's Kitchen. From here, the apparently unfashionable but most attractive path descending beside the Afon Las leads back to the Pass of Llanberis. To return to the car park, it is a simple walk back up the road, but much safer and more enjoyable to quit the tarmac for the little path alongside the bank of the stream on the right.

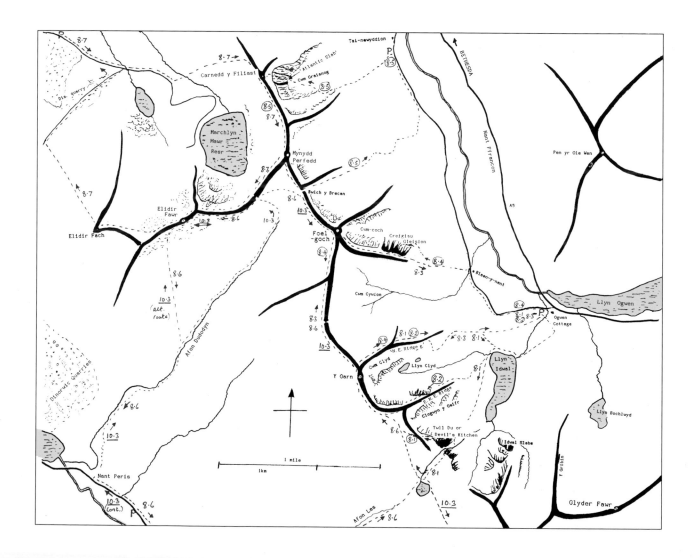

# 8: West Wall of the Nant Ffrancon

| BEST MAPS: | OS 1:50,000 Landranger 115 Snowdon & surrounding area | | | | | |
|---|---|---|---|---|---|---|
| | OS 1:25,000 Outdoor Leisure 17 Snowdonia: Snowdon area | | | | | |

| Approx Distance | Approx Time | Highest Elevation Reached | Height Gained | Star Rating | Scramble Difficulty Grade | Scramble Height Gain |
|---|---|---|---|---|---|---|
| **8.1 Y Garn via the Sheep Walk** | | | | | | |
| 4 miles/6.4km | 3–4 hours | 3106ft/947m | 2113ft/644m | * | — | — |
| **8.2 Y Garn via scramble on east-north-east ridge** | | | | | | |
| 3¼ miles/5.2km | 3 hours | 3106ft/947m | 2113ft/644m | */** | 2 | 262ft/80m |
| **8.3 Round of Y Garn and Foel-goch** | | | | | | |
| 4½ miles/7.2km | 3–4 hours | 3106ft/947m | 2379ft/725m | ** | — | — |
| **8.4 Scramble on Foel-goch by Needle's Eye Arête** | | | | | | |
| 4½ miles/7.2km | 4½ hours | 3106ft/947m | 2379ft/725m | */** | 2/3 | 525ft/160m |
| **8.5 Scramble on Carnedd y Filiast via Atlantic Slab** | | | | | | |
| 3 miles/4.8km | 4 hours | 2697ft/822m | 1975ft/602m | *** | 2/3 | 700ft/213m |
| **8.6 A Round of Y Garn and Elidir Fawr from Llanberis Pass** | | | | | | |
| 9 miles/14.5km | 5–6 hours | 3028ft/923m | 3684ft/1123m | ** | — | — |
| **8.7 A Round of Carnedd y Filiast and Elidir Fawr from Marchlyn** | | | | | | |
| 6 miles/9.7km | 4 hours | 3028ft/923m | 2034ft/620m | ** | — | — |

The peaks, fine main ridge and deep cwms that form the west wall of the Nant Ffrancon are essentially a continuation of the ridge of the Glyders, as a glance at the map will show. Especially towards the northern end, however, the ridge-top walking is much more likely to be on grass than rock and there is generally less traffic. This allows for more peaceful contemplation of some marvellous scenery as well as the indulgence of hard activity without the competitiveness that creeps in whenever there are too many people on the same walk or scramble. The main peaks covered in this chapter are Y Garn, Foel-goch, Elidir Fawr and Carnedd y Filiast and they each have their own cwms, some with crags suitable for scrambles and each cwm providing a walker's horseshoe round in its own right. My selection of walks and scrambles is not exhaustive but will give a good choice.

Before beginning with three routes which each involve the peak of Y Garn, a few introductory remarks about the mountain may be helpful, especially to a newcomer.

Y Garn is the elegant mountain, only a little lower in altitude than Glyder Fawr, whose symmetry is well seen from near Ogwen Cottage at the west end of Llyn Ogwen, or better from the North Ridge of Tryfan, when the view is enhanced by the waters of Lyn Bochlwyd and part of Llyn Idwal. Two fine curving ridges enfold a high cwm, Cwm Clyd, carved out by glacial action and containing two llyns obviously once joined together as they are known by the single name Llyn Clyd. Much of the direct ascent of the left-hand ridge (the ENE ridge) of the cwm is really an easy scramble in its lower reaches but it is blocked by a crag straddling it higher up, so that walkers, when they do approach Y Garn from this direction, normally avoid it altogether, using a path up the centre of the cwm to Llyn Clyd, then traversing below the crag to outflank it and then reach the summit. It is not a popular way for walkers and so I am not dealing with it in detail. For scramblers, however, the ridge and crag provide

a good route, which I have described in **8.2**. The right-hand ridge encircling Cwm Clyd is much more amenable for walkers and is thus used as a means both of ascent and descent. I have used it as an ascent and combined it with a visit to Foel-goch (**8.3**). The third possibility with Y Garn is to dodge round the back of the left-hand encircling ridge of Cwm Clyd by walking up to Lyn y Cwn via Twll Du (the Devil's Kitchen) and then up long but easy slopes to the summit of Y Garn from the south. This route, exactly the same as **7.5** as far as Llyn y Cwn, can be varied with a bit, a tiny bit, of scrambling by way of the 'Sheep Walk' before continuing to the summit of Y Garn. Let us begin with this last one.

### 8.1 Y Garn via the Sheep Walk
*4 miles/6.4 km        3–4 hours*

The start is from Ogwen Cottage (grid ref 651603) and the well-signed path then leads up to Llyn Idwal, to the outlet from the lake. From here the black cleft of Twll Du, the Devil's Kitchen, is well in view on the other side of the water, and well-worn paths lead round the shore to either side. Then a rough ascent through large boulder debris leads to the foot of the main gully (*see* **7.5** for further details).

Scrambling up the main gully of the Devil's Kitchen is really only an expedition for masochists who enjoy getting wet and slithering about in precarious places. Making progress requires strenuous effort, exit from the back of the Kitchen is a graded rock-climb (Very Difficult) and it is best left to those both enthusiastic and competent enough to tackle it, even if you do retreat from the exit pitches. On the other hand, there is an alternative to the normal path going up below the cliffs to the left of the Kitchen; it is almost its mirror image.

From Tryfan's North Ridge over Cwm Bochlwyd to Cwm Idwal.

Y Garn seen from Tryfan's North Ridge.

Starting from just below the actual lowest point of the rocky cleft of the Kitchen itself, the 'Sheep Walk' curves to the right and upwards. If in any doubt as to the start, go up the normal path to the left to gain about 15ft/4.6m of height and then look back: two or three rock ledges forming a little staircase will then be clearly seen, with a path winding out of sight beyond them. The path leads into an overhung bay, with dripping water and black cliffs above, then continues up rubble-covered ledges to a rubble-filled gully which itself splits into three smaller gullies. Previous parties have clearly been indecisive here because what was a well-defined path lower down now disappears. It doesn't matter greatly which gully you choose, although the right-hand

one is perhaps the best. This scrabbles up scree to a collapsed cairn just below an area of rust-coloured rocks on the right-hand side. It's not much of a route really and the actual rock scrambling is very short. However, under winter conditions and with winter gear, it could be a very different story, of course.

A grassy depression now leads steadily upwards and you should soon spot a ladder-stile over the wire fence and be able to join the path that climbs the broad grassy slopes to the north to the edge of Cwm Clyd and then follow it round and upwards to the circular stone shelter on the summit of Y Garn.

To return to the valley via the other encircling ridge of Cwm Clyd, you need to descend about 60ft/18m to the north to a collapsed cairn which marks the start of the path down the ridge. This now takes an attractive line, curving round almost in a semi-circle towards the two little llyns in the cwm and then turning away again to descend steeper and more boulder-covered ground. Its direction is never really in doubt, although there is a choice as to whether you return to the outlet of Llyn Idwal or go the slightly shorter way across to Llyn Ogwen without crossing the river.

### 8.2 Y Garn via scramble on east-north-east ridge

SUMMARY: 270ft/82m of Grade 2 scrambling, north-east-facing; 3¼ miles/5.2 km, 3 hours. Looking from Ogwen towards the summit of Y Garn, two ridges run towards you encircling Cwm Clyd. The route goes up the left-hand ridge with short bits of scrambling lower down but the scrambling proper is concentrated on the buttress straddling the ridge high up. The steep bottom buttress is avoided by a gully on the left overlooking Cwm Idwal; this leads to a horizontal neck of rocks and a short further ascent beyond to reach easy ground.

The start is again from Ogwen Cottage (grid ref 651603), then take the signed track to Llyn Idwal to reach the outlet from the lake. Cross the footbridge and circle westwards round the shore to reach the stream flowing down from Cwm Clyd. Seen from here, the left-hand ridge doesn't look like a ridge at all; it looks more like a triangular rounded buttress of rock and grass, with another flatter topped buttress rearing up quite some distance behind it – the Castell y Geifr.

The triangular buttress of rock and grass mentioned above and to the left of the path does need to be avoided and this is best done to the left by way of some tedious, though short, heathery runnels to reach the crest of what proves to be a generally easy angled and clearly defined ridge beyond. This is quite long, has two little 15ft/4.6m sections of actual scrambling on it and, as it gains height, a little path develops along the spine. When it runs out onto a flatter area, littered with boulders, the steeper rocks of the main ridge rise beyond, slanting across from bottom right towards top left so simply trend over to the left towards the lowest rocks which are ended by a steep triangular buttress, split vertically in the middle. There is a definite path at the bottom of this crag, curving under these steep rocks to the left, where it ends with a fine view down into Cwm Idwal. A gully goes back right from here for about 100ft/30m; it's fairly steep but a lot less steep than round on the face of the buttress, and the holds are generally good. The gully reaches the ridge above and then 50ft/15m of easy ground leads to a connecting neck of rock with steeper rock rearing up beyond. This neck is about 50ft/15m across, almost level but with a little step in it halfway, and it leads to a large buttress made up of columnar blocks. It is easiest to go right, climbing some easy blocks and then, in an exhilarating and fairly exposed position, climb up the sharp edges of some enormous blocks, keeping to the right, with a final few paces over boulders. It's only about 80ft/24m above the neck and about 270ft/82m from the start of the sustained scrambling, but though short it is very enjoyable.

The 'neck' and crags on the ENE Ridge of Y Garn.

A grassy ridge now leads easily to the top of Y Garn and a convenient descent would be down the normal right-hand ridge (*see* **8.1**).

### 8.3 A round of Y Garn and Foel-goch
*4½ miles/7.2km*     *3–4 hours*

North of Cwm Idwal, the superb ridge that runs from Y Garn to Carnedd y Filiast and overlooks the Nant Ffrancon has no fewer than six cwms gouged out of its eastern flank. The ridge itself gives a fine skyline walk (*see* **8.6**) but for a shorter day or for a change, try an ascent of Y Garn followed by a descent from Foel-goch which, as a walk, is the better way round. For competent scramblers, a grand day's outing is to try the same, but in reverse, ascending by way of the Needle's Eye Arête of Foel-goch, in Cwm-coch.

For a walk (or the scramble, **8.4**) the best start is from Ogwen Cottage (grid ref 651603) at the west end of Llyn Ogwen where there is parking, or park along the roadside of the A5. Behind the buildings, take the well-worn track which climbs south-east and then swings south-west to the gate near the outflow from Llyn Idwal at the entrance to the Cwm Idwal Nature Reserve. Leave the main track here, cross the outlet by the footbridge and curve north-west to west on a grassy path, keeping to the north of the stream issuing from Llyn Clyd out of sight above. This leads through a gateway in a wall and then winds up much steeper and rockier hillside towards the right-bounding arm of Cwm Clyd. The initial steep rise leads to a shoulder above the two little llyns in Cwm Clyd, with splendid views both down the Nant Ffrancon and over Cwm Idwal to the Glyders and Tryfan, and then swings to the south-west for the final pull. Little spikes

*The ridge to Foel-goch, with Pen yr Ole Wen, from Elidir Fawr.*

of slate mark the last bit where the path reaches the main ridge at a collapsed cairn. The summit of Y Garn itself is about 30ft/9m higher to the south, and has a low circular stone shelter.

The continuation to Foel-goch is straightforward. Go back to the collapsed cairn and then easily downhill for half a mile/0.8km to the bwlch at the lowest point of the rim of Cwm Cywion. Easy grassy slopes beside a wire fence lead over a little hump and then up to the little pile of stones, and the end of the fence, on Foel-goch. The descent is back south, past a deep-cut rocky gully piercing the rim of Cwm-coch to a wider gully at the lowest point of the rim and leading down into the cwm. Continue down the slopes keeping south of the crags of Creigiau Gleison, through the area of rocky stumps and little pinnacles called 'The Mushroom Garden' on the OS 1:25,000 map, to reach the old road just below the farm of Blaen-y-nant. From here it is a pleasant walk back to Llyn Ogwen.

### 8.4 Scramble on Foel-goch by the Needle's Eye Arête

SUMMARY: 525ft/160m of Grade 2/3 scrambling, north-east-facing; 4½ miles/7.2 km, 4½ hours. This route finds a way, after an awkward start, up the longest and most continuous of the ridges amidst the maze of towers and pinnacles. Once located, however, the route is followed fairly naturally, with some exciting situations.

The southern or left-bounding arm of Cwm-coch below Foel-goch is made up in part of a maze of towers and pinnacles which are much more extensive than is apparent from near Llyn Ogwen. The route goes up the longest continuous rocky ridge amidst them and, after an awkward start, gives fine rock scenery and exciting scrambling. The rock is mostly excellent but the lower section would not be pleasant in the wet.

From Ogwen Cottage (grid ref 651603) walk along the old
road (directly in front of the Youth Hostel) as far as the bridge
just above Blaen-y-nant Farm. Here the road turns steeply
downhill but a faint path strikes north-west up the hillside
beside a little stream and a collapsed wall to rise above two
rocky bluffs and reach a wire fence. Cross the fence, then cross
the better path reached just beyond it and the collapsing wall
beyond that; continue in the same north-westerly direction up a
rock-strewn grassy slope towards the pinnacles seen on the skyline above. Just before reaching them, you also reach a good
path contouring the hillside at about the 500m contour. Turn
right here; the path leads into Cwm-coch, but only go just far
enough along it to reach a definite corner where it turns into the
cwm. Just above this spot is a wall and a sheepfold, although the
sheepfold isn't immediately spotted from below. On a bearing of
240° magnetic from this corner, you will be looking straight up
the twisting East Gully winding a way through the towers and
pinnacles, with a lighter coloured scree chute emerging from its
foot. The Needle's Eye Arête is the ridge to the immediate right
of the gully and the footpath crosses the scree chute about a
hundred paces further on towards the cwm.

Go easily up the grassy East Gully, with the first big rock
tower or buttress on your right until, level with its top, you are
stopped by a smooth and wettish rock barrier on either side of
which grassy ledges lead up to little cols on both sides of the
gully. Turn right here and then cross back left on ledges above
the rock barrier into the gully bed again. In another 60ft/18m or
so (100ft/30m from the bottom of the first rock pillar) of easy
scrambling, the grassy part of the gully you are in merges with
another scree-filled part, with pinnacles and towers up ahead.
Now traverse rightwards for 30ft/9m to the base of the obvious
steep tower which has a little 'window' near its base where a
small rock has jammed between two bigger ones. I would recommend a rope be used here to safeguard the next passage where

you creep round under the overhung tower, with good hand-holds but rather flaky footholds, to scramble back left up a heathery runnel beyond and reach a notch on the arête over-looking the east gully. Immediately above, on excellent rock, good holds lead up a very short slab to an airy perch straddling the arête and then, 10ft/3m further along it, there is the hole through the ridge, like a little cave and which you can sit in: the Eye of the Needle.

Above looks intimidating and loose; a traverse left for 40ft/12m is much easier and enables the arête to be regained and at an easier angle. The hardest part is now over but much good scrambling without anxiety remains. Two tiny pinnacles are taken directly, then a groove starting on the right and finish-ing on the left gets you up the next bigger pinnacle and over-looking the East Gully again. At the next bigger one, it looks as though a way could go round to the right but a short groove straight up its front gets you up nicely and onto the crest of the ridge again, past a couple of spiky bits onto a grassy part. One area of steeper rock only remains, in two tiers. The bottom tier has a slightly overhanging bit but excellent holds lead easily to the last easier-angled section, which ends just where the top of the East Gully merges into the hillside on the left.

The easy ground above leads to grassy slopes and then it is an easy walk to the top of Foel-goch. From here there are splendid views along the continuation of the ridge to Mynedd Perfedd, to Elidir Fawr and to the seamed east flank of Pen yr Ole Wen, with the highest tops of the Carneddau beyond, seen across the Nant Ffrancon. From here, it is a grand return to continue to Y Garn and then descend from there (the reverse of Walk **8.1**) on the well-marked path down the north-east ridge, back to Ogwen Cottage.

Ogwen, Tryfan and Nant Ffrancon from the 'Needle's Eye Arête'.

## 8.5 Scramble on Carnedd y Filiast via Atlantic Slab

SUMMARY: 700ft/213m of Grade 2/3 scrambling, south-east facing; 3 miles/4.8 km, 4 hours. The route takes the lower, outside edge of the enormous Atlantic Slab, the huge one with the clearly rip-pled surface to the right of a prominent curving gully in Cwm Graianog. Higher up, moves into the grooves right of the main overlap give the easiest line. The exposure is exhilarating but the angle easy.

The great ridge of the Glyders terminates in the north with Cwm Graianog and Carnedd y Filiast, but far from fizzling out tamely in grassy slopes as you might have expected, the north side of the cwm is dominated by a huge expanse of the most extraordinary gritstone slabs. These are clearly in view from the A5 road but perhaps because they look so improbable, so smooth, so holdless and indeed so unusual, they are seldom vis-ited. It is a great pity for here there is both solitude and atmos-phere, as well as at least one first-rate scramble of about 700ft/213m.

Start by parking beside the old Nant Ffrancon road just south of Tai-newyddion Farm; there is space for three or four cars about 100 yds/91m away from a cattle-grid and gate (grid ref 632634). Beyond the cattle-grid, you have direct access to the hillside and a climb up steep bracken- and grass-covered slopes leads into Cwm Graianog about 600ft/183m higher. Going left up the grassy ridge which is the cwm's left-hand retaining wall enables you to get a good view of these extraordinary overlap-ping slabs opposite. Ignoring the slab which is the lowest down the cwm and further away from the others, the two main ones which catch the eye are Waved Slab, which is above and to the right of a scree fan; its surface is clearly rippled, almost horizon-tally. Further left is a tremendous crescent-shaped gully, curving bottom right to top left from top to bottom of the entire crag: this is The Runnel. It marks the lower and left-hand boundary of the enormous Atlantic Slab. This is rippled, like Waved Slab (though with more vegetation on it) but it also has about sixty narrow veins of white quartz running across its surface at almost equal intervals and almost horizontally. This tremendous slab is like a static ocean breaker surging from left to right and its crest breaks onto another line of slabs at a slightly lower level. This crest gives the line of the route. It is broken up and irregular and an extraordinary number of the broken blocks are either edged or faced with quartz. As a final guide to check that you are in the right place, a wall runs along the bottom of the entire belt of slabs; go horizontally about 100yds/91m to the right from the point where it abuts against the overlap below the much smaller Russet Slab. The key, I must emphasise, is that crescent-shaped gully, The Runnel. Atlantic Slab is to its right and the route goes up the right edge of Atlantic Slab.

The route starts with a slight degree of uncertainty because, lower down, there are several edges to the right-hand side of Atlantic Slab; the best scrambling is found by sticking as near as possible to the furthest right-hand edge, although it won't be long before you find yourself moving into the grooves to the right below the overlap to dodge what look like hard moves on the edge of the slab itself. When you do, you will forsake solid rock for a mixture of rock and bilberry. It is impossible to give you precise directions beyond saying: 'Just find the easiest way up the edge of this extraordinary slab.' It is delightful scrambling, airy but at an easy angle and always there are good holds. Higher up, the height of the overlap diminishes and so it makes little difference whether your progress is up the groove to the right or on the slab itself. In dry conditions, it is a delight; dry gritstone always is. On the other hand, although you can get up it under wet conditions, gritstone tends to be a bit slimy and you may find yourself using knees rather than feet on the occasional tricky bit. On a fine day, the route is first class, really enjoyable.

Heading south from Carnedd y Filiast, a ladder-stile leads over a wall and there is a good view of the dammed Marchlyn Mawr, with the rocky Pillar of Elidir rising from the scree slopes just above the water's edge. A gentle descent follows, down a stone-studded grassy slope followed by an equally gentle rise to a circular stone shelter on Mynydd Perfedd. There is virtually no path along this part of the ridge, but after Mynydd Perfedd the slope declines noticeably to the col of the Bwlch y Brecan, on the far slope of which is the dangerous-looking notch, and slope above, of Foel-goch.

From the bwlch, a simple descent down grass slopes leads easily but fairly steeply back to the valley bottom, where you can turn left along the old road back to the car.

### 8.6 A Round of Y Garn and Elidir Fawr from Llanberis Pass
*9 miles/14.5km      5–6 hours*

It is no doubt fashionable to climb to the shapely peak of Y Garn from Llyn Ogwen, but to continue the ridge to the north, the west wall of the Nant Ffrancon, and then go out to the peak of Elidir Fawr as well is not so often done in this direction. For a change, and for a strikingly different view of the Llanberis Pass, I suggest you try this fine round.

There is a large and free car park at Nant Peris (grid ref 607583), then walk the half mile south-east up the Pass to find the 'public footpath' sign on the left, just after crossing the Afon Las, beside the camp site, bus stop and post-box at Cae Perthi (grid ref 614577), just north-west of Beudy-mawr.

(I'm sorry that I could not quite fit all the walk on the sketch map.)

Yr Elen and the Carneddau seen from Carnedd y Filiast.

The path leads up a lane with a wired slate-spike fence, continuing past several cottages to the highest one up the slope. Here there is a ladder-stile, and walking-man signs lead you up sheep pastures on the right-hand side (as you look up) of the wooded ravine of the Afon Las to reach a metal footbridge crossing a subsidiary of the main stream. A stonier section follows, climbing quite steeply and gaining height rapidly to a ladder-stile over a transverse fence, then trending to the right and round a little rock outcrop, just over 1000ft/305m above the start and on the level of some waterfalls over to the left. The views back to the pass below are exceptionally fine from up here, particularly to the magnificent Cwm Glas and Cwm Glas Bach and are ample compensation for the effort.

The continuation is still steep but the going becomes easier now as the path climbs to a gentle lip and then onto a wide and rather boggy plateau almost 2000ft/610m above the valley, leading to where Llyn y Cwn lies below the steep slopes and outcrops of the northern flank of the Esgair Felen.

It is a dreary trudge from here up to Glyder Fawr and best forgotten today; the path up to Y Garn to the north on the other hand isn't very exciting either but it is on firm ground and the stone windbreak on the top is sooner reached than you might think. Now you have the superb views down the cwms and airy ridges on the north side of the Nant Ffrancon to make you revel in being on the high tops again. Whether the wind is blowing soft breezes or squalls of rain or sleet in your face now hardly matters; I know of few feelings of exhilaration to match those that flow from a good tramp along a fine mountain ridge – and this is a fine one.

An easy descent to Bwlch y Cywion follows, but you will scorn the traversing path used by the 'Welsh Threes' walkers (because Foel-goch doesn't reach the magic 3000ft/914m) and keep near to the edge overlooking the Nant Ffrancon as you climb up to Foel-goch, for more splendid views. Now you can descend the slope to the north-west and join the traversing path if you like; it avoids Mynydd Perfedd and Carnedd y Filiast, which are consequently left in seclusion for those who know about the wonderful scrambling on the great Atlantic Slab of the latter (see **8.5** and **8.7**), and curves out to the west to Bwlch y Marchlyn. From here you have the strange sight of the Marchlyn Mawr Reservoir, with the crags of the Pillar of Elidir rising almost from its surface, and can wonder at the technology that sends all that water swooshing up and down tubes inside the mountain on which you stand.

The path climbs the crest of a sharp and slaty ridge to a false summit, giving exciting views to the east, to the Carneddau, and then leads up more open grassy slopes to reach the rocky summit crest of Elidir Fawr. This is a jumble of tilted slabs and blocks and the summit cairn is a little way along it.

To return to the valley, you could return to Bwlych y Marchlyn first but a more direct way is to continue along the ragged crest until you reach a point where the easier ground on the southern slopes of Elidir Fawr is almost free of boulders and slabs, then slant down the slopes to reach the path beside the Afon Dudodyn. This path leads without further incident to Nant Peris.

### 8.7 A Round of Carnedd y Filiast and Elidir Fawr from Marchlyn
*6 miles/9.7km        4 hours*

The construction of a road, rising to about 1200ft/366m, to the Marchlyn Mawr Reservoir has made a round of Elidir Fawr, one of the 'Welsh Threes', noticeably easier. There is a car park at Grid ref 597631 (just south of Talywaen on the OS 1:25000 map) reached by turning off the B4547 north of Deiniolen at Blaen Cae and following signs for 'Marchlyn'. Walk up the road beyond the gate to the first obvious bend (grid ref 611626) then across country to the north-east and up open slopes to reach a broad col, then up steeper but short slopes ending in boulders to the stone windbreak on Carnedd y Filiast.

Now head south over a ladder-stile and skirt the edge of the amazing Atlantic Slab rising out of Cwm Graianog. A slight descent, then rise, lead to another windbreak on Mynydd Perfedd, from where you can see the sharp-edged ridge rising towards Elidir Fawr. Another gentle descent leads to Bwlch y Marchlyn then a path up the sharp and slaty edge above the reservoir leads to a false summit. Easier grassy slopes lead to the shattered real summit crest and the cairn.

To complete the round, continue south-west along the crest to its end then strike west down shaly slopes to a cairn on Elidir Fach. A 1000ft/305m of grassy slopes to the north-west lead to a junction with a metalled road and a right turn (north-east) along this quickly leads to the reservoir access road again.

The amazing Atlantic Slab on Carnedd y Filiast.

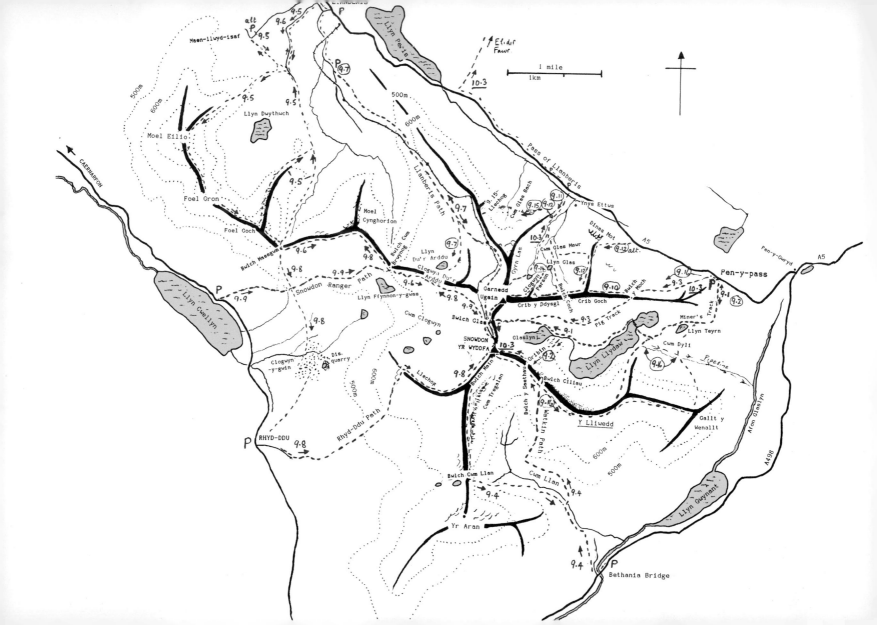

# 9: The Snowdon Group

| BEST MAPS: | OS 1:50,000 Landranger 115 Snowdon & surrounding area | | | | | |
|---|---|---|---|---|---|---|
| | OS 1:25,000 Outdoor Leisure 17 Snowdonia: Snowdon area | | | | | |

| Approx Distance | Approx Time | Highest Elevation Reached | Height Gained | Star Rating | Scramble Difficulty Grade | Scramble Height Gain |
|---|---|---|---|---|---|---|
| **9.1 Snowdon by the Miner's Track** | | | | | | |
| 9 miles/14.5km | 5 hours | 3560ft/1085m | 2382ft/726m | */** | — | — |
| **9.2 Scramble to Snowdon by Cribau (The Gribin)** | | | | | | |
| 9 miles/14.5km | 5 hours | 3560ft/1085m | 2382ft/726m | *** | 1 | 656ft/200m |
| **9.3 Snowdon by the Pig Track** | | | | | | |
| 9 miles/14.5km | 5 hours | 3560ft/1085m | 2382ft/726m | ** | — | — |
| **9.4 Snowdon by the Watkin Path, return by the south ridge** | | | | | | |
| 8 miles/12.9km | 5 hours | 3560ft/1085m | 3363ft/1025m | ** | — | — |
| **9.5 Moel Eilio and the round of Cwm Dwythwch** | | | | | | |
| 7½ miles/12.1km | 4½ hours | 2382ft/726m | 2415ft/736m | **/*** | — | — |
| **9.6 Snowdon by Moel Eilio and Moel Cynghorion** | | | | | | |
| 12 miles/19.3km | 6 hours | 3560ft/1085m | 4990ft/1521m | **/*** | — | — |
| **9.7 Llanberis Path to Snowdon (with optional scramble on Clogwyn Du'r Arddu)** | | | | | | |
| 8 miles/12.9km | 5–6 hours | 3560ft/1085m | 2674ft/815m | * | 1 | 250ft/76m |

| Approx Distance | Approx Time | Highest Elevation Reached | Height Gained | Star Rating | Scramble Difficulty Grade | Scramble Height Gain |
|---|---|---|---|---|---|---|
| **9.8 Snowdon from Rhyd-Ddu, return by Moel Cynghorion** | | | | | | |
| 9½ miles/15.3km | 7 hours | 3560ft/1085m | 3553ft/1083m | **/*** | — | — |
| **9.9 Snowdon by the Snowdon Ranger Path** | | | | | | |
| 8 miles/12.9km | 5–6 hours | 3560ft/1085m | 2936ft/895m | * | — | — |
| **9.10 Crib Goch by the East Ridge** | | | | | | |
| 7 miles/11.3km | 5 hours | 3560ft/1085m | 2382ft/726m | *** | — | — |
| **9.11 Crib Goch via Cwm Glas Mawr and Bwlch Coch** | | | | | | |
| 3½ miles/5.6km | 3–4 hours | 3028ft/923m | 2484ft/757m | ** | — | — |
| **9.12 Crib Goch via the North Ridge** | | | | | | |
| 4 miles/6.4km | 3–4 hours | 3028ft/923m | 2484ft/757m | **/*** | — | — |
| **9.13 Garnedd Ugain via Cwm Glas** | | | | | | |
| 5 miles/8km | 5–6 hours | 3494ft/1065m | 3035ft/925m | * | — | — |
| **9.14 Garnedd Ugain by scramble on Clogwyn y Person Arête** | | | | | | |
| 5 miles/8km | 5–6 hours | 3494ft/1065m | 3035ft/925m | *** | 2/3 | 800ft/244m |
| **9.15 Scramble on Llechog Buttress to Clogwyn Station** | | | | | | |
| 3½ miles/5.6km | 4 hours | 2526ft/770m | 1936ft/590m | * | 2/3 | 600ft/183m |

The only thing to a mountain-walker that may sometimes be a disappointment about Snowdon is the summit itself, called Yr Wyddfa, The Tomb, although any evidence of an ancient grave that may have once existed there has long since vanished. The stink from the diesel oil generator at the café on the summit is enough in itself to ensure that any stay there is a brief one. But in winter, when the snows obliterate the orange peel and the café is shut, or during the week when the crowds are absent, even the summit is a glorious place. I've got used to the Snowdon Railway. I'm old enough to realise that there are many people who are quite incapable (including elderly and disabled) of actually walking up to Yr Wyddfa by their own unaided effort and, since it is now there anyway, they might just as well use the railway. The new pipeline out of Cwm Dyli is a different matter, a monstrosity that should never have been allowed to happen.

Tourists, who simply want to climb to 'the top' (and they too have a perfect right) under their own steam, have a different requirement. They shouldn't but do sometimes wear shoes with sling-backs or wellies, and are like accidents-waiting-to-happen. They need what is quite explicitly called in the Alps a 'tourist route' which is as short and safe as possible and on which they won't get lost. If you discount walking up beside the railway track itself (although you are in great danger of being knocked over by mountain-bikes on any of the ways from Llanberis nowadays) there almost is a tourist route now. I say 'almost' although by the time this book is in print the last top bit of the Pig Track will have been pitched and tidied up, and as near as perfect a 'tourist route' as is possible on this superb massif will be completed. Certainly those who use it will never experience the simple pleasure that comes from safely crossing an awkward passage, but fewer of them will slither down those iced-up slopes in winter. I will describe it shortly; in poor conditions it may give a good escape for everybody.

The name 'Snowdon' really means the whole mountain massif, the 'Creigiau Eryri' or 'crags of the eagles', not just the bit at 'the top'. In fact, Snowdon's 'top' is a curved ridge about half a mile/0.8km long with a dip in the middle. At one end is Yr Wyddfa and at the other is Garnedd Ugain, just 66ft/20m lower. From this summit ridge, subsidiary ridges with their own tops radiate from both ends, curling round magnificent cwms left by the retreating glaciers and with great cliffs at their heads. So the choice for the mountaineer, competent in all aspects of the sport, is almost endless. For the hill-walker who is strictly a walker only, it is more limited, but for the hill-walker not afraid of using his or her hands occasionally and who can thus cope with a scramble as well, there is a lot more choice. I will therefore deal with the walking ways first, but attach the nearby scrambling variations as they arise. Some of the paths overlap where they converge near the summit ridge and this needs to be borne in mind when reading the descriptions.

### 9.1 Snowdon by the Miner's Track
*9 miles/14.5km        5 hours*

I choose this route to begin with because it is the most popular 'tourist route', formerly used to bring copper from the mines in Cwm Dyli and with some superb mountain scenery. The first drawback to it being the 'tourist route' is that you pay quite dearly to park at Pen-y-pass, the head of the Pass of Llanberis (grid ref 647556) and it will pay you in the other sense to get there early. There is a large café and Youth Hostel there too.

From the lower left-hand car park, make for a broad stony track leading south round a broad shoulder with the land falling away on the left to the Gwynant valley. The first and smallest of the three lakes, Llyn Teyrn, is soon passed, often mirroring the dramatic cliffs of Y Lliwedd's twin peaks, which are however much better seen once a corner is turned. Then the much larger

reservoir of Llyn Llydaw comes into view, bridged by a causeway which effectively turns it into two lakes. The summit ridge comes dramatically into view from here, although it is the highest cone of Yr Wyddfa which inevitably draws the eye.

Once across the causeway, the track winds beside the shore to pass some derelict copper mine buildings, but gains only about 260ft/79m in the 2½ miles/4km from Pen-y-pass. The next half mile/0.8km or so up to the superb upper cwm, with Yr Wyddfa's graceful cone rising sheer above, is steeper but still on a smooth track as far as the outlet from the hidden upper lake of Glaslyn, whose waters are sometimes a startling green-blue colour, the effect of the copper ore in the underlying rocks. It is the next section, the 1300ft/396m or so rise to Bwlch Glas, the lowest point on the summit ridge, which is the crunch. A steep climb, with some made steps, leads to the junction with the Pig Track (also coming from Pen-y-pass, see **9.3**) and then a rising traverse with some final zigzags leads to a large rock finger (with the Snowdon Railway track just beyond), on Bwlch Glas. These zigzags gave the section which could – and no doubt will still – be tricky in winter conditions especially, although the considerable work done in pitching and improving it has made it vastly easier and tamer than it ever was. The rock finger, about the height of a man, is a most useful landmark and may be a vital one in poor visibility, appreciated by even the most experienced climbers and walkers. It is well worth noting its position.

From Bwlch Glas it is only ten minutes or so but still 302ft/92m to the trig point on Yr Wyddfa and 'the top'. The safest return is by the route of ascent, although you could vary the descent by taking the traversing line of the Pig Track instead of descending to Glaslyn (see **9.3**).

Snowdon reflected in Llyn Llydaw, Crib Goch on right. The sunlit ridge below Snowdon is Cribau (the Gribin).

## 9.2 Scramble to Snowdon by Cribau (The Gribin)

SUMMARY: 656ft/200m of Grade 1 scrambling, north-east-facing; 9 miles/14.5km, 5 hours. This easy scramble takes the obvious spur or ridge extending from the outflow of Glaslyn towards Bwlch y Saethau, starting up slabs and continuing by rock flakes and ledges, rising to the right. It can also give a useful descent for competent scramblers (see **9.16**).

This first-class and easy scramble is a superb alternative to the last part of the Miner's Track and the zigzags on the approach to the summit ridge of Yr Wyddfa. (It also gives a useful descent from Bwlch y Saethau for a shortened version of the 'Snowdon Horseshoe' if needed, see **9.16**.) The rock is sound, the situation

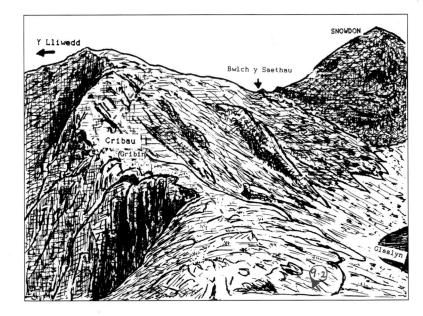

exhilarating without being exposed and the route clambers up the easy-angled ridge of rock which forms part of the rim of Cwm Glaslyn.

Start from Pen-y-pass (grid ref 647556), and then follow the Miner's Track (see **9.1**) beyond Llyn Llydaw to Glaslyn. Cross the stream from the outlet of Glaslyn and immediately make for the smoothed slabs on the left. These start north-east of the point marked 'Cribau' on OS 1:25,000 but the ridge is generally anglicised to 'Gribin' or 'The Gribin'. Don't confuse this one with the other one, 'Y Gribin', anglicised to 'The Gribin Ridge' which leads up to the main Glyders ridge (see **7.6**). The slabs quickly lead by a shallow groove to the top of what is now seen to be the end of a mostly grassy and almost level spur which leads in 200 yards/183m or so to the main upthrust of the ridge separating the upper cwm from the lower. Here the strata tilt bottom right to top left, giving a long curving slope with many short, blunt and smooth ribs of excellent rock. There is a choice of ways but the most obvious use shallow grooves between the rock ribs. Hands are definitely needed but the angle is very easy; it's similar to the north ridge of Tryfan but with much less exposure. The angle eases still further for a while after reaching a rock rib with a prominent quartz vein in it, then steepens again with more grooves to reach easy ground at a cairn. What a delightful way to gain about 650ft/198m of altitude.

Just above, up easy ground, is the col of Bwlch y Saethau. The summit of Yr Wyddfa is still about 900ft/274m above and you can now choose to either follow the well-worn (but treacherous in winter) scree slopes at the top of the Watkin Path or, more in keeping with the scramble below but only advisable in clear weather and good conditions, stay as close as possible to the right-hand edge of the blunt ridge above Glaslyn and complete the scramble to the top. It isn't anything like as good as The Gribin you have just ascended but it's more interesting than the last section of the Watkin Path (see **9.4**). A descent to Bwlch Glas and then down the Pig Track (see **9.3**) gives a good return to Pen-y-pass.

## 9.3 Snowdon by the Pig Track
*9 miles/14.5km        5 hours*

This is really a shorter version of the Miner's Track, although it is significantly rockier and rougher in its early stage than the latter. I must admit that, for years, I thought it was the PYG track, named after the Pen-y-Gwryd Hotel, well-known for its Everest associations, but I now believe that it is named after Bwlch y Moch, the Pass of the Pigs.

Starting from Pen-y-pass (grid ref 647556 – if you're lucky enough to find a space to park – see **9.1**) instead of taking the Miner's Track, the path leads out of the top car park at its right-hand side and heads west below the line of the long ridge leading towards Crib Goch. Although much improved of recent years, it is still a rough way of gaining about 700ft/213m of height. On the col, the path forks, the right-hand one heading for Crib Goch's east ridge (and the spectacular traverse that follows, see **9.10**) while the left-hand one descends slightly; this is the Pig Track, traversing well below the slopes of Crib Goch. It has also been levelled, pitched and generally improved for much of its way in recent years so that it is now a very simple proposition in all but the worst weather. As it passes below the cliffs of Crib y Ddysgl and above the waters of Glaslyn, the continuation of the Miner's Track (which really ends at Glaslyn) rises to join it.

The combined track then zigzags upwards to Bwlch Glas and the exit onto the summit ridge is marked by a large and solitary rock finger. Store it in your memory for future descents. Turn left (south) now and follow the line of the railway to the summit.

Glaslyn and north-east face of Snowdon seen from Bwlch Glas.

The best return at the same level of difficulty is to reverse the route of ascent although a longer and easier return could be made by completing the descent from the rock finger mentioned above as far as Glaslyn and then using the Miner's Track back to Pen-y-pass (see **9.1**).

I would only suggest that, as a better start to either the great Snowdon Horseshoe (see **9.16**), or as an approach to the Gribin Ridge (see **9.2** above), instead of following the hordes along the normal path, turn off the path almost as soon as you leave the car park. A scramble over a few boulders and an easy climb on grass onto the end of the ridge (known, very appropriately, as the 'First Nail in the Horseshoe') above the path soon gives you enough height to enjoy a fine view along the line of five or six grass-sided rocky pimples backed by Crib Goch's east ridge and also an even finer one into Cwm Dyli. You will reach Bwlch y Moch almost as quickly as the hordes anyway.

### 9.4 Snowdon by the Watkin Path, return by the south ridge
*8 miles/12.9km       5 hours*

This is a most attractive round and the best on the south side, ascending via Cwm Llan from the beautiful Gwynant valley and marred only by the final slope up to Yr Wyddfa, although even that can be avoided in good weather. (It is also a very good round in the reverse direction, that is, using the south ridge as the way of ascent from Bwlch Cwm Llan and descending the Watkin Path.) The Watkin Path was named, incidentally, after Sir Edward Watkin, a Victorian railway owner, who constructed the path as a donkey track. As on the ascent to Scafell Pike in the Lake District, many Victorians preferred their fellwalking to be assisted.

The north-east face of Snowdon from Bwlch Glas in winter. The stone finger marks the start of the Pig Track/Miner's Track.

The start is from the Bethania Bridge car park at grid ref 628506. Then go down the road and cross the bridge itself to the signed track at the foot of slopes covered in mature oaks. Shortly turning off the farm track, the way ahead soon curves round into Cwm Llan, with rocky bluffs on its right-hand side crowned by a mixture of pines and deciduous trees. Then, just before reaching a series of attractive waterfalls, it crosses over the remains of a dismantled tramway, an indication of what to expect higher up the cwm. The track passes close by the stream where it flows through a little gorge and there is a first ruined building on the far bank, with another at the top of the gorge. A path goes off to the left at the top of the gorge; this is the way of the descent (or to Bwlch Cwm Llan if you were doing the route by climbing the south ridge of Snowdon first).

In the wide basin above the gorge on the side of the path, there are some sheepfolds made in a typical Welsh way from blades of slate held together by wire. There are also the ruins of the substantial house of Plascwmllan, which was the home of the manager of the South Snowdon Slate Works whose quarries are shortly to be seen above. About 250 yards/229m further on in this tremendous amphitheatre is the Gladstone Rock, on which a plaque commemorates the visit of Mr Gladstone in 1892; then eighty-three years old and Prime Minister for the fourth time, he 'addressed the people of Eryri on justice for Wales. The multitude sang hymns and *Land of my Fathers*'. It must have been a moving occasion in this tremendous natural arena.

The track continues past a large and steep slab. It looks as though the right-hand edge, and particularly the stony curving ridge beyond and above on the left edge of Craig Ddu, could give a good easy scrambling line towards Y Lliwedd, and it does, but only for a short distance. The line fizzles out on steep slopes some way below Y Lliwedd's top, after which it is just rough grass and stones, so I don't recommend it. The track continues past two large spoil heaps and some more ruined buildings. Then on the left can be seen the place where the dismantled tramway ends, with the graceful cone of Yr Aran on the south ridge on the other side of the cwm. The height gain from the car park to here is about 1000 feet/305m.

The next section, to Bwlch Ciliau, is almost 1000 feet/305m as well, but the track degenerates now to a rougher path and you'll be breathing rather more sharply than you did lower down as it swings to the north-east and zigzags uphill past many cairns of quartz-speckled rock to reach a great heap of stones, a collapsed cairn (which I have heard called Carnedd Arthur), just below Bwlch Ciliau: this is the lowest point on the ridge linking Yr Wyddfa (Snowdon's highest peak) to Y Lliwedd. Before reaching it, it passes through the upper part of Cwm Llan, called Cwm Tregalan, whose wall opposite is buttressed by a forbidding-looking shattered crag, Clogwyn Du (one of many such 'black cliffs'). I had harboured thoughts that this might give a good scramble but having looked at it more closely (the south ridge path goes along its top), I don't think that there is anything there that could justify one. Steep rock with solid holds where you can stay nicely in balance is one thing; steep loose rock is quite another.

The path reached at the pile of stones runs just below the crest of the ridge but it's far more interesting, except under bad conditions, to go left along the actual crest, for there is a tremendous view down to Llyn Llydaw and you can draw a mental veil over the sight of that hideous pipeline running out of Cwm Dyli. Even though it is so hateful, it will take more than that pipeline to ruin this superb cwm.

Staying on the crest as far as Bwlch y Saethau (the Pass of the Arrows, another of King Arthur's legendary battle sites), where there are a couple of tiny llyns and a good view down to Glaslyn, gives very easy but delightful scramble-walking, with dramatic retrospective views to the great cliffs of Y Lliwedd. At the bwlch, the crest rears up towards Yr Wyddfa but it also broadens, is a lot steeper and the line is not so clear, so that, although it is a more satisfying ascent that way in good weather, if it is misty it is better to follow the fairly well-marked and cairned path slanting up unpleasantly steep shale, earthy runnels and grooves. This gives 700ft/213m of either drudgery or awkward ascent, depending on conditions; in winter, you could quite definitely need crampons and ice-axe; in summer, be prepared to dodge dislodged debris from careless parties above. The point of arrival on the south ridge is marked by a bottle-shaped finger of rock, about 6ft/1.8m high, which is a key marker to look for in a descent, then another 200ft/61m of ascent up more solid ground leads to the summit.

Return back down the south ridge to the finger of rock but do not turn off here; continue south beyond it along the ridge. This is quite sharp and pinnacled but a good path winds round from one side to another and the ridge remains interesting for quite a long way, losing over 500ft/152m in height quite gently until it steepens and fades into broader slopes. Now, although the sharpness of the ridge has been lost, the path runs above the crumbling cliffs at the head of Cwm Tregalan for a way, before descending a rather rockier and spikier section by means of a little gully, then continuing steadily to where two small llyns lie in folds of land just to the west of the col of Bwlch Cwm Llan. Rocks with vertical bands of quartz mark the point where the path turns left (east) and downhill. There is only an intermittent path continuing from Bwlch Cwm Llan towards the peak of Yr Aran further along the ridge, although Yr Aran looks superb when seen from near Llyn Gwynant in the valley. If you do visit Yr Aran, it would probably be advisable to return by much the same route back to the col as the slopes on the Gwynant side of

Looking down Snowdon's South Ridge from near the summit.

Yr Aran are uniformly steep and forbidding and the subsidiary spurs run into little woods which would complicate the descent.

The normal path from Bwlch Cwm Llan quickly descends easy slopes to join the grassy way of the dismantled tramway opposite the Gladstone Rock, but near its end it is advisable to turn down a slanting path towards the little gorge and so avoid the tramway's final precipitous descent. From here the ascent route is rejoined.

### 9.5 Moel Eilio and the round of Cwm Dwythwch
*7½ miles/12.1km        4½ hours*

A long ridge extends to the north-west from the summit of Snowdon, giving the longest but in some ways the most attractive of all the approaches to the reigning peak. Three of the tops along its length form a separate cirque around Llyn Dwythwch and the skyline gives a short but delightful walk. Most of the going is on grass, the views are fine and it is certainly not as well-known as many of the other walks hereabouts; it should be.

The distance and heights given in the specification at the beginning of this chapter assume that you park in Llanberis: there is a large car park on the side of the by-pass at grid ref 582600 and other places also. Walk along the main street and turn up Fford Capel (from the east and near the Royal Victoria Hotel, this is the second road on the left, grid ref 578601). Keep going up here, ignoring a side road on the right, past the Youth Hostel and wind up the hill for just under a mile/1.6km, including going through a gate, until you reach the end of the tarmac at a second gate (grid ref 573591). Here you meet the old track leading over the Bwlch Maesgwm to Rhyd-Ddu. Now turn right (north-west) and go immediately over a ladder-stile beside a gate and along the track for only 50 yds/46m or so, then look up the hillside to the left (south-west) and you will spot a ladder-

stile over the wall a little higher up the slope. Make your way up the field to this and you are on the broad north-east ridge coming down from Moel Eilio by way of Braich y Foel.

(You may be able to avoid road-walking and gain a little over 500ft/152m of altitude if you drive up to the derelict farm at Maen-llwyd-isaf (grid ref 567595) which is where the tarmac road ends and a track contours round the northern end of Moel Eilio. There is room for a couple of cars here without causing any obstruction. Walk back down the road for 100yds/91m and then turn right (south-east) along the contouring track (which leads to the end of Fford Capel, *see* above). Follow this track for about 100yds/91m to a ladder-stile and gate, then turn up rough pasture and alongside the fence on the right to reach a ladder-stile over the wall. Continue up the field to reach the north-east ridge of Moel Eilio, as above.)

A wall runs up the crest of the ridge, with ladder-stiles at the tranverse walls, and when the wall ends, a wire fence takes over and continues the line. What path there is is very faint but it is easy walking, going steadily uphill on grass alongside the fence all the way to a last stile almost on the top of Moel Eilio. Just beyond is a round stone windbreak, a good place from which to look across the valley below to the hills of the Nantlle Ridge to the south-west. To the north-east, there is a view of the tremendous Dinorwic slate quarries, tier upon tier of terraces running out onto steep slopes of slate spoil.

The descent from here is easy and grassy, with just one stile over the wall and then down the ridge to the SSE, with views ahead now to Snowdon. Bwlch Gwyn will be passed without noticing it but Bwlch Cwm Cesig is definitely noticed because there is a short rise immediately beyond it to a fence-post at the 2064ft/629m spot height. On the descent from here, Llyn Cwellyn comes into view for the first time, down below on the right; and on the left is a line of shattered and vegetated crags, high above the much smaller Llyn Dwythwch far below. A very short rise leads to the cairn on Foel Gron, lower than the unnamed top you've just left, then a simple descent to the col beyond follows. On the rise up the far slope, the path meets and runs alongside a wire fence to reach two ladder-stiles on a broad shoulder of Foel Goch, avoiding the highest point. In fact the actual top is a short distance away and a little higher to the north-east.

From here, you could make the sharp descent (alongside the wire fence going in that direction) to Bwlch Maesgwm and get onto the track going back north down the sheltered valley of Maesgwm towards Llanberis, to the east of Llyn Dwythwch, but it is much more in keeping with the open and windswept nature of this walk to descend the long grassy ridge projecting to the north-east from Foel Goch. So it is better to avoid crossing either of the two ladder-stiles near the top of Foel Goch and turn north up the last bit of slope to Foel Goch, then descend alongside the fence, with two more stiles on the way down then, on a broad col just before a last rise, trend right (north-east) to avoid a steep slope and reach the valley track.

This is alternately grassy and stony, passes various derelict farms and quickly leads northwards, past an extraordinary concrete block structure just above the bank of the Afon Hwch, to reach a small stand of trees and a couple of buildings at the road end. If you walked up from Llanberis you will just go through the gate and turn downhill to follow Fford Capel back to town. If you parked up at Maen-llwyd-isaf, don't turn downhill but go straight ahead over the stile beside the gate. The track contours round and reaches the metalled road again within minutes and your transport should be just up the slope.

Looking north-westwards to Moel Eilio from the summit of Snowdon.

## 9.6 Snowdon by Moel Eilio and Moel Cynghorion
*12 miles/19.3km        6 hours*

Snowdon's longest ridge winds in elegant and graceful curves giving mostly easy walking over grass, but with a fair amount of undulation also, meaning that the total ascent is almost 5000ft/1524m. There is little doubt but that is the main reason why this superb ridge is not used more often than it is, for in some ways it is the best way of all up this great mountain, allowing fine views on the approach and splendid ones when you get there. If the weather deteriorates or the flesh proves weaker than you hoped, it is always possible to make a sheltered descent to the north either from Bwlch Maesgwm, after descending Foel Goch, or from Bwlch Cwm Brwynog, after traversing Moel Cynghorion.

The way as far as Foel Goch has already been covered in detail in the previous walk (**9.5**) although it is best to park in Llanberis for this route. Then walk up Fford Capel as described above to reach and traverse the Moel Eilio–Foel Gron–Foel Goch ridge, crossing the ladder-stile on the shoulder (not the top) of Foel Goch and descending the steep grass slopes alongside the fence to the south-east to Bwlch Maesgwm, where there is another ladder-stile at a junction of three walls/fences. The continuation of the path, fainter now but obvious alongside the wire fence, can be seen from the descent, leading up the ridge beyond to the wide grassy summit of Moel Cynghorion. Follow the wire fence over the top and down the edge of precipitous slopes to the south-east, crossing a final ladder-stile shortly after leaving the summit. The descent is nearly 600ft/183m but it is very easy, heading towards the little reservoir of Llyn Ffynnon-y-gwas, to reach the col of Bwlch Cwm Brwynog. Now join the Snowdon Ranger Path, seen just below the col and which now climbs in zigzags up the right (south) flank of the main ridge leading towards Snowdon itself. The easy grassy walking has been left now for a stony way, but detours to the left of the main path allow breathtaking views down the steep cliffs of Clogwyn Du'r Arddu and to the right hand the view is into the wide Cwm Clogwyn with its several little lakes. As the angle eases the path reaches the railway line at a vertical marker stone, on the left of the line as you are looking down it, then runs alongside the railway line to reach the summit station and café. (The other, larger marker stone, a little further away and on the other side of the line, marks the start of the descent of the Miner's and Pig Tracks to the east.) The summit trig point is, of course, a little higher to the north-east and you will not want to linger there for very long, I don't suppose.

To return, head back down the railway line but keep on its right (east) side on the Llanberis Path as far as Clogwyn Station. From here, you could of course simply continue down the Llanberis Path, busy and stony and the best way in poor visibility. But a more attractive way, much easier on the feet, infinitely more peaceful and with some superb views over the Llanberis Pass, is to descend the Llanberis ridge. Some of the best views are seen from the summit of the cliff of Llechog, which is traversed immediately after leaving Clogwyn Station. Thereafter, just ramble easily down the grassy ridge-top, over several minor eminences en route and then, as the ridge tends to the west, pass down the grassy slopes to join the main Llanberis Path just before it reaches the metalled road and the last steep tarmac descent to the town.

## 9.7 Llanberis Path to Snowdon (with optional scramble on Clogwyn Du'r Arddu)

SUMMARY: 249ft/76m of Grade 1 scrambling, east-facing; during a walk of 8 miles/12.9km, 5–6 hours. This scramble is up the Eastern Terrace of Clogwyn Du'r Arddu, the route used as a descent by rock-climbers. Slant in from the left to reach the bottom of the Terrace. Easy but has a very impressive and, to some, intimidating atmosphere.

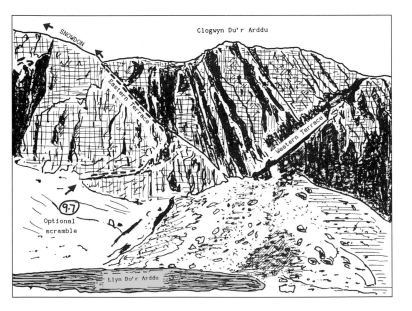

After the Miner's Track (9.1) and Pig Track (9.3) to Snowdon, probably the most popular route to the summit shadows the line of the Snowdon Mountain Railway from Llanberis. It always *seems* a long way and although the return could be varied by descending the Snowdon Ranger Path as far as Bwlch Maesgwm (*see* 9.9) and then returning down Maesgwm, that descent is just short of 2 miles/3.2km longer than the return down the Llanberis Path and is only likely to appeal if you have parked in Llanberis town rather than further up the hill at the start of the Llanberis Path. Consequently, most walkers descend the same

way. Apart from reaching the top, of course, a highlight of the walk up the Llanberis Path is the sight of the great cliffs of Clogwyn Du'r Arddu. For scramblers who do not feel that they may be put off by the tremendous atmosphere and aura of 'Cloggy', there is even a short but interesting route using the Eastern Terrace and which adds some variety to the simple ascent and descent by the ordinary walking route.

Clogwyn Du'r Arddu, generally known to the rock-climbing world as 'Cloggy' is the finest crag in Wales and a good case could be made out for it being one of the very best in Britain. To stand near the little black llyn, Llyn Du'r Arddu, that lies in the hollow beneath these precipices and to look up at them, is to experience a great sense of awe at their most impressive architecture. It seems an impossibility that men can climb such rocks, yet Cloggy has seen several waves of climbing exploration and the cliff now has many magnificent routes which weave intricate ways across the overlapping and steeply angled slabs of the West Buttress or take even steeper lines up the near vertical walls elsewhere.

The Victoria Hotel in Llanberis is at grid ref 584597 and there is a minor road directly opposite, with a cattle-grid just before it starts to climb steeply. You can walk up here if you like, but you'll save yourself about 500ft/152m of uphill trudge on a tarmac road if you drive up to where the road levels off and there is an obvious space immediately after the large sign for the Llanberis footpath: about fifteen cars can park here (grid ref 582588). The heights and distances given in the spec at the beginning of the chapter assume that this is what you do: if not add 1¹/₂ miles/2.4km. The path itself is generally stony and a bit hard on the feet but is well-made and is at an easy angle, slanting across gentle slopes; this is just as well because the summit of Snowdon looks a disconcertingly long way away. Shortly after having passed through a tunnel under the Snowdon Railway, at about 2000ft/610m, you will pass the Halfway House. I remember buying lemonade there years ago, then it seemed to go through a period of disuse, but I noticed a new roof recently and that it seems to be open for business again.

A little further on, the main path turns uphill and shortly reaches Clogwyn Station, where it goes under the railway line again. It then climbs the rather exposed lower slopes below Crib y Ddysgl and traverses them to Bwlch Glas, finally going up alongside the track to the summit. In summer, it is a section walked over almost without noticing it; in winter, the path and the railway line both get filled with snow and ice, and a slip on the section before the path joins the track could send you hurtling down for a too-close look at the precipices of Cloggy below. It is the longest of the paths to the top and probably the least interesting, apart from the views of Cloggy from the slopes below Clogwyn Station.

For a controlled look at the cliffs of Clogwyn Du'r Arddu and

Snowdon and Cwm Clogwyn seen from the path to Rhyd-Ddu.

its scramble, however, do not continue uphill beyond Halfway House up towards Clogwyn Station but take a level grassier track to the right which leads into the great cwm and continues contouring directly below the cliffs. Seen from opposite them, there is a giant triangular-shaped buttress to the right of centre of the cliffs, with the point of the triangle at the base, on scree. The Western Terrace takes a slanting line from the bottom of the triangle to top right, the Eastern Terrace takes a slanting line almost from the bottom of the triangle to top left of it. Both are used as ways of descent for rock-climbers but normally only on summer days. The Western Terrace has a much harder start to it and then degenerates rapidly into a scrabble up loose shale and earth. I don't think it is an attractive way; the Eastern Terrace is better and finishes higher up towards Snowdon.

The slanting and easy-angled rake of the Eastern Terrace (*see* sketch) comes to an end about 70ft/21m above the base of the cliffs and a direct ascent to it is for rock-climbers only, as will be obvious as you approach. It is necessary to avoid this lower section by traversing in from left to right on a slanting line across well-marked quartz ledges, followed by some steeper steps leading towards a deep gully ahead. Don't go up the gully (feasible but harder) but make a step up and then a traverse across to the right to reach easier ground. This is a bit exposed, but the holds are big and everything above now is easier as a little zigzag path leads quite definitely onto the Terrace itself which, at this point, is a boulder-strewn and overhung ledge. The ledge leads into a little corner which is often a bit wet but good holds quickly overcome this problem; then trend left by way of a simple groove to reach easier-angled ground. You now look up a huge glacis, a big flat plane of rock inclined at an easy angle, and the way goes up this: little slabs and little ledges on it give delightful progress, sadly for only about 100ft/31m before they lead onto more open and rubble-strewn ledges, so be careful not to dislodge anything onto climbers who may be below.

The best part of the ascent is little more than 250ft/76m in total, but it is a most interesting variation on the Llanberis Path. What remains of the Terrace is really little more than scree before the cairned route of the Snowdon Ranger Path is reached at about 2750ft/838m, so there is still a bit to go to the top at 3560ft/1085m. A big standing stone marks the point where this crosses the railway line and then it merges with the Llanberis Path to the top. As mentioned in the introduction to this walk, the Snowdon Ranger Path could be taken as far as Bwlch Maesgwm but most parties will prefer to return by the Llanberis Path as it gives a straightforward and fast descent.

### 9.8 Snowdon from Rhyd-Ddu, return by Moel Cynghorion
*9½ miles/15.3km        7 hours*

A pleasant start, a rather uninteresting middle section but a dramatic and exciting finale would be a fair brief summary of this route. A return to Rhyd-Ddu from Yr Wyddfa could quite logically be made by descending the south ridge towards Yr Aran and turning west at Bwlch Cwm Llan, but my favourite way is to descend by the Snowdon Ranger Path along the top of Clogwyn Du'r Arddu and then bag Moel Cynghorion as well before returning to Rhyd-Ddu by a delightful cross-country route that avoids using any roads. This gives a magnificent round that is only marginally less good than the great Snowdon Horseshoe (**9.16**).

Start from the SNP car park at Rhyd-Ddu (grid ref 571527) and follow the signs out of its north end onto a stony track which quickly leads past a former small slate quarry. Pass through two gates while skirting the nearby farm to reach a third gate/ladder-stile over a wall and then, in a further 100yds/91m reach a junction with the path climbing eastwards towards Yr Aran. Swing left through a kissing-gate here, going north-east towards Snowdon, whose summit is just visible over the left end of the crags at the head of the still hidden Cwm

Clogwyn. The path now winds through much rockier ground towards a long ridge with a wall running up it and which forms the southern rim of Cwm Clogwyn. Before reaching the foot of the ridge you pass through another gate in a wall and the path is then excessively cairned (there is one about every five yards/4.5m) over a broad shoulder, before it swings noticeably to the left (north), climbing steadily now and with fine retrospective views back to Llyn y Gader and the Nantlle Ridge. At about 2000ft/610m you reach another kissing-gate, with a grand view down to Llyn Cwellyn and in another 450ft/118m of steady upward plod quite suddenly reach the rock-rimmed edge of Cwm Clogwyn.

The wall that comes up the ridge ends on the very edge of the crags of Llechog and yet another kissing-gate enables you to pass through the wall and skirt the edge of this fine cwm. Very shortly the sharpness of the edge fades into a more rounded shoulder with some loose rock and the section of route that follows is up a zigzag path channelled by a strong wire fence away from what could be, in high winds or icy conditions, a dangerous place. At just over 3000ft/914m the fence ends and the path passes across the face of the upper part of the cwm to join the south ridge at Bwlch Main, a col between two pinnacles.

The bunker-like summit café is now clearly in view ahead as the path crosses onto the east side of the ridge and, about 200ft/61m below the summit, reaches the bottle-shaped marker-stone that indicates the point where the Watkin Path starts the descent to Bwlch y Saethau; it also allows your first view over into Cwm Dyli and to Llyn Llydaw. A last short pull up rocky grounds leads to the summit, just above and behind the café.

Apart from the grandeur of the prospect down Cwm Dyli to the east, I think the finest views from the summit are those to the west, over Moel Cynghorion to Moel Eilio. It is a superb landscape of elegant cwms and ridges which improves the nearer you approach it; which is why it is my favourite descent.

The last section of Snowdon's South Ridge, with the eyesore café.

Leave the summit and go down beside the railway line, keeping it on your right hand, as far as the marker stone on the left of the track; this marks where the Snowdon Ranger Path turns downhill to the north-west. Just a few feet away from this marker stone there is also a notice erected by the railway company which states, on its bottom line, 'The company accepts no responsibility for anyone bitten by a poisonous snake whilst trespassing.' So you have been warned. As it descends, the cairned path understandably keeps well back from the dramatic crags of Clogwyn D'ur Arddu, but in good conditions you should not fail to peer over to Llyn Du'r Arddu and linger over the marvellous views to the west. The Snowdon Ranger Path now zigzags down the stony ridge towards Bwlch Cwm Brwynog but turns downslope at the last moment, just before reaching it, to make towards the reservoir of Llyn Ffynnon-y-gwas. Here, at the Bwlch, I suggest you leave the path to complete the traverse of Moel Cynghorion. (Your eventual descent from Moel Cynghorion will intersect with the route taken by the path anyway, at grid ref 575553; the Snowdon Ranger Path will continue downhill to the west but you will head south towards Rhyd-Ddu.)

The climb up Moel Cynghorion is steep but easy going, mostly on a grassy path up the edge of steep rocky slopes falling to the right, reaching a ladder-stile just below the summit and then continuing beside the wire fence to the rounded grassy top. The expected backward prospect of the great cliffs of Cloggy never really appears from here, even when it is late in the afternoon when they may be illuminated by the sun, but once you are walking along the top of Moel Cynghorion, the landscape on the Llanberis side is really superb, across ridges and cwms lit by western light and well worth the extra little effort to come up here instead of taking the main path traversing the slopes below. Just over the top, heading for Bwlch Maesgwm and still following the fence line, you reach the curious sight of some particularly large boulders, one perched on spikes of slaty rock, which are so incongruous in this grassy landscape that they can only have been deposited there by moving ice. After a gentle descent to Bwlch Carreg y Gigfran and slight rise beyond, the descent continues beside the fence to the Bwlch Maesgwm, where three walls/fences meet at a point (two of the walls are collapsing and so have been replaced by fences). From here descend about 100ft/30m in 200yds/183m to reach a ladder-stile at a collapsed wall and wire fence. Cross the stile but then shadow the edge of the fence to the SSE and you will reach the Snowdon Ranger Path again at a gateway by a little stream. Turn left here, back

towards Snowdon for just 50yds/46m and you will see a ladder-stile on your right. This, as mentioned above, is the start of the path back to Rhyd-Ddu.

Easy walking across sheep pasture, directed by wooden marker posts, leads in a curving descent towards the former slate quarry grounds seen ahead. Reaching the edge of the great spoil-tips, the path crosses a rough track, then a lively stream by a metal footbridge and adjacent wall by a stile into the property of Clogwyn-y-gwin. The marker posts lead below the bottom edge of a big tip and then, somewhat disconcertingly, turn back uphill to the east towards a man-made cutting in the midst of millions of tons of slate spoil. Just beyond a roofless ruin on the left, the marker posts climb up the edge of a tip and lead you quickly to another ladder-stile and back onto mountain pasture again. Now it all becomes clear again as the path winds towards Rhyd-Ddu between some fine rugged outcrops and down more sheep pasture to cross an old incline and reach a metal gate partly hidden in some small trees. Turn left (SSW) here along an old grassed-over railway embankment. This gives an easy level walk, with a last look back to Snowdon all golden in evening light, leading precisely back to the car park and the end of a superb day.

### 9.9 Snowdon by the Snowdon Ranger Path
*8 miles/12.9km          5–6 hours*

This is a long and fairly boring way up Snowdon and I really only include it for the sake of completeness. It is, however, comparatively easy and still seems to enjoy popularity on that account. The ascent starts from the Snowdon Ranger Youth Hostel (grid ref 565551) beside the lovely Llyn Cwellyn, where there is a car park just opposite the building. A signed path from the left side of the hostel (as you face it) leads up a farm track before zig-zagging steeply up grassy hillside behind the farm. As

the angle eases, the main track crosses the path heading north-wards to Bwlch Maesgwm and then goes through a gateway in a wall beside a little stream. From here it contours, sometimes rather boggily, round the lower slopes of Moel Cynghorion and just fails to make the last little bit of ascent to Bwlch Cwm Brwynog, from where you might at least have had a change of view down the other side. It then zigzags up the edge of the great cliffs of Clogwyn Du'r Arddu, one of the finest crags in Britain, and sadly avoids the excellent views again (which you can easily rectify by a slight diversion) before trudging across a bare slope towards the railway line, which it meets at a marker-stone and notice-board (see **9.8** above). The summit, as you might expect, is at the end of the railway, on the left.

There isn't much of a choice for a return, unless it is high summer and you can make use of the Sherpa bus service to be collected from any of the main points around the mountain, so you will need to return the same way as you ascended. I would strongly recommend the slight detour over Moel Cynghorion to vary the journey (again, see **9.8** above for a reversal of the ascent route etc).

### 9.10 Crib Goch by the East Ridge
*7 miles/11.3km       5 hours*

This, the normal first half of the Snowdon Horseshoe, must be the most popular ridge walk in Wales and understandably so. Its attraction never seems to wane, even for old hands who may have done it many times, for to stand at the east end of the Crib Goch ridge with the prospect of Garnedd Ugain, Yr Wyddfa and Lliwedd, seen over the two llyns of Llydaw and Glaslyn, is to view a superb alpine mountainscape in miniature. Few ridges in

*Looking along the rim of Clogwyn Du'r Arddu to Snowdon's NW Ridge.*

Scotland rival it and, while in summer conditions (except for high wind) it can be traversed by any reasonably active person who does not suffer from a fear of heights, under snow and ice or high wind at any time it may become a major undertaking; then it requires experience, proper equipment and the know-ledge of its use. These comments are equally applicable to any of the major ridge lines, of course; I merely repeat them here because of the particular likelihood that inexperienced people may be tempted to push their luck on this one. Very few acci-dents in fact occur, but that there are not more is sometimes far more due to good luck than good judgement.

The start is at the head of the Llanberis Pass, at Pen-y-pass (grid ref 647556) where there is a car park, toilets and a good café opposite the Youth Hostel. Be sure to get early to the car park for it is very popular. (In summer, there is a 'Sherpa' bus service that runs from the large car park in Nant Peris at the bottom of the Pass and it could be worth while checking there before going up to Pen-y-pass.)

The path you need to begin the day is the Pig Track which leads out of the top car park at its right-hand side and heads west below the line of the long ridge towards Crib Goch (see **9.3**). Having gained about 700ft/213m of height and reached the col, Bwlch y Moch, where the Pig Track turns downhill at the col before traversing across the flank of Crib Goch, your way turns uphill instead, up the East Ridge. It is very well marked, an excellent scramble-walk up a broad face leading to a steeper section about halfway up, where some grade 1 scrambling is needed, then narrowing to a ridge thereafter. It is an ascent of nearly 1200ft/366m to what is generally considered to be the summit of Crib Goch; there is a platform at its east end from where the spectacular traverse ahead – inspiring either fear or exhilaration – can be clearly seen. The next almost level section can seem quite a long way; the confident will be able to skip along with their feet on the actual crest; the nervous will tend to

use the crest for handholds, with their feet on rock footholds just below the crest on the Cwm Dyli (south) side, passing by Crib Goch's actual summit (6ft/2m higher than at the east end) just before the edge dips a little to an obvious path, beyond which the pinnacles begin. It is exhilarating scrambling along the crest of these but more normal to drop down a little to the left of the first two and then scramble back up to a gap beyond which is an obvious 20ft/6m scramble upwards onto the top of a big pinnacle. A short descent down the other side quickly leads to a grassy col where there is a short length of wire fence. This is Bwlch Coch; it is also an escape route into Cwm Glas Mawr if needed (see **9.11**).

Beyond the col, the ridge rises again and a path follows the crest which rises over a minor hump on rockier ground, then on grass again until it rises once more towards the pinnacles blocking the ridge ahead. The main path goes left here, on the level, but then seems to be quite uncertain where to go and it is not uncommon to hear shouts from parties who have kept too low and found themselves endlessly traversing the sides of these pinnacles. I think the best way is to go just left of the first rocks, and then slant initially to the right and so up to the crest; there is only about 40ft/12m of actual scrambling, much less than on Bristly Ridge for instance. Then just continue along the top for a short way until the section ends at a shaly col where there is a big cairn and a path goes off downhill, slanting back right towards the Clogwyn y Person Arête (see **9.14**). The ridge ahead is still well defined, rocky, with little pinnacles that you just walk round; then there is another 20ft/6m scramble up a slightly steeper section and down the other side. One last slightly steeper rocky rise follows and then an almost level bit leads to the trig point on Garnedd Ugain.

The East Ridge of Crib Goch seen from near Bwlch Moch.

It is a gentle enough descent now to reach the point where the Llanberis Path merges with the one you are on and you spot the railway track rising alongside and see the big vertical stone on Bwlch Glas that marks the point where the Pig Track starts its descent down Cwm Dyli. I'm sure you won't be able to resist the ten-minute walk from here up to Yr Wyddfa, at least I never can, even though I may just rush up to it and off again as fast as possible.

After the visit to the summit, assuming you do not plan to continue towards Lliwedd and the rest of the Horseshoe (see **9.16**), the best descent is down the Pig Track. So return to Bwlch Glas, ensure that you have found the rock finger on the right-hand side (east) of the railway line (a bit of advice that will seem totally superfluous on a clear day but can be vital if mist closes in) that marks the top of the joint Pig Track/Miner's Track descent and follow it down the zigzags until just above Glaslyn. From here you will see that the Pig Track takes a level traversing line across the lower slopes of Crib Goch and returns you to Bwlch y Moch. Here you cross over the crest of the ridge and follow your outward route back to the start.

### 9.11 Crib Goch via Cwm Glas Mawr and Bwlch Coch
*3½ miles/5.6km        3–4 hours*

Apart from the superb Cwm Dyli, the northern wall of the Snowdon massif has a much more neglected but still magnificent cwm, that of Cwm Glas Mawr. Above a lip lies the little Llyn Glas and then it forms into two upper cwms. The right-hand one, Cwm Glas, is the direct continuation of Cwm Glas Mawr and has its own delightful little Llyn Bach directly below the cliffs of Crib y Ddysgl. The left-hand one is Cwm Uchaf, which has several little unnamed llyns and is walled in by the steep slopes of Crib Goch's North Ridge and the crags below

Crib Goch's ridge and pinnacles. Apart from a few rock-climbers on the crags it is usual to find yourself alone in this magnificent cirque. Perhaps it is because it is north-facing and sees less sun (and therefore, of course, holds snow longer); or perhaps because the initial impression from below is of a wilderness of tumbled rockfalls overhung by black crags; or perhaps because it has such an apparently steep climb into it. But for those who love the splash of running water, the croak of the raven and the pleasure of sitting on those great ice-smoothed slabs near Llyn Glas, or those who have waited in thick swirling mist in Cwm Glas itself for the sun to burn it off and leave the great prow of the Clogwyn y Person Arête bathed in sunlight, the rough ascent is well worth the little extra effort.

A simple walking route into the cwm starts from the Llanberis Pass; there are numerous laybys all down the Llanberis Pass. Find a free one, then make for and cross the bridge at grid ref 623570, about a hundred yards/91m below the Climbers' Club hut of Ynys Ettws. Don't turn into the camp-site field on the left but go ahead over a stile, followed by

Crib Goch from Glyder Fawr; E Ridge on left, N Ridge on right.

another bridge and then the path will be seen heading fairly steeply up grass and through boulders up the right bank of the stream. It leads up into Cwm Glas Mawr, going over an ill-defined lip into a more level basin below the cliffs of Gyrn Las, then continues just left of those cliffs in a zigzag track up rough scree, still beside the stream, to reach Cwm Glas. At the top of the first rise beyond Gyrn Las, a few widely scattered cairns indicate the best line to take, swinging south-west beside Llyn Glas and making for the col on the skyline at the right-hand (west) end of the almost level skyline of Crib Goch. A short scrabble up scree lands you on Bwlch Coch, recognisable even in mist by a short length of wire fence on the col itself.

Now turn left (east) and reverse the normal route over Crib Goch's pinnacles (see **9.10**) and the almost level section of ridge which follows, to the point where the East Ridge starts its abrupt descent. (This is the point usually considered to be the summit of Crib Goch; it is certainly the point where waverers coming in the opposite direction contemplate the knife-edge traverse that you have just crossed.) The North Ridge descends from here, appropriately enough to the north. A few steps down in that direction will disclose a narrow path snaking along the crest of the North Ridge which, with one short scrambling section, leads onto easier ground from where a descent path down scree leads easily and obviously back into upper Cwm Glas. Here you rejoin the ascent route.

Few people ever seem to use this as an ascent route (except in winter), but it enables you to avoid Crib Goch until later in the day when it is usually quiet, avoids the busy Pig Track/North Ridge route, and gives an opportunity to savour this splendid amphitheatre. Its merits as an escape route from the Crib Goch ridge should not be under-estimated either; that short scree descent into the cwm from Bwlch Coch enables you to traverse back right below the rocks of Crib Goch and very rapidly reach easy ground.

## 9.12 Crib Goch via The North Ridge
*4 miles/6.4km        3–4 hours*

The North Ridge of Crib Goch is less popular than the East Ridge and this is probably fair because it isn't quite of such high quality and it is not so accessible. For a change from the 'normal' route or as a descent with a difference, it is nevertheless an excellent way. There is less actual scrambling on the North Ridge than on the East, but the ridge is more sharply defined at its top.

I did try to find a scrambling route much lower down in the cwm, on what looks like an easy-angled rocky rib to the right of the nasty wet gullies which are themselves to the right of the cliff of Dinas Mot (i.e. as you look up the cwm from below, near Ynys Ettws). I failed: the little problems I encountered were too hard to classify as scrambling and I finished up simply going into the cwm and then trending far left to get above Dinas Mot and then working up easy ground to the North Ridge. Some other enthusiast may well succeed. The other alternative, Jammed Boulder Gully, as it is known to rock-climbers, is far too precarious, wet and generally nasty to be acceptable as a scramble in my opinion.

The two most commonly recognised ways up to Crib Goch's North Ridge are as follows. First, as in **9.11** above, starting from the laybys low down in the Llanberis Pass, crossing the bridge at grid ref 623570 just north (i.e. lower down the Pass) of Ynys Ettws, head for Llyn Glas but then trend left (east) to a path at the bottom of a red scree slope at the end of the North Ridge. About 200ft/61m kicking up the scree leads to the ridge itself. Secondly, from further up the Llanberis Pass, although parking places are few and far between there, it is better to outflank the prominent rock nose of Dinas Mot which terminates the North Ridge of Crib Goch very abruptly, on its east side. To do this, leave the road almost anywhere in the region of the little crags of Dinas Bach and walk up into Cwm Beudy Mawr. A path, not worn but cairned, can be picked up which leads to a shoulder above Dinas Mot. From here, the extension of the North Ridge is very easy and this path goes out right then back left above Dinas Mot to a big cairn at about 2100ft/640m. Ahead rock-studded grassy slopes lead up the broad ridge until, nearly 500ft/152m higher, it suddenly sharpens into a crest of tiny rock splinters. For the next 300ft/91m or so, it is just a simple path but then it becomes a solid rock crest. A tiny notch, with a little steeper bit just past it, is soon reached and gives the best scrambling but then it is easier again on a good crest (or even easier if that is dodged for a path just below on the left). A final easy scramble over the left end of a noticeable band of white quartz (a useful marker in mist) leads in 30ft/9m to what is generally accepted as the top of Crib Goch, although the true top is at 3028ft/923m just across the sharp-edged arête towards the pinnacles. You could then descend the East Ridge to Bwlch y Moch and return to Pen-y-pass for a final walk down the road, which is the way assumed in the specs above.

Crib Goch and its pinnacles from the ridge of Crib y Ddysgl.

### 9.13 Garnedd Ugain via Cwm Glas
*5 miles/8km        5–6 hours*

Start from laybys in the Llanberis Pass, cross the bridge at grid ref 623570 just below Ynys Ettws and then follow the path up into Cwm Glas Mawr. It leads to a point below the great cliffs of Cyrn Las (spelled Gyrn Las on the OS map) and then forks. Take the right fork winding up very rough and rocky ground close to the stream issuing from Llyn Bach above. This is a delightful little llyn and a place to linger for a while, with splendid views across to the pinnacles on Crib Goch and, much nearer, to the fine rock nose and ridge of Clogwyn y Person.

The rest of the ascent, in summer, is a matter of simply walking up rather dull and somewhat loose slopes going due west from the llyn. A fairly short climb leads to the broad shoulder of Garnedd Ugain's north ridge. Turn up it to reach the summit trig point, at the west end of the Crib y Ddysgl Ridge. Under winter snow the last pull out of Cwm Glas can be quite exciting but should *only* be attempted by walkers equipped with the right gear, including ice-axe and crampons. In any clear conditions, the splendid views of the Clogwyn y Person Arête, backed by Crib Goch, is well worth seeing.

Looking west down the Llanberis Pass from the lip of Cwm Glas.

From here the natural continuation is to traverse the Pinnacle Ridge of Crib y Ddysgl (see **9.10**) remembering that the best way down from the actual pinnacles is at their very end, on the right side (south). After that, you will know you have reached Bwlch Coch when you spot the short length of wire fencing before the rise up towards the Crib Goch pinnacles. You can either descend down scree slopes from here, the col, into Cwm Uchaf or, more interestingly, continue over the pinnacles of Crib Goch, followed by the traverse of the level section to the point where the obvious descent begins down the East Ridge. Here turn north (left hand down a bit) and after a few steep steps on a well-marked way you will join the sharp crest of the North Ridge of Crib Goch. There is only one little section of scrambling on this ridge and you are soon at the point where you can see the descent path off to the left (west) down a red scree slope into the upper reaches of Cwm Glas. Descend rough ground over superb rock slabs now to pick up the path back to the road.

### 9.14 Garnedd Ugain by scramble on Clogwyn y Person Arête

SUMMARY: 800 ft/244m of Grade 2/3 scrambling, north-east-facing and often in morning sunshine; 5 miles/8km, 5–6 hours. A superb route, high on the mountain and on perfect rock. It avoids the nose at the end of the obvious arête or spur by good holds on the right-hand wall of the gully to the right of the nose. About 50ft/15m above the notch, go right and then up a short chimney (crux). Easier but always interesting scrambling follows to reach the main summit ridge just west of the Crib y Ddysgl pinnacles.

Cwm Glas: the Clogwyn y Person Arête, with Crib Goch.

This is the last and finest of the ways out of Cwm Glas Mawr to reach the summit ridge. It is an almost alpine scramble, and of absorbing interest. From the start of the route to the summit ridge it is about 800ft/244m, of which about 450ft/137m is on perfect rock and virtually continuous. In winter conditions, of course, it becomes a mountaineering route requiring all the appropriate equipment. As a summer scramble, it is a delight.

The arête or ridge of Clogwyn y Person is the one which divides the upper cwm above Cwm Glas Mawr into the two separate ones of Cwm Glas and Cwm Uchaf and it is quite unmistakable when seen from below, or even better from near Llyn Bach. From this latter point, it can be seen that the solid rock end of the ridge is almost separated from the rest of the ridge by a gully on each side of the nose. This rocky end is known, appropriately enough, as The Parson's Nose and there is a rock climb straight up it. The scrambling way avoids this by using the gully to the right of the nose (the west gully) as seen from Llyn Bach. The altitude at start is about 2500ft/762m.

Reach Llyn Bach in Cwm Glas from the laybys in the Llanberis Pass, crossing the bridge at grid ref 623570, following the footpath up into Cwm Glas Mawr and then alongside the stream, to the left side of the huge cliff of Cyrn Las, to where it issues from Llyn Bach. From here, the gully which almost separates the nose from the rest of the ridge will be very obvious.

Make your way over to the gully from Llyn Bach and it will soon be found that there is a virtual staircase of excellent square-cut holds leading steeply but easily up the right wall of the gully for about 80ft/24m to reach the big stone jammed in the notch. A couple of moves above this are slightly harder but then 50ft/15m of easier ground follows to a little corner. It looks a bit steeper and more strenuous here and you will need to consider the situation. Going right leads into a little chimney; going left looks easier, enabling you to climb up a large flake to a ledge, but then you find yourself at the top of the little chimney anyway so you might just as well have stuck to the chimney in the first place. If this makes you puff a bit, take consolation from the fact that everything is easier from now on.

The angle eases and gentler scrambling follows on superb rough rock. There are odd little problems on the way but all are either avoidable or just add to the scramble's interest as you solve them. The last 300ft/91m or so is just an easy walk for, although the ridge is buttressed by sentinels of rock on the right, where they drop sheer to Cwm Glas, on the left there is a definite path; this merges with the summit ridge at the big cairn just west of the main pinnacle (see **9.10**). A descending traverse of the Pinnacle Ridge of Crib y Ddysgl (see **9.10**) going east, then a traverse of Crib Goch followed by a descent of its North Ridge (see **9.12**) will bring you down from the heights. Turn off to the left (west) down a path of red scree at the end of the sharp section of the North Ridge (about grid ref 625556) and then across superb slabs towards Llyn Glas. From here it is a straightforward descent down Cwm Glas Mawr to the road again.

The eastern traverse of Crib Goch has another advantage: the procession of walkers on the Snowdon Horseshoe all tend to leave Pen-y-pass in the morning and to have crossed Crib Goch before you are thinking of going the opposite way. And if you are able to experience, as I have done, the delight of traversing alone, with not another walker in sight, from Garnedd Ugain over to Crib Goch on a summer evening, as the shadows lengthen and deepen in Cwm Dyli and the hills lie silent and listening, you will know how lucky you are.

### 9.15 Scramble on Llechog Buttress to Clogwyn Station

SUMMARY: 600ft/183m of Grade 2/3 scrambling, east-facing; 3½ miles/5.6m, 4 hours. A vegetated gully cutting through two bands of broken rocks leads to a heather terrace and the main buttress. Grooves lead to a vertical wall which is avoided by going right directly below it to reach easier-angled rock ribs which lead to the top of the buttress.

Just a little lower down the Llanberis Pass than the magnificent Cwm Glas Mawr is Cwm Glas Bach. Seen from the valley, trains on the Snowdon Railway can occasionally be seen chugging along the skyline just to the left of the top of an easy-angled rock buttress crowning a long broken ridge which extends into the cwm. This buttress, Llechog, is east-facing, receives morning sunlight and gives a good scramble of about 600ft/183m on excellent rock on the main buttress, to finish almost at Clogwyn Station. The detailed description of the route will make it sound more complex than it is, so don't let that put you off.

Start as if going up into Cwm Glas (*see* **9.11**) by crossing the bridge at grid ref 623570 just below Ynys Ettws, but instead of crossing the stile to go up into Cwm Glas, turn right along a track which leads past the other Climbers' Club hut (named 'Cwm Glas'). The track soon runs out but seen directly ahead across the cwm is the Llechog Buttress. Below its upper part is a band of vegetated and broken rocks, with two easy ramps slanting across it. A gully running up the middle of the band leads straight to the toe of the lowest rocks of the upper buttress and gives an obvious approach to them.

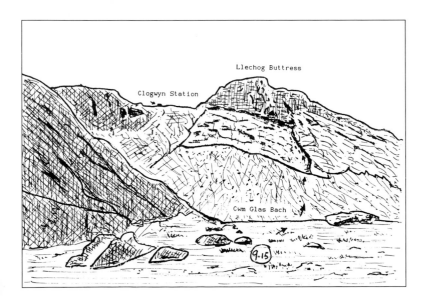

A rather scruffy start to the route, gaining about 200ft/61m, leads up this gully (which is here more like a rubble-filled trench), dodges a jammed flake on the left to regain a more grassy trench ahead, dodges another jammed boulder on the left and then leads up the remainder of the gully, now choked with boulders. Easy ground follows, then an easy-angled rock rib leads to a broad rock-strewn heather terrace to reach, at last, the main buttress. A large perched block overhangs a vegetated groove and marks the start of the route proper.

Go easily up the groove for about 25ft/7.6m to a ledge beside the block and then for a similar distance up another groove just beyond and to the left, which has an obvious capstone. Continue, veering right, for another 20ft/6m up a grassy groove and then back left towards a second obvious perched block with a distinctively jagged left-hand edge. Just behind this jagged-edged block, a corner-groove with an awkward start (avoidable on its right) leads past a quartz-faced block (on the right) to a small chockstone and a large spiky boulder jammed amongst others below an almost vertical rock wall. This wall is obviously a major obstacle and needs to be by-passed, which is done by going to the right, as follows: scramble up to the jammed spike and then go right on big holds onto a large sloping platform a little higher up but still below the steep wall. Now cross a boulder-filled depression just a little further right, towards another grassy gully, but just before reaching it go up a little rock rib leading into another narrower grassy groove. Gain about 70ft/21m up this groove on good holds and then traverse left onto the main line of the ridge again, having by-passed the vertical wall below. Easier rock now leads to a large platform with a big rock spike next to a large boulder. From here you can either go round to the right and up a 15ft/4.5m crack on good holds, or go left behind the spike and take a slanting rock groove which leads more directly again to the main crest of the ridge. The continuation is easy but delightful scrambling up little spikes,

grooves and walls, coming out onto the main ridge just a short distance from Clogwyn Station.

Several alternatives are now available. You could join the Llanberis Path to Snowdon (Yr Wyddfa); you could follow that path but then bear off along the Crib y Ddysgl ridge; you could go just a short way towards Clogwyn Station and then descend steep scree into the head of Cwm Glas Bach; or perhaps most

Llechog Buttress on Snowdon's Llanberis Ridge. The train has just left Clogwyn Station for Llanberis.

interestingly, you could descend a little and then traverse across to the long ridge bounding Cwm Glas. Here you will enjoy superb views into Cwm Glas and also find a path going easily down the crest and leading back to the road and the start.

## 9.16 The Snowdon Horseshoe
*7¹/₂ miles/12km        5–7 hours*

This is the most popular ridge traverse in Snowdonia and understandably so. It is best done anti-clockwise, so that you have the scrambling sections in ascent and the scruffy section, from the top of the Watkin Path from Yr Wyddfa to Bwlch y Saethau, in descent. Normally a magnificent scramble-walk, under winter conditions of snow and ice it becomes an alpine-style expedition. It then requires full winter equipment and, at least as importantly, the ability to use it. I still see walkers with ice-axes without wrist-loops in their hands; if they slip they will lose their axe in seconds.

The normal start is from Pen-y-pass (grid ref 647556) and, because of the popularity of the route, it is well to be there early. Most walkers then go by way of the Pig Track to Bwlch y Moch at the foot of the east ridge of Crib Goch, but I would suggest that it avoids what is sometimes a mad rush if you turn off the path almost as soon as you leave the car park and scramble up boulders and grass onto the true end of the ridge. Here you may spot the curious rock known, most appropriately, as the First Nail, but you will also enjoy early views into Cwm Dyli. Now a short traverse over half a dozen rocky pimples leads to Bwlch y Moch and the scramble up the east ridge of Crib Goch (*see* **9.10**), over the two lots of pinnacles (those of Crib Goch and Crib y Ddysgl) to reach the trig point on top of Garnedd Ugain.

The short descent to Bwlch Glas, where the Pig Track emerges at the big marker-stone, follows, then the short ascent to the summit of Snowdon (Yr Wyddfa). Descend about 200ft/61m down the south ridge to the bottle-shaped marker stone and then traverse the loose slopes to the east, losing about 700ft/213m of height, to stony Bwlch y Saethau. If conditions deteriorate, *competent* scramblers (but only those who must also be sure of their position) could descend from here by reversing the ascent of Cribau (the Gribin) (*see* **9.2**). Otherwise it would be as well to reverse **9.1** or **9.3** (i.e. the Pig Track /Miner's Track routes) and to make that decision before starting down the south ridge from the summit.

In normal conditions, the continuation from Bwlch y Saethau, undulating over rocky ground to the large cairn at Bwlch Ciliau is perfectly obvious and on a well-worn path. The scramble-walk ascent up the north-west ridge and on the edge of the superb cliffs of Lliwedd now follows and is almost the last ascent of the day. There are two summits on Lliwedd, West Peak being only a bit lower than East Peak just beyond it; then a stony descent leads over the little lump of Lliwedd Bach. Just beyond, a well-worn, fairly loose and unpleasant path descends down ruts through rubble, rock and earth to the north-east and towards the east end of Llyn Llydaw and the Miner's Track. This is the normal descent and it is the fastest.

Walkers with a little energy still in hand will, however, appreciate a gentler and full completion of the Horseshoe by walking out on a grassy, undulating path to the little cairn on the true end of the ridge, Gallt y Wenallt, the Last Nail. From here the descent is down grassy slopes to Cwm Dyli, trying to avoid losing more height than necessary, for an ultimate surge of energy is needed for a final, but short climb back to the last section of the Miner's Track just east of Llyn Teyrn. The car park will be just round the corner.

# 10: Three Classics and Two Outliers

BEST MAPS:  OS 1:50,000 Landranger 115 Snowdon & surrounding area
OS 1:25,000 Outdoor Leisure 17 Snowdonia: Snowdon area, plus 16 Snowdonia: Conwy Valley area
• for Moel Famau: OS 1:50,000 Landranger 116 Denbigh and Colwyn Bay
• for the Limestone Edges of Llangollen: OS 1:50,000 Landranger 117 Chester, Wrexham and surrounding area

| Approx Distance | Approx Time | Highest Elevation Reached | Height Gained | Star Rating | Scramble Difficulty Grade | Scramble Height Gain |
|---|---|---|---|---|---|---|
| **10.1 The Cwm Bochlwyd Horseshoe** | | | | | | |
| 3³/₄ miles/6km | 4–6 hours | 3261ft/994m | 2972ft/906m | *** | 1 | 950ft/290m |
| **10.2 The Idwal Skyline** | | | | | | |
| 6¹/₂ miles/10.5km | 5–7 hours | 3277ft/999m | 4012ft/1223m | *** | 1 | 950ft/290m |
| **10.3 The Welsh Three-Thousanders** | | | | | | |
| 31¹/₂ miles/50.7km | 14–15 hours | 3560ft/1085m | 11800ft/3597m | *** | — | — |
| **10.4 A Round over Moel Famau in the Clwydian Hills** | | | | | | |
| 6 miles/9.6km | 3–4 hours | 1818ft/554m | 1227ft/374m | * | — | — |
| **10.5 The Limestone Edges of Llangollen (The full round)** | | | | | | |
| 11 miles/17.6km | 5–6 hours | 1608ft/490m | 1247ft/380m | **/*** | — | — |
| **(The shorter version, requiring a transport pick-up)** | | | | | | |
| 7 miles/11.2km | 3–4 hours | 1608ft/490m | 787ft/240m | *** | — | — |

This chapter collects together three great walks (two on the Glyders, plus the traverse of all the summits over 3000ft) together with two walks which, although they are outside the area covered by the rest of this book, are well worth a visit.

## 10.1 The Cwm Bochlwyd Horseshoe
*3¾ miles/6km       4–6 hours*

This excellent round of the skyline of Cwm Bochlwyd was not included in Chapter 6 (Tryfan) because it continues onto the ground covered separately in Chapter 7 (Glyders). It is, however, too important to be overlooked as it gives a fine day's scrambling and walking, taking in two of the area's best low-difficulty scrambles and the descent of a third. I have marked the route (**10.1**) on both the map for Chapter 6 and Chapter 7.

Start from the car park at the foot of the Milestone Buttress of Tryfan (grid ref 663603), or anywhere in parking places further west along the edge of the A5. Now take the path slanting below the Milestone Buttress and rising up a broad gully to the shoulder on the North Ridge of Tryfan. The scramble up the North Ridge now follows (*see* **6.2**) which gives about 500ft/152m of Grade 1 scrambling if you take the easiest line, which turns steeper sections on the left, except at the top where you trend rightwards below the North Peak. A short walk across the depression beyond leads to the well-known twin summit rocks of Adam and Eve. If you take the most direct line up the upper part of the North Ridge, there are short sections of Grade 2 scrambling. The route in all its variations is well-marked, but avoid traversing into the amphitheatre on the East Face in poor visibility, not because there are any particular difficulties but because it is much more confusing.

From the summit of Tryfan (Main Peak), continue the short distance to the South Peak and then down the rocky south ridge to Bwlch Tryfan. The way is well-marked and obvious enough, down rocky ledges and grooves, but avoid any temptation to stray too far right onto jumbled sharp-edged rocks on the descent.

From the bwlch, the Bristly Ridge of Glyder Fach rising directly ahead, with a wide scree slope on its left side, looks more like a broad buttress than a ridge, but a walk up alongside the wall that rises towards it will disclose, up on the left side of the main mass of the rocks, a well-scratched gully which quickly leads to a shoulder. From here the route continues up the crest, well-marked and obvious, with an entertaining section winding round several pinnacles. The ridge ends on easy ground, with the scree slope mentioned earlier leading back down to the foot of the ridge. A short walk over rocky ground soon leads to Glyder Fach (*see* **7.2** for more details for Bristly Ridge etc). Continue over Glyder Fach's summit, keeping right (north) of the summit rocks, shortly afterwards passing by the spiky rock formation of the Castell y Gwynt on their left (south) side.

Beyond here, the path leads to the col at the head of Cwm Bochlwyd, the Bwlch y Ddwy-Glyder, where a main path climbs easy slopes to the WSW towards Glyder Fawr's summit. A secondary path curves away from this to the north-west, initially rising but only for a short distance as it then curves downhill gently to the north, reaching a circular stone windbreak (a useful marker if the visibility has worsened) at the end of the ridge called Y Gribin (the Gribin Ridge).

The descent of the Gribin Ridge (*see* **7.6** for the ascent of this) is very straightforward and the easiest route is little more than a walk: if you want to enjoy the scramble you will need to keep to the rocks on the crest itself. At the end of the rocky section the path continues downhill, just off the crest, and then down a grassy groove to a broad shoulder. If you have parked along the edge of the A5 or near Ogwen Cottage at the west end of Llyn Ogwen rather than at the foot of the Milestone Buttress, you may turn left and descend an easy grassy gully to reach

Tryfan's south ridge seen from the upper slopes of Glyder Fach.

Cwm Idwal and then take a good path back to the A5 and Ogwen Cottage.

If you have parked, as I suggested, at the foot of Milestone Buttress, there is a short cut which avoids the descent to Ogwen Cottage. For this, from the shoulder on the Gribin Ridge turn right instead of left and descend easy slopes on an obvious path to the outflow from Llyn Bochlwyd. Now make a very slightly rising traverse over somewhat boggy ground towards Tryfan's West Face. You will soon pass over a slight col and will intersect with the fast descent route from Tryfan which passes below the rocky ground of the West Face and soon leads you back to the road and parking place.

## 10.2 The Idwal Skyline
*6½ miles/10.5km        5–7 hours*

Another superb round, and a bit longer and harder (nearly 3 miles/4.8km and an extra 1000ft/305m of ascent) than the round of Cwm Bochlwyd described above, is the round of Cwm Idwal. I have marked the route with the number 10.2 on the sketch map for Chapter 7 (Glyders and Gallt yr Ogof).

The start is from the car park areas at the bottom of the Milestone Buttress of Tryfan (grid ref 663603) or from Ogwen Cottage (grid ref 651603), which has the advantage of toilets and a handy snacks kiosk. However, if you use the latter, you will then need to walk eastwards along the side of the A5 to the path below the foot of the Milestone Buttress. From here, take the path up the broad gully to the shoulder on Tryfan and then complete the scramble up the North Ridge to the twin rocks of Adam and Eve on the summit. Descend the South Ridge to Bwlch Tryfan, continue with the scramble up the Bristly Ridge of Glyder Fach to its summit and then the gentle descent to Bwlch y Ddwy-Glyder, passing the spiky rocks of the Castell y Gwynt. (All this is a repeat of the first part of **10.1** above.)

From the bwlch, do not turn off to the north as if heading for the Gribin Ridge (Y Gribin) to descend and return to the start, but continue up the broad path beyond to reach the several rock castles on the summit of Glyder Fawr. If you are lucky with the light, you will have a superb view from here across the trench of the Llanberis Pass to the great Snowdon massif.

Descend the shaly slopes beyond Glyder Fawr and then down the slanting shaly groove that leads to Llyn y Cwn (this is all in **7.2**) where you are on the rocky shelf above the damp black cliffs of Twll Du, the Devil's Kitchen. In case of need, an escape can be made here by descending the path to the right (south) of the stream that flows from Llyn y Cwn and down the gash of the Kitchen (also in **7.2**) to reach the base of the cliffs and then reach the much-used path down to Llyn Idwal and so to your parking place.

Assuming no escape is necessary, the final ascent of the walk is that from Llyn y Cwn up the grassy slopes to the top of Y Garn, with its splendid views across the Nant Ffrancon towards the highest tops of the Carneddau. From here the start of the way down the north-east ridge, the one to the north of the two llyns in Cwm Clyd far below, is a little distance to the north and about 60ft/18m lower in altitude below the summit cairn. Here you will find a second collapsed cairn marking the start of the descent path, turning north-east down the ridge. It's obvious enough in good visibility, but in mist it is very easy to miss the start of this path.

This leads easily downhill, curving round almost as if to visit the two llyns of Llyn Clyd en route, but turning away again as it approaches them to descend bouldery ground to the foot of the ridge. From here, paths lead either to the north end of Llyn Ogwen or more directly to Ogwen Cottage. If you parked at the Milestone Buttress car park, this is a golden chance for some tea and a butty before the last walk along the road. If you parked at Ogwen, you will be glad of some anyway.

## 10.3 The Welsh Three-Thousanders
*31½ miles/50.7km        14–15 hours*

This book is essentially based on the assumption that walkers almost always want to return to their starting-point at the end of the day and consequently traverses have been avoided. The Welsh Three-Thousanders is the one great one that I dare not omit. I have completed it three times myself (in boots and with a rucksack) and failed once (in trainers and lightweight clothes, although the weather was the problem then, not the equipment). I hope I shall do it again.

I have indicated the clockwise route of the walk, **10.3**, on the relevant maps for Chapter 9 (Snowdon), 8 (West Wall of Nant Ffrancon), 7 (Glyders), 6 (Tryfan), and on the two maps for the Carneddau, south and north, in Chapter 5. For anybody who is not sure which are the peaks involved the lists is as follows, going clockwise, which is the way in which personally I have always done the walk: Crib Goch, Garnedd Ugain, Yr Wyddfa (Snowdon summit), Elidir Fawr, Y Garn, Glyder Fawr, Glyder Fach, Tryfan, Pen yr Ole Wen, Carnedd Dafydd, Carnedd Llewelyn, Yr Elen (the outlier, which really should be included even though it is a diversion from the main ridge), Foel Grach, Garnedd Uchaf (although this one, being just a bump on the ridge rather than a real top, is often not counted) and Foel-fras. It will only need a few minutes with the map to realize that a lot of distance and height gain are involved and so, unless you are very fast and fit, it is a walk that can really only be done during the months of high summer when the days are long.

For some reason the 'traditional' distance for this walk is calculated from the first summit (normally Snowdon/Yr Wyddfa) to

Crib Y Ddysgl Ridge seen from the summit of Snowdon.

the last (Foel-fras) for which a distance of about 24 miles/39km is given, with an average time in good conditions for that distance of between 11 hours and 13 hours. But you have to ascend Snowdon and descend from Foel-fras as well as complete the 'official' traverse and for the complete journey as described below the total distance (in map miles) is about 31$^1$/$_2$ miles/50.7km. The overall altitude gain for the complete journey is about 11,800ft/3597m. I have also read elsewhere that it is 'traditional' to start this ascent of all the fourteen Welsh peaks over 3000ft in height (that is 914m for anybody who doesn't know what a good English foot is!) from the summit of Snowdon at dawn. That simple statement avoids answers to important questions such as how you got up there in the first place, whether you spent the night on the summit, and so on. If you do bivouac on the top, you will have unnecessary weight to carry the next day, unless you arrange to drop it off somewhere in the Llanberis Pass, to be collected later. If you start at dawn without bivouacking you will have to walk up in the dark, which is perfectly feasible from Llanberis up the railway, but very boring.

We, that is I and my friends, have always started from Pen-y-pass (grid ref 647556) at 6 a.m., climbing Snowdon by the East Ridge of Crib Goch and the Crib y Ddysgl Ridge while fit and fresh to enjoy the ascent. (Alternatively, you could reach Snowdon by the Pig Track and then return to the Pass of Llanberis by going out to Crib Goch and then descending the North Ridge into Cwm Glas and so to the road.) From Snowdon we have descended rather unstable slopes into Cwm Glas Bach, although my most recent experience suggests that it is better to continue towards north-west Llanberis, down the long ridge shadowing the railway, as far as Derlwyn (grid ref 588587) and then down much shorter slopes north-east to the road just west of Nant Peris. You have gained about a quarter of the distance and altitude when you reach Nant Peris and will be ready for a second breakfast.

The next section, the long grind to Elidir Fawr, is a real energy-sapper and what follows is no easier, for from Nant Peris to the foot of Tryfan (about 9 miles/14.4km) is only 1 mile/1.6km further than that needed to traverse Snowdon, but the altitude gain is almost twice as much at about 5330ft/1625m.

In Nant Peris, turn up the metalled lane alongside the chapel (grid ref 605585) and follow it until a footpath sign points uphill to a ladder-stile, beyond which the Afon Dudodyn can be seen emerging from the cwm above. Above the stile a good path climbs to the lip of the cwm and then crosses the Afon Dudodyn by a footbridge (grid ref 608596). From here a faint path (appearing and disappearing and crossing a ladder-stile about half way up the hill) climbs virtually due north up the grassy slopes and eventually reaches the shattered rock crest just west of the actual summit of Elidir Fawr.

Having ticked-off Elidir Fawr, you can enjoy the undulating grassy walking on the path that skirts below the summit of Foel-goch (it doesn't reach 3000ft/914m and so can be by-passed today), then goes over Y Garn and descends to Llyn y Cwn. The way from here to the top of Glyder Fawr is just donkey-work, hard going up those slithery, stony, earthy slopes. It does not get any easier underfoot on the traverse to Glyder Fach, the rapid descent down the scree slope by the side of Bristly Ridge or on the subsequent ascent to Tryfan by the South Ridge, but the prospect of a longer halt in the Ogwen valley before tackling the Carneddau will be spurring you on now. The descent from Tryfan can be very rapid and straightforward if you go beyond Adam and Eve towards North Peak, trend left to a rocky bay and then down the shaly gully leading from it to reach the path flying down to the north below the West Face. All other ways cross much rocky ground and are consequently much slower. Having

The ridge above Ysgolion Duon (the Black Ladders).

reached the foot of Tryfan you will have done a little over 17 miles/27km and almost 8200ft/2499m, that is just over half of the miles but 70% of the total altitude gain. You are likely to be feeling in need of rest and food.

On all our three successful traverses, my friends and I have stopped in the Ogwen valley in order to stoke up with food and drink and have then tackled Pen yr Ole Wen from Glan Dena by its east ridge above Cwm Lloer. This is easier-angled than the brutal south ridge and you don't run so much risk of cramp in your legs. On the first two occasions, however, I reached the cairn on Pen yr Ole Wen and collapsed, feeling violently sick. It took nearly half an hour to recover but it was only after the second occasion that I realised that the sickness was the result of over-eating at Glan Dena, piling the rice-pudding on top of the honey butties and fruit cake and sweet tea! The lesson, more easily said than done, is to eat little and often.

Once you are on top of Pen yr Ole Wen, assuming the weather is still in your favour, you know that, although there is a lot of distance still to put beneath your feet (just over 13 miles/21km), the amount of uphill walking that remains is limited to about 1400ft/427m and it is all at an easy angle. From Carnedd Dafydd round the rim of Cwm Llafar and up to Carnedd Llewelyn is glorious scenically but straightforward and, although it may seem an interruption to the flow of the walk to go out on the narrow ridge to Yr Elen and then to have to return, it is a fine summit and worth visiting. In mist you will curse it as a time-wasting deviation.

The easy descent and gentle climb to Foel Grach follows; the refuge shelter is a good place to hide from wind or weather for a little more sustenance before heading for the rocky little bump of Garnedd Uchaf. Although it qualifies on altitude, its relative insignificance as a summit means that it is not normally counted; if you do include it then your summit total rises to fifteen, instead of the normal fourteen.

Foel-fras is the last of the 'Threes', a much bigger swelling hump of grass and stones just a mile/1.6km away and with a solid stone wall, the only one in sight, visible on its summit. It also has an OS trig point, the site of many congratulatory handshakes over the years since Esme Firbank walked out of the mist on the first successful traverse back in the 1930s.

On the long descent to the north-east, the wall soon gives way to a wire fence leading to the little stone wind-break on top of Drum, then a jeep track helpfully heads towards Aber (which is the usual pick-up point at the end of the traverse) but only for a short way. After those miles of easy walking on the high ridges of the Carneddau, with the 'official' traverse completed, this final section can be something of a trial unless it is planned. My experience has been that it is best to stay on the jeep-track until it turns north just before reaching Foel-ganol (at grid ref 695713) and then descend the slopes to the west to reach the rough track running down the valley from Llyn Anafon. (Alternatively, stay on the Foel-ganol ridge above.) The track leads to the metalled road a mile/1.6km from Bont Newydd and I hope your transport is waiting for you there when you arrive.

Over the years, our times for the complete journey as described, from Pen-y-pass to Aber, have ranged from 13 hours to 14 hours; more importantly, we never came off the hill in the dark and we always enjoyed the day. Later.

### 10.4 A Round over Moel Famau in the Clwydian Hills
*6 miles/9.6km        3–4 hours*

North of the delightful limestone edges above Llangollen (*see* **10.5**), the course of the Offa's Dyke path leads along the rolling Clwydian Hills, the highest point of which is Moel Famau, at 1818ft/554m. There is little drama about these hills; they are made up of Silurian slates and shales which rarely outcrop into

anything resembling a crag, while above the farmland the slopes are covered in bracken until heather takes over at the top. Nevertheless, they allow panoramic views up to thirty-five miles away, to the major hills of Snowdonia and as far as the River Dee and the Wirral. This walk is a horseshoe round, mostly within the area of the Moel Famau Country Park, climbing up to Moel Famau itself and traversing a short distance along the sum-

Climbing heather slopes from Cilcain towards Moel Famau.

mit ridge before returning to the valley. It is easy going underfoot, on good paths and tracks and well worth a few hours to visit, especially for Mersey-bound visitors driven off the higher hills by poor weather.

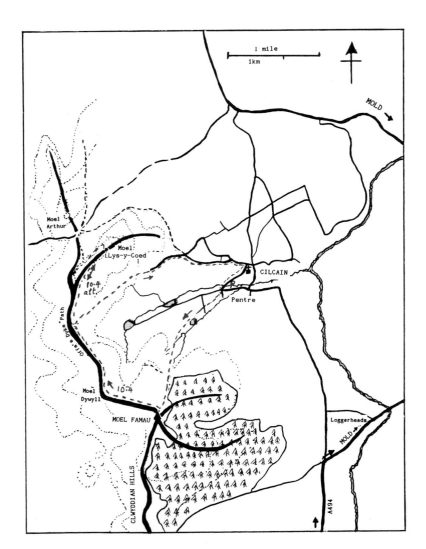

The start is from Pentre, on the edge of the village of Cilcain, a few miles south of Hendre, and it is signed off the A494 between Ruthin and Mold, near the Loggerheads Country Park. Pentre is just south-west of Cilcain and there is plenty of parking space at a road junction (grid ref 172647). From the road junction, a bridleway leads up a hedged lane to the south-west, but a footpath is also signed to the SSW and this is the one to take. Walk no more than a few yards up the track to the south from the junction and then take the stile on the right. The path is not very clear on the ground just here but it leads up the left-hand side of a field to the SSW and in about 400yd/365m reaches another stile, crosses one lane and continues in the same direction up the lane beyond (signed with the arrows).

This soon becomes a delightful path beneath horse chestnut trees and leads into a wide basin with slopes of gorse and bracken, passing a little reservoir on the left. In a short while, the path starts to climb more steeply, then zigzags uphill through the bracken, which soon gives way to heather as height is rapidly gained. After about 1 mile/1.6km, having gained about 800ft/244m above the start, the path crosses a bridleway by the edge of a conifer plantation and the strange Jubilee Tower on the top of Moel Famau is clearly visible on the skyline ahead.

A last short pull puts you on the summit, where the view-indicators on the four-sided structure will enable you to distinguish a remarkable number of distant places; then head slightly downhill to the north-west along the Offa's Dyke Path. The path is perfectly obvious, with the initial gentle descent soon followed by a change of direction to the north and a sharper pull up to the big cairn on the top of Moel Dywyll. Just over the other side, you reach the end of a track rising from Cilcain (grid ref 145641) and it is as well to turn north-east now and follow it downhill.

If you do decide to go a little further before turning downhill for home, the Offa's Dyke path continues obviously enough, climbing the gentle slope beyond to the north and then contouring the slopes of Moel Llys-y-coed to give a good view of the hill-fort site of Moel Arthur. This is partly ringed by a wall, like a circlet round its highest slopes and is apparently one of the best preserved of the chain of hill-forts which were built along the Clwydian Hills. Once you've gone this far there is a tempting-looking path shown on the map curving round the northern slopes of Moel Llys-y-coed which seems to lead simply back to Cilcain, but you must lose height descending to the road and cattle-grid below Moel Arthur and then regain it once you have located the path. I can only say that I tried to cut a corner by avoiding the descent and became entangled in walls, fences and deep heather and failed abysmally. And that is why I suggest you either turn downhill before your problems start or just go for a view of Moel Arthur and then return to the track I have suggested. This leads pleasantly down the south-east flank of Moel Llys-y-coed and becomes metalled just before some cross-roads. Turn right (south-east) here and follow the lane down to Cilcain church; I'm afraid you'll seek in vain for that short-cut path shown so clearly on the map. At the church turn right (south-west) and a short ramble downhill brings you back directly to the parking-place.

## 10.5 The Limestone Edges of Llangollen
*11 miles/17.7km or 7 miles/11.2km*
*5–6 hours or 3–4 hours*

One of the most scenic sections of the Offa's Dyke path passes below a series of superb limestone escarpments above the famous little town of Llangollen. To walk along the escarpments themselves is even better than on the path below, a truly delightful expedition known locally as the 'Panorama Walk'. If you can organise transport so that you can be collected (or two cars, one starting at one end and the other at the other end and

swapping keys midway) you can enjoy the very best of this superb walk. If not, then a round is perfectly possible, though the last four miles of the return are a bit of an anticlimax after what has preceded them. The round is essentially a circuit of Ruabon Mountain starting near Mountain Lodge but if it is to be cut short, then transport should be arranged for a pick up near the sharp bend in the minor road below Trevor Rocks (grid ref 235432).

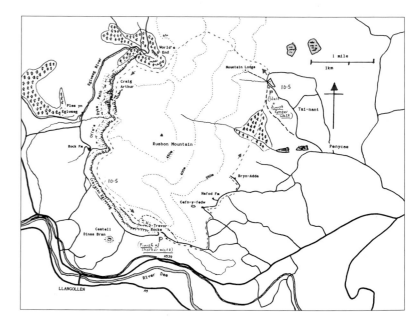

Ruabon Mountain is a domed plateau whose western edge consists of tiers of gleaming white limestone, the rest being managed grouse moor. A few cars can park at grid ref 263469, reached by driving from Ruabon up the road (signed) for Penycae, then to Tai-nant (also signed). Continue north-west up a narrow, single-track road to reach a little sheepfold (and the first chance to park anyway) on the left. Park here and walk up the road a little further, past a small reservoir on the right and a private tarmac strip leading up to 'Mountain Lodge' on the left. Just beyond, the road turns sharply right uphill and the path leaves the road here, heading north-west. A gate with stile leads to a grassy way up the right (north) bank of a little stream and wood, with a derelict ruin on the far side of the stream, then, continuing north-west, gently climbs onto the rolling, heather- and bracken-covered moor. Mountain Lodge, seen sheltering in a circle of beech trees is quickly passed and about half an hour's walking on this obvious path leads to the top of the moor.

Now the path leads downhill (with minor paths which all return to it anyway) to reach a major track which runs around the head of the afforested valley of World's End (grid ref 237477). (This doesn't accord with the path on the OS map which is shown as further north incidentally.) Follow the track around the very edge of the wooded valley until the trees suddenly end and there is a fine view of the valley with a three-tiered limestone buttress and a road seen running below.

The path leads to the very edge of an escarpment of little limestone cliffs and just beyond the first obvious cliff a grassy path slants down to join the Offa's Dyke path, which can now be seen winding along below the crags. Don't descend but stay on the high edge now, for the views along it and across the lovely valley of the Eglwyseg River below are outstanding. The situation becomes more impressive still (and care may be needed on the slippery limestone in windy or wet weather) as the way leads over the top of the highest of the crags, Craig Arthur, a 100ft/30m-high vertical wall. This is a modern rock-climbing ground, but it isn't really visible until you have continued beyond it and skirted round the head of the first little side-valley, when its vertical face and scalloped edge come clearly into view as you look backwards. Descending a little, the path continues round the head of a second side-valley, with Plas Yn Eglwyseg Farm directly below, while the escarpment from here looks like a series of ledges and there are more paths to choose from. All however curve round the head of the third side-valley, with some straggling pines seen across the far side. Another path climbs up to the edges from Rock Farm below this point (which looks as though it could provide a quick way home to the east down Ruabon Mountain if necessary but will miss out some of the best walking) but cross it and keep on beyond it, curving round south-east now, until Llangollen comes into view below. The paths are not so obvious now but it is easy walking and ahead is the unmistakable and dramatic ruin of Castell Dinas Bran, crowning its own separate hill overlooking the town. It must have been a near-impregnable fortress for the eighth-century Princes of Powys.

Stay on the edge, on the highest land, allowing fine views down the valley of the River Dee; keep above a gully well furnished with larch and pine trees, to reach and follow the level grassy way beyond. This runs between escarpment and trees and alongside a wire fence, continuing on a gentle slope beyond to reach a sharp bend in the unfenced road just below the old quarry (and climbing area) of Trevor Rocks. This is where your transport should be if you are ending the walk here.

To complete the round, walk up the quiet minor road to the south-east (on the Offa's Dyke path) to the top of the hill (grid ref 248428) where you turn north. Stay on the lane, passing Prospect Place, Cefn-y-fedw and Hafod Farm. At the next junction, turn left (north) to Bryn-Adda and, encouraged by the 'Public Footpath' sign, continue a further hundred paces to reach it. It's there all right, but not very visible on the ground which is wild and virtually untrodden heather moorland, and you'll have to climb a little fence even to get onto that.

Persevere! These paths have a curious habit of getting blocked unless we use them. A compass bearing NNE across the heather leads to the end of a walled lane. Continue beyond it down a slope into the forestry plantation to intersect with a good path which runs from the Wrexham Waterworks reservoirs. Turn left (north) here and it is a straightforward and pleasant return to the little sheepfold and the car.

*Left:* Castell Dinas Bran, above Llangollen, seen from Trevor Rocks.

*Opposite:* The limestone edge of Craig Arthur above Llangollen.

# Index

*Page numbers in italics refer to illustration captions.*

Aber Falls 93–4, 94
Aberglaslyn Pass 65
Adam and Eve 122, 126, 131, 212
Afon Aber 93
Afon Cadair 3
Afon Caseg 104
Afon Colwyn 74
Afon Cwm-llefrith 82
Afon Cwm-y-foel 63
Afon Disgynfa 28
Afon Dudodyn 174, 216
Afon Dwyfor 80, 82, 84
Afon Gam 94
Afon Glaslyn 56, 64
Afon Goch 87, 93
Afon Gyrach 100
Afon Las 161, 172, 174
Afon Llafar 98, 103, 104
Afon Llugwy 50
Afon Maesgwm 61
Afon Ogwen 109
Alphabet Slabs 142
Aran (range) 19, 20
Aran Benllyn *22*, 22, 24
Aran Fawddwy 20, 22, 24
Arenig Fach 31
Arenig Fawr 31–2, *32, 34*, 34

Atlantic Slab 172, *175*, 175

Bastow Gully 128
Beddgelert 65, 72, 74
Beddgelert Forest 73–4, 81
Bera Bach 94
Bera Mawr 94
The Berwyn 26
Bethania Bridge 56, 185
Bethesda *94*, 104
Bont Newydd 93
Braich Ddu 8
Braich y Ddeugwm 136, 146
Bristly Ridge 122, 138, *139*, 139, 140, 142, 159, 211, 213
Bryant's Gully 159–61, *161*
Bryn-Adda 221
Bwlch Carreg y Gigfran 195
Bwlch Ciliau 186, 209
Bwlch Coch 199, 201, 205
Bwlch Cowlyd 106
Bwlch Cwm Brwynog 190, 195, 197
Bwlch Cwm Cesig 188
Bwlch Cwm Llan 185, 186, 188, 193
Bwlch Cwm-trwsgl 72, 80, 82, 83
Bwlch Cyfryw-drum 104, 110, 117
Bwlch Dros-bern 77, 78
Bwlch Drws-Ardudwy 41, 42
Bwlch Glas 181, 182, 192, 199, 209
Bwlch Gwyn 188

Bwlch Maen Gwynedd 26, 28, 30
Bwlch Maesgwm 188, 189, 190, 191, 195, 197
Bwlch Main 194
Bwlch Meillionen 72, 81, 82, 83, 84
Bwlch Mignog 106
Bwlch Stwlan 63
Bwlch Trimarchog 108, 118
Bwlch Tryfan 122, 124, 128, 138, 139, 140, 211, 212
Bwlch Tyddiad 43, 45
Bwlch y Battel 54
Bwlch y Brecan 172
Bwlch y Cywion 174
Bwlch y Ddeufaen 98
Bwlch-y-Ddwy-elor 74, 76, 78, 80, 84
Bwlch y Ddwy-Glyder 140, 159, 211, 212
Bwlch y Marchlyn 175
Bwlch y Moch 185, 197, 199, 202, 209
Bwlch y Rhosydd *59*, 62, 63
Bwlch y Saethau 181, 182, 186, 209
Bwlch-y-Sygyn 64
Bwlych y Marchlyn 174
Bwrdd Arthur (Arthur's Table) 28

Cadair Berwyn 28, *30*, 30
Cadair Bronwen 28, 30
Cadair Idris 2, *3*

Cae Perthi 172
The Cannon 124, 125
Cantilever Rock *138*, 138, 140
Capel Curig 105–6, 108, 148
Capelulo 100
Carneddau 93, 103, 117, *172*
Carnedd Dafydd *96*, 104, 105, 110, 111, 112, 117, 217
Carnedd Fach 110
Carnedd Llewelyn *96*, 98, 104, 110, *112*, 112, 117, 217
Carnedd y Filiast 171–2, *175*, 175
Castell Dinas Bran 221, *223*
Castell y Bere 16–17, *17*
Castell y Geifr 167
Castell y Gwynt 138, 140, 159, 211, 212
Ceunant Ciprwth 79, 84
Cilcain 219, 220
Clogwyn Du 154, 186
Clogwyn Du'r Arddu 190, 191, 192, 193, 194, *197*, 197
Clogwyn Station 190, 192, *208*, 208
Clogwyn y Grochan 159
Clogwyn y Person Arête 199, 203, *205*, 205–6
Clogwynyreryr 119
Clogwyn y Tarw 152
Clwydian Hills 217–20
Cneifion Arête *154*, 154, 155
Cnicht 51, *53*, 53–4, 63, *65*
Craig Arthur 221, *223*
Craig Cau 3, *12*, 12, 14, 16
Craig Cwm-llwyd 8
Craig Cwm Silyn 77, 78, 79, 84

Craig Cywarch *24*, 24
Craig Ddu 185
Craig Llugwy 111
Craiglwyn 106
Craig Pennant 77
Craig-wen *106*, 106
Craig Wion 45
Craig y Bera 86, 87, *88*, 88, 91
Craig-y-llyn 8
Craig yr Aderyn 16–17
Craig yr Ysfa *109*, 110, 112, 117, 118
Craigysgafn 61, *62*, 63
Creigiau Gleision 106, 169
Cribau *see* Gribin Ridge
Crib Goch *181*, 182, 197, *199*, 199–200, *200*, 201, *202*, 202, *205*, 205, 206, 209, 215
Crib y Ddysgl 182, 192, 203, 205, 206, 208, 209, *213*, 215
Crib-y-Rhiw *36*, 39
Crimpiau 106
Croesor 51, 61, 63, 64
Cwm Beudy Mawr 202
Cwm Bochlwyd 138, 141, 144, 152, *164*, 211
Cwm Bochlwyd Horseshoe 211
Cwm Bychan 43, 45, 64–5, 108
Cwm Cau *12*, 12, 14, 15
Cwm Ciprwth 78, *79*, 79, 84
Cwm Clogwyn 190, *192*, 194
Cwm Clyd 164, 166, 169
Cwm Cneifion 149, 152, *154*, 154, 155, 159
Cwm-coch 169, 170

Cwm Croesor 54, 61, 62–3
Cwm Cywarch *20*, 20, 22, 24
Cwm Cywion 169
Cwm Du 84, 86
Cwm Dyli 179, 186, 194, 199, 209
Cwm Eigiau 110, 112, 118
Cwm Eigiau Horseshoe 106, 117–19
Cwm Glas 159, 199, 200, 201, *203*, 203, *205*, 205, 206, 208, 215
Cwm Glas Bach 206, 208, 215
Cwm Glaslyn 182
Cwm Glas Mawr 199, 201, 203, 205, 206
Cwm Graianog 171, 175
Cwm Idwal 149, 155, *164*, 166, 167, 212
Cwm Llafar *103*, 103, 104, 110, 217
Cwm Llan 185, 186
Cwm Llefrith 81, 82, 84, 85
Cwm Lloer 108, 111, 114–15, *117*, 117
Cwm Maen Gwynedd 28, 30
Cwm Pennant *ix*, 70, 74, 76, 78, 79, 80, 81–2, 84
Cwm Rhwyddfor 10, 15
Cwm Silyn 77
Cwm Tal-y-braich 108
Cwm Tregalan 186
Cwm Trwsgl 72, 78, 80, *83*, 83
Cwm Tryfan 122, 128, 129, 139, 159
Cwm Uchaf 199, 205, 206
Cwrt Isaf 84, 85
Cyfrwy 3, *5*, 5, 6, 7, 7
Cyfrwy Arête 5, 7
Cyrn Las 201, 203, 206

Dduallt 67
Devil's Kitchen *see* Twll Du
Diffwys 35, 39
Dinas Bach 202
Dinas Mawddwy 24
Dinas Mot 201, 202
Dinas y Cromlech 161
Dog Lakes *see* Llynnau'r Cwn
Dolgellau 16
Dolmen Buttress 144, 146
Drosgl *94*, 94
Druids Circle *91*, *98*, 100
Drum 98
Drws Bach 20, *22*
Drysgol *20*, 20, 24

East Gully (Foel-goch) 170, 171
East Gully (Glyder Fach) 142, 143
Elidir Fach 175
Elidir Fawr 174, 175, 215
Esgair Felen 159

Ffestiniog Railway *66*, 66–7
Ffestiniog, Vale of 66, 67
Fford Capel 188, 190
Ffynnon Caseg 104
Ffynnon Lloer 108, 109, 115, *117*, 117
Ffynnon Llugwy *i*, 108, 110, 111, *112*, 112, 118
Foel Boethwel 54
Foel Cynwch 16
Foel-fras 98, 216, 218
Foel-ganol 98, 218

Foel-goch 164, 169, 171, 172, 174, 215
Foel Goch 189, 190
Foel Grach 96, 117, 118, 217
Foel Gron 189
Foel Rudd 87

Gallt yr Ogof *146*, 146, 148–9
Gallt y Wenallt 209
Garnedd-goch 77, 78, 79, 84
Garnedd Uchaf 94, 98, 218
Garnedd Ugain 179, 199, 203, 205–6, 209
Garreg Wastad 159
Gau Graig *10*, 10, 12, 15
Gerlan 103, 104
Gilfach copper-mine *79*, 79, 84
Gist Ddu 19
Gladstone Rock 185, 188
Glan Dena 108, 111, 112, 115, 127
Glaslyn 181, *182*, 182, 185, 199
Gloyw Llyn *45*, 45
Glyder Fach 136, *138*, 138, 139, 141–5, *144*, 146, 149, 150, 152, 159, 211, *212*, 212, 215
Glyder Fawr 87, 141, 149–50, 155, 157, 161, 174, 211, 213, 215
Glyders (range) 136, 157
Golygfan 67
Great Gully 14
Green Gully 128, 131
Gribin Ridge (Cribau) *181*, 182, 185, 209
Gribin Ridge (Y Gribin) 141, 142, 150, *152*, 152, 211

Gwern Gof Isaf 108, 111, 112, 136, 139, 146, 148
Gwern Gof Uchaf 127, 128, 129
Gyrn Las *see* Cyrn Las

Heather Terrace 126–8, 129, 131, 133
Hendwr 26
Hengwm 20, *22*, 24
Horned Ridge 114

Idwal Slabs 150, 155, 156

Little Gully 130, 131
Little Tryfan 127, 139
Llanarmon Dyffryn Ceiriog 30
Llanberis 188, 189, 190, 191
Llanberis Pass 157, 159, 161, 172, 197, 200, 201, *203*, 203, 206, 215
Llanberis Path 190–3, 199, 208
Llanberis Ridge *208*
Llangollen 220
Llanrhaeadr-ym-Mochnant 30
Llanuwchllyn 22, 24
Llech Ddu *103*, 104, 104–5
Llechog 190, 194, 206–7
Llechog Buttress *208*
Lliwedd 209
Llyn Anafon 98
Llyn Arenig Fawr 31
Llyn Bach 199, 203, 206
Llyn Bochlwyd 122, 124, 140, 141, 150, 152, 212
Llyn Bodlyn 36, 39

Llyn Caseg-fraith 122, *127*, *136*, 138, 139, 146, 149, 159
Llyn Cau 3, *12*, 12
Llyn Celyn 31
Llyn Clyd 164, 169
Llyn Cowlyd 105, 106, 108
Llyn Crafnant 106
Llyn Cwellyn *86*, 86, 188, 195
Llyn Cwm Bychan 43, 45
Llyn Cwmffynnon 157, 159
Llyn Cwmhosan 42
Llyn Cwm-y-foel 54, 63
Llyn Cynwch 16
Llyn Cyri *8*, 8
Llyn Dinas 59, 64
Llyn Du 41, 43, 45
Llyn Du'r Arddu 191, 194
Llyn Dwythwch 188
Llyn Edno 54, 56, *59*
Llyn Eigiau 117, 118
Llyn Erddyn 39
Llyn Ffynnon-y-gwas 190, 195
Llyn Glas 199, 200, 206
Llyn Hywel *38*, *41*, 42
Llyn Idwal 141, 150, 152, 154, 164, 166, 167, 169, 213
Llyn Llagi 54, 56
Llyn Lliwbran 24
Llyn Lluncaws 28, *30*, 30
Llyn Llydaw *181*, 181, 182, 209
Llyn Mair 67
Llyn Morwynion 45
Llynnau Cerrig-y-myllt 54, *56*
Llynnau Gregennen 8

Llynnau Mymbyr *ii*
Llynnau'r Cwn 54, 56
Llyn Ogwen 108, 122, 140, 166, *169*
Llyn Pen Aran 24
Llyn Teyrn 179
Llyn y Bi 42
Llyn y Biswail 54
Llyn y Coryn *106*, 106
Llyn y Cwn 141, 150, 155, 161, 164, 174, 213, 215
Llyn y Foel 48, 50, 51
Llyn y Gadair 3, *5*, 5, 6, 7
Llyn yr Adar 54, 56, 63
Llyn yr Arddu 54

Maen-llwyd-isaf 188, 189
Maes-y-garnedd 39
Main Gully (Glyder Fach) 142
Marchlyn Mawr Reservoir 174
Melynllyn 117, 119
Milestone Buttress 124, 126, 129, 211, 212, 213
Miner's Track 122, 138, 139, 140, 149, 152, 159, 179, 182, 185, 209
Moel Arthur 220
Moel Cynghorion *87*, 190, 193, 195, 197
Moel Defaid 106
Moel Dywyll 219
Moel Eilio 188, *189*, 190
Moel Famau 217, *218*, 218, 219
Moelfre 39, 100
Moel Hebog 70, 72, 82, 83, 84
Moel Lefn 72, 80, 81, *83*, 83
Moel Llyfnant 34

Moel Llys-y-coed 220
Moel Meirch 51, 56, *59*
Moel Pearce 26
Moel Siabod *i*, *48*, 48, *50*, 50–1
Moel Sych 28, 30
Moel Wnion 94
Moelwyn (range) 59, 61
Moelwyn Bach 59, 61, *62*, 63–4
Moelwyn Mawr 59, *61*, 61–2, 63
Moel-yr-hydd 62
Moel yr Ogof *70*, 72, *73*, 81, 83
Mynydd Drws-y-coed 74, 76, 78, 84
Mynydd Du 104
Mynydd Mawr 70, *86*, 86, 87, *88*
Mynydd Moel 10, 12, 14–15
Mynydd Pencoed 16, *17*
Mynydd Perfedd 172, 175
Mynydd Tal-y-mignedd 76, 77, 79, 84

Nameless Cwm *see* Cwm Cneifion
Nantcol 39
Nant Ffrancon 164, *171*
Nantgwynant 51, *53*, 70
Nantlle 87
Nantlle Ridge 70, *74*, 74, 77–80, *85*
Nant Peris 157, 172, 215
Nant y Geuallt 106
Nant y Gors 148, 149
Nant y Llyn *28*, 28
Needle's Eye Arête 169, 170–1
Nor' Nor' Gully 124, 125, 126, 128
North Gully (Tryfan) 128, 130–1, 133
North Ridge (Tryfan) 124–6, *125*, *129*, 129, 130, 131, 211

Offa's Dyke Path 217, 219–20, 221
Ogwen 140, *152*, 152, 154, 171
Ogwen Cottage 164, 166, 169, 170, 212, 213

Pen Bryn-du 98
Pen Llithrig-y-wrach 105, 106, 108, 117–18, *119*
Pentre 219
Penygadair 2–3, 5–8, 12, 14, 15–16
Pen-y-Gwyrd 122, 157, 159
Pen-y-pass 157, 159, 179, 182, 197, 209, 215
Penyrhelgi-du 108, 110, 111, 118, *119*
Pen yr Ole Wen 108–10, 111, 112, *113*, 113–14, 115, *117*, *150*, *169*, 217
Pig Track 179, 181, 182, 197, 199, 209, 215
Pistyll Rhaeadr *26*, 26, 28
Plas-y-pennant 78, 82, 84
Pont Cyfyng 50, 51
Pont-Scethin 39

Rhaeadr-bach 94
Rhinog (range) 35–6
Rhinog Fach 35, *38*, 41, 42
Rhinog Fawr 35, *38*, 41–2, 43, 45
Rhiw Gwredydd 3
Rhyd-Ddu 74, 77, 78, 86, 87, 193
Rhydymain 19
Roman Steps 41, 43, 45
Ruabon Mountain 220, 221

Senior's Ridge 155, 156, 157
Sentries' Ridge 88
Sheep Walk 166
Snowdon *54*, *59*, *122*, 179, *181*, 181–2, *182*, *185*, 185–6, *186*, 188, *189*, 190–1, *192*, 193–5, *194*, *197*, 197, 199, 209, 213
Snowdon Horseshoe 181, 185, 197, 209
Snowdon Mountain Railway 179, 191,
Snowdon Ranger Path 190, 191, 193, 194, 195–6
South Gully (Tryfan) 128, 133
South Ridge (Tryfan) 122, 124, 128, 129, 211, 212
Stwlan Dam *61*, 61
Sychnant Pass 98, 100
Sygun Copper Mine 64, 65

The Table 6, 7
Table Buttress 5, 6, 7
Tal-y-bont 36–8, 117
Tal y Fan 98, 100
Tal y Llyn Ogwen 108, 114
Tan-y-bwlch 66–7
Tanygrisiau 67
Tan-y-pistyll 26, 28
Trevor Rocks 221, *223*
Trum y Ddysgl 74, 76, 78, 84
Tryfan 121–2, *122*, 124–31, *125*, *127*, *129*, *133*, 133, *139*, *143*, *171*, 211, *212*, 212, 215, 217
Twll Du 141, *149*, 149, 150, 155, 161, 164, 213

Tyddyn Mawr 85
Ty-nant 2, 7
Tyn-y-ddôl 16
Tyrau Mawr 8, 8, 108

Watkin Path 182, 185–6, 194, 209
Welsh Three-Thousanders 213, 215, 217
West Gully (Glyder Fach) 144, 146
West Highland Tunnel 64–5
World's End 221

Y Braich 108, 111
Y Diffwys 72
Y Foel Goch 146
Y Garn 74, *76*, 78, 84, 164, *166*, 166, *167*, 167, 169, 171, 172, 174, 213, 215
Y Gribin *see* Gribin Ridge
Y Gyrn 84
Y Llethr 35, *36*, 39, 41, 42
Y Lliwedd 179, 185
Ynys Ettws 200, 201, 203, 207
Yr Aran 186, 188
Yr Aryg 94
Yr Elen *96*, 103, 104, 118, *172*, 217
Yr Orsedd 98
Yr Wyddfa 179, 181, 182, 185, 186, 193, 199, 209, 213
Ysgafell Wen 54
Ysgolion Duon 104, 110, 111, 117, *215*

*aber* – river-mouth, confluence

*aderyn* (pl. *adar*) – bird

*afon* – river

*allt, gallt* – height

*bach, fach* – small

*bedd* – grave

*betws* – chapel (bede-house)

*beudy* – byre, cow-house

*blaen* (pl. *blaenau*) – head of valley

*bod* – home (abode)

*bont, pont* – bridge

*braich* – arm

*brith* – speckled

*brwynog* – rushy

*bryn* – hill

*bwlch* – pass, defile

*bychan* – little

*cadair, cader* – chair

*cae* – field

*caer* – fort

*canol, ganol* – middle

*capel* – chapel

*carn, carnedd* – heap of st...

*carreg* – rock

*caseg* – mare

*castell* – castle

*cau* – deep hollow

*cefn* – ridge

*celli, gelli* – grove

*ceunant* – ravine

*cidwm* – wolf

*cigfran, gigfran* – raven

*clogwyn* – precipice

*coch* – red

*coed* – woodland

*congl* – corner

*cors, gors* – bog

*craig* – rock

*crib* – narrow ridge

*croes* – cross

*cwm* – cirque, valley

*deg, teg* – fair

*dinas* – fort

*dol, ddol* – meadow

*drum* – ridge

*drws* – door

*dwr* – water

*dwy* – two

*dyffryn* – valley

*eglwys* – church

*eira* – snow

*esgair* – shank, mountain shoulder

*fach, bach* – small

*fawr, mawr* – big

*fechan* – little

*felin, melin* – mill

*ffordd* – road

*ffridd* – mountain pastur...

*ffynnon* – well, spring

*filiast* – greyhound

*foel, moel* – rounded hill

*fraith* – speckled, pied

*fynydd, mynydd* – mount...

*gadair, gader* – chair

*gafr, afr* – goat

*gam* – crooked

*gigfran, cigfran* – raven

*glan* – bank, shore

*glas, las* – blue or green

*glyder, gludair* – heap

*glyn* – glen

*goch, coch* – red

*gors, cors* – bog

*grach* – scabby

*gribin* – serrated ridge

*grug* – heather

*gwastad* – plain, level ground

*gwern* – marsh

*gwrach, wrach* – witch

*gwyn, wyn* – white